walking with purpose

Dear Friend,

You are an extraordinary woman. How can I write that, never having met you? Your desire to unpack the riches that are contained in the Gospel of John thrills the heart of God. As you open your study guide, many Christians are busy doing good works and feeling as though that is sufficient in their Christian walk. You might be feeling tempted, even now, to get up and get something done. Yet, with Bible in hand, you are choosing the better option: to give some time to your Creator. He has amazing things in store for you. God tells us in Jeremiah 33:3, "Call to me and I will answer you, and will tell to you great and hidden things which you have not known." As we open the pages of Holy Scripture, the Holy Spirit is going to be with us, whispering God's Truth to our souls. Isn't that exciting?

I wish that I could sit across my kitchen table from you and discuss these study questions face-to-face! I'd make you a cup of tea (and it would be good—I'm married to a Brit), or a cup of coffee (it might taste nasty—I don't drink coffee), and I'd enjoy every minute of our time together! More than likely you live far from me, and so I content myself with praying for you. I pray for you each morning. I pray that "the eyes of your heart [would] be enlightened, that you may know what is the hope that belongs to his call" (Ephesians 1:18). This study of John's Gospel is meant to touch your heart and fill you with hope. We're going to learn a great deal along the way. The more we learn about Jesus, the more we are going to love Him. And that's what it's all about. It's about seeing how amazing our God is, falling in love, and being loved passionately in return.

This was John's experience. He referred to himself as "the one whom Jesus loved" (John 20:2). What a perfect guide for us as we set out on this adventure of *Touching the Divine*!

I am blessed to be on the journey with you.

Lisa Brenninkmeyer
Founder and Chief Purpose Officer, Walking with Purpose

Touching the Divine

A Study of the Gospel of John

SECOND EDITION

Lisa Brenninkmeyer

Touching The Divine

Lisa Brenninkmeyer

walking with purpose
~ SO MUCH MORE THAN A BIBLE STUDY ~

www.walkingwithpurpose.com

Authored by Lisa Brenninkmeyer

IMPRIMATUR   + William E. Lori, STD, Archbishop of Baltimore

The recommended Bible translations for use in Walking with Purpose™ studies are: The New American Bible, which is the translation used in the United States for the readings at Mass; The Revised Standard Version, Catholic Edition; and The Jerusalem Bible.

Any internet addresses (websites, blogs, etc.) in this book are offered as a resource and may change in the future. Please refer to www.walkingwithpurpose.com as the central location for corresponding materials and references.

22 23 24 25 / 12 11 10 9 8 7 6 5 4 3 2 1

ISBN: 978-1-943173-36-5

Touching the Divine: A Study of the Gospel of John (Second Edition)

Printed in the United States of America

TABLE OF CONTENTS

INTRODUCTION

LESSONS

APPENDICES

ANSWER KEY

PRAYER PAGES

Welcome to Walking with Purpose™

You have many choices when it comes to how you spend your time—thank you for choosing Walking with Purpose™. Studying God's Word with an open and receptive heart will bring spiritual growth and enrichment to all aspects of your life, making every moment that you've invested worth it.

Each one of us comes to this material from our own unique vantage point. You are welcome as you are. No previous experience is necessary. Some of you will find that the questions in this study cause you to think about concepts that are new to you. Others might find much is a review. God meets each one of us where we are, and He is always faithful, taking us to a deeper, better place spiritually, regardless of where we begin.

The Structure of *Touching the Divine*

Touching the Divine is a twenty-two-session Bible study that integrates the Gospel of John with the teachings of the Roman Catholic Church to help us know Christ in a deeper, more intimate way. This Bible study is designed for both interactive personal study and group discussion.

If you are going through *Touching the Divine* with a small group in your parish, most weeks will be spent in the small group discussing one of the lessons from the *Touching the Divine study guide*. Once a month you'll gather for a Connect Coffee, which consists of social time, a video presentation of one of the related Bible study talks, and small group discussion of selected questions that relate to the talk.

If you're going through this study either on your own or in a small group, you are welcome to order the DVDs, but you might find it simpler to watch the talks online. The URL for each talk is listed on the Connect Coffee talk outline within the study guide.

Study Guide Format and Reference Materials

The *Touching the Divine study guide* is divided into three sections:

The first section comprises the Bible study lessons. Most lessons are divided into five "days" to help you form a habit of reading and reflecting on God's Word regularly. If you are a woman who has only bits and pieces of time throughout your day to accomplish tasks, you will find this breakdown of the lessons especially helpful. Each day focuses on Scripture readings and related teaching passages and ends with a "Quiet your heart" reflection. In addition day five includes a lesson conclusion; a resolution section, in which you set a goal for yourself based on a theme of the lesson; and short clips from the *Catechism of the Catholic Church*, which are referenced throughout the lesson to complement the Scripture study. Each lesson ends with a relevant verse study. Instructions for how to do a verse study can be found in appendix 3.

For the Connect Coffee talks in the series, accompanying outlines are offered as guides for taking notes. Questions are included to guide your group's discussion following the video.

The second section, the appendices, contains supplemental materials referred to during the study, as well as an article about Saint Thérèse of Lisieux, the patron saint of Walking with Purpose.

The third section contains the answer key. You will benefit so much more from the Bible study if you work through the questions on your own, searching your heart, as this is your very personal journey of faith. The answer key is meant to enhance small group discussion and provide personal guidance or insight when needed.

At the end of the book are pages on which to write weekly prayer intentions.

Bible Recommendations

What were your thoughts the first time you picked up a Bible? Perhaps you got one as a gift for Confirmation or graduation. Maybe it was a copy you found lying around at home. It could be that the first time you held a Bible was in a classroom setting. Which of these two statements better reflects how you felt in that moment: "I just can't wait to dive into these pages because I know it'll be life-changing" or "This looks boring and inaccessible. I'm sticking it on my shelf"? For most of us, it was the latter.

One of our goals at Walking with Purpose is to teach women how to use the Bible as a practical, accessible tool. There are some obstacles to that happening. One problem is how we approach the Bible. If we open it up to Genesis and start reading through from start to finish, we will likely have trouble understanding what is going on (and we'll probably quit once we get into Leviticus). One of the reasons this method can be confusing is because Scripture is not a book; it's a library. This library is filled with many genres: poetry, letters, historical narrative, and apocalyptic writings. When we don't know what genre we are reading, we can quickly become frustrated. For example, reading Genesis as a science book instead of as inspired poetry will cause us to see faith and science at odds. Far too many people write off Christianity because they feel it can't possibly be true after seeing discrepancies between things proven by science and the way those same things are described in the Bible. This is a consequence of not recognizing the Bible as a *library* of Truth, utilizing many genres of literature to lead us to the heart of God, understand His story, and see our place in the epic tale of redemption. Catholics don't read everything in the Bible literally. We read some things literally, but not everything.

Another obstacle to using the Bible as a practical, accessible tool for spiritual growth is not knowing where to begin. This is exactly why Walking with Purpose has created Bible studies and programs like BLAZE. Being guided through Scripture, being led to the passages that are most applicable to life in the twenty-first century, helps readers feel the Bible come alive.

You may also want to consider Bible tabs as a resource. It takes about thirty minutes to put tabs into a Bible, but it makes it so much easier to find your way around Scripture. You can find Bible tabs at Catholic bookstores or online. Be sure to get the Catholic version, as Protestant versions of the Bible are missing seven books. (At the time of the Reformation, the books of Sirach, Tobit, Wisdom, Judith, 1 and 2 Maccabees, and Baruch, as well as portions of Daniel and Esther, were removed in order to embrace a canon of Scripture that reflected Protestant theological beliefs. Books were never *added* to the Catholic Bible—they have always been there.)

We recommend using either the NABRE (New American Bible, Revised Edition) or the RSVCE (Revised Standard Version, Catholic Edition) translations.

Walking with Purpose™ Website

Please visit our website at www.walkingwithpurpose.com to find additional free content and supplemental materials that complement our Bible studies, as well as a link to our online store for additional Bible studies, DVDs, books, and more!

WWP *Scripture Printables* of our exclusively designed verse cards that compliment all Bible studies. They are available in various sizes and formats, perfect for lock screens or emailing to a friend.

WWP *Playlists* of Founder Lisa Brenninkmeyer's favorite music accompany each Bible study.

WWP *Videos* of all Connect Coffee talks.

WWP *Blog* for a weekly dose of inspiration and encouragement from our bloggers. Subscribe for updates.

WWP *Leadership Development Program* for those who long to see more women touched by the love of Christ but aren't sure how to help. We are here to help you learn the art of creating community. It's easier than you think! God doesn't call the equipped; He equips the called. If you love God and love women, then you have what it takes to make a difference in the lives of people around you. Through our training, you'll be empowered to step out of your comfort zone and experience the rush of serving God with passion and purpose. You are not alone, and you can become a great leader. We offer the encouragement and the tools you need to reach out to a world that desperately needs to experience the love of God.

Join Us on Social Media

facebook.com/walkingwithpurpose

twitter.com/walkingwpurpose

instagram.com/walkingwithpurpose_official

youtube.com/walkingwithpurpose_official

pinterest.com/walkingwpurpose

Lessons

NOTES

Lesson 1: Connect Coffee Talk 1

INTIMACY AND IDENTITY

The accompanying talk can be viewed via DVD or digital-download purchase or accessed online at walkingwithpurpose.com/videos.

Key Verses

"And the Word became flesh and dwelt among us, full of grace and truth; we have beheld his glory, glory as of the only Son from the Father" (John 1:14).

"The light shines in the darkness, and the darkness has not overcome it" (John 1:5).

"Therefore, if anyone is in Christ, he is a new creation. The old has passed away, behold, the new has come!" (2 Corinthians 5:17).

I. **Introduction**

   The purpose of the book: John 20:30–31

   Why can we trust this book?

   - The trustworthiness of an eyewitness account

   - The integrity of the writing

II. **The Pursuit of Intimacy**

   Jesus invites us to…

   A. Receive the Holy Spirit in our hearts and become His dwelling place.

   From the very beginning, God has desired closeness with the people He created. When Jesus ascended into heaven, God came to dwell in the hearts of His people through the indwelling Holy Spirit. Our hearts become tabernacles of God.

B. Experience precious intimacy with Him through the Eucharist.

As if that were not enough, He invented the Eucharist; a God who makes Himself into bread, a little host, in order to descend onto our lips and into our hearts, to bridge all distance between Himself and us.[1]

C. Be transformed by our closeness to Him.

Jesus' light gives us hope—hope that we can overcome our past and our present failings, hope that we can have a fresh start.

Like the apostles, we can stop identifying ourselves in terms of what our culture values and begin to identify ourselves by our relationship to Jesus. We receive a new identity in Christ.

III. The Bestowal of Identity

Who am I? I am God's beloved daughter. I belong to the Lord.

A. Identity is received and not achieved.

B. Nothing can take away God's love for you. Nothing is beyond the scope of His mercy.

As we study Scripture, more than anything else, we are pursuing a *person*, and that person is Jesus Christ.

---

1   Father Jean d'Elbee, *I Believe in Love: A Personal Retreat Based on the Teaching of St. Thérèse of Lisieux* (Manchester, NH: Sophia Institute Press, 2001), 9.

Questions for Discussion or Journaling

1. What are some words you would use to answer the question, "Who are you?"

2. Have you been confused by any of the three identity lies described by Henri Nouwen? (I am what I have. I am what I do. I am what others think of me.)

3. In what way would you most like to grow in your spiritual life through this Bible study?

NOTES

Lori Z.
Kathy
Karen
Paula
Biffie
Adel
Claudia
Mary Theresa

Lesson 2

JESUS, THE WORD OF GOD

Introduction

I have a real weakness for paper products (as in stationery, not paper towels). I jump at any excuse to have something printed up on pretty paper! When I got married and moved to Germany, I had little "At Home" cards made up with my new name and address. Thinking I was exhibiting some serious paper style, I mailed them out to all my new acquaintances there. I was shocked when I was told that the cards were confusing; people couldn't figure out who I was. *They can't figure out who I am when my name is right on the card? What's wrong with them?* I thought. The problem was that in Europe, a woman often keeps her maiden name, and it is hyphenated after her married name. I hadn't done this, and no one could figure out what family I was from. They wanted to know my roots, my origin.

The Jews had a similar fascination with a person's background and genealogy. Because of this, Matthew's Gospel introduces Jesus by describing His family tree. And John goes a step further. His introduction of Jesus takes us back in time to creation and to before creation. He provides the answer to the question "Where did Jesus come from?" in the first verse of his Gospel: "In the beginning was the Word, and the Word was with God, and the Word was God." When John talks about the Word, he's talking about Jesus.

Jesus was there at the very beginning. Everything that exists has its source in Him. Everything that we see originated with Him. He was there at the time of creation. As the second person of the Holy Trinity, Jesus took part in creation. When the first molecule was made, Jesus was already there. There is nothing greater, older, wiser, or more amazing than Jesus. "He is before all things, and in Him all things hold together" (Colossians 1:16).

"word" (Jesus)
God (Jesus) @ creation
John wasn't killed
4 most important Gospels ?

13

Tradition holds that John was the last of Jesus' disciples to die. He was writing at the end of his life, which means his Gospel is one of the last living testimonies to Jesus. How was he to introduce his Friend to his readers?

John chose to begin at the beginning, bringing us back to creation. Through his words he taught that Jesus was the agent of creation. "All things were created through Him and for Him" (Colossians 1:16). Unlike plant and animal life, human beings are the only creatures who can enter into this relationship with Jesus. We are the only ones on the planet who can understand that He is our origin and destiny. He created us too. This is our meaning in life. If we reject Jesus, we will never find the true meaning or the real purpose of our lives.

We often search for meaning in life through relationships, accomplishments, and possessions. It's so easy to look for our purpose in life in the wrong places. What's your purpose in life? What is your reason for living?

We were created by God and for God. Only as we tune our hearts to Him will we truly be fulfilled.

Let's pray that we would read these Scriptures with fresh eyes and with hearts open and willing to receive a touch from the Divine.

Day One: The Prologue

Read John 1:1–9.

1. A. What do we learn from John 1:1–3 about "the Word"?

    B. What additional insight do you gain into "the Word" from CCC 291?

It's incredible to think that everything in existence is here and held together because of the creative power of God. And God didn't create in the way that a sculptor, painter, or carpenter does. They take existing things and create something new from them. A carpenter doesn't create the wood or the nails he uses in a chair's construction. He has some material to work with. But it's different with God. He creates something out of nothing. He brings something into existence where nothing was. What difference does that make to you and me? Frank Sheed explains:

> God made us of nothing, but by the mere act of His will He made us into something. And the same will that brought us into existence is required to keep us in existence. Think hard about this, for in it is the primary truth about ourselves; without it we shall not know the first thing about ourselves…

> A carpenter makes a chair. He leaves it, and the chair continues to exist. Why? Because the material he made of it preserves the shape he has given it. In other words, when the maker of a thing leaves it, it is kept in existence by the material used in its making. If God, having made us, left us, we should be kept in existence by the material used in our making—namely nothing…

> [Not to know this truth] is to be wrong about everything. If we omit God, we see nothing as it is but everything as it is not—which is the very definition of insanity.[2]

    C. People turn to many different sources of information when they seek to answer questions like "Who am I?" and "Why am I here?" Few people see God as the explanation of everything—the answer to life's biggest questions. But when He is omitted in the search for truth, confusion results. Can you see evidence of this in our society today?

2. A. We have learned in John 1:1–3 that Jesus is "the Word." What else do we learn about Him in John 1:4?

    B. What does John 1:5 teach us about the power of light versus darkness?

Thomas Jefferson - wrote own bible! - stated Montecello

---

2   Frank Sheed, *Theology for Beginners* (Mansfield Center, CT: Martino, 2016), 64–65.

C. The world is so accustomed to the darkness that spiritual light can hurt our eyes. Where has God put you as a light in the darkness, and where do you need to keep shining even though it's difficult to do so?

3. A. The "man sent from God, whose name was John" (John 1:6) was John the Baptist. What was his purpose and mission? See John 1:7–8.

   B. According to John 1:9, what was the reason the true light (Jesus) came into the world?

   C. What insight can we gain from Isaiah 42:16 regarding the illumination Christ's light provides?

Quiet your heart and enjoy His presence…Take a moment to contemplate God's presence with you, shining light into your circumstances.

God often takes us down paths that seem unclear. When all seems unfamiliar, we are tempted to run back to the last place that felt certain. But if we insist on staying in comfortable and predictable places, our spiritual growth will be impeded. It's a comfort to know that God promises to turn darkness into light before us and to make rough places smooth. In my experience God usually lights the path directly in front of me, step by step, but He doesn't show me very far ahead. If He did, I could walk by sight instead of walking by faith. But "without faith, it's impossible to please him" (Hebrews 11:6).

When a clear path forward is obscured and you aren't sure where to go next, remember that God is with you and can bring good out of the darkest hour. As you wait, ask for Christ's light to illuminate your path. He won't show you far into the future, but He will light the way, moment by moment. Ask Him to show you the next right thing, and thank Him for holding you together even when things feel out of control.

Day Two: The Word Became Flesh

Read John 1:10–18.

1. When Jesus started His earthly ministry at the age of thirty-three, how was He received by the world He had created? (See John 1:10–11.) How is He received in our world today? What is the effect when a person brings up Jesus at a dinner party? What are some reasons that many reject or resist Him?

Many people believe Jesus was a great teacher, but they reject His divinity. Some people choose to make Him into a "god of their liking," embracing some of His teachings but ignoring others. Others don't think about Him at all.

As painful as it is to admit, many people reject Jesus because of negative experiences with Christians and the Church. As followers of Christ, we have a great responsibility to represent God's mercy and goodness to a world that desperately needs His love. We must soak in the grace of the Lord so that we can radiate His healing love to our hurting and broken world.

2. A. According to John 1:12, to whom did Jesus give power to become children of God?

   B. God desires that every person He has created becomes His child. He wants every one of us to know our true identity and to live out that reality. Because of this, God is the protagonist of each of our stories. He pursues us and helps us to find Him. How is this help described in CCC 1996?

   C. God does His part in giving us grace—the help we need to respond to His call. Our part is to receive Him and believe in His name. Read **appendix 4, "Conversion of Heart,"** where this process is described in greater detail. Have you experienced a conversion of heart? Journal your thoughts here.

   - Matthew Kelly—Next right thing
   - hold His hand 24 hrs

3. A. How does Saint John describe Jesus in John 1:14?

If this verse was boiled down into one word, it would be *"incarnation."* This means that the divine Son of God (Jesus) took on a human nature. Jesus is truly God and truly man.

B. How is the Incarnation described by Saint Paul in Philippians 2:5–8?

The Incarnation was prophesied in Wisdom 18:14–15: "For while gentle silence enveloped all things, and night in its swift course was now half gone, your all-powerful word leaped from heaven, from the royal throne, into the midst of the land that was doomed." The Word leaped from heaven, was made flesh, and changed everything. What was really happening is described in *The Christian Cosmic Narrative*:

> The invasion of earth by all the powers of heaven, the celestial attack upon the dark forces that had held the human race enslaved, the fulfilment of a thousand-year old promise to undo the ancient curse, was inaugurated by the power of God and the willing cooperation of one of his creatures. The most momentous act since the creation of the world took place in the secret silence of a young girl's heart and womb.[3]

Through His perfect life and sacrificial death, Jesus was going to upend everything and achieve a victory beyond our imaginings. And Mary, His mother, played an absolutely critical role in this cosmic battle to set us free.

4. A. What have we received from Jesus according to John 1:16?

B. What is the source of the grace we receive?

Worship in all you do
- paint
- sing
-

---

[3] Foreword by Fr. John Riccardo, *The Christian Cosmic Narrative* (Detroit, MI: ACTS XXIX Press, 2021), 78.

Habit of gratefulness

C. When John 1:16 talks about Christ's fullness, it's referring to the fact that in Jesus "the whole fullness of deity dwells bodily" (Colossians 2:9). This means that Jesus is fully God, fully divine. Before you put this in the box of theological truths that are good to know but don't necessarily impact your daily life, hear me out. Are you facing a challenge, and you're worrying that you don't have what it takes? Do you feel you don't have time to do all that is requested of you? Do you have a relationship that requires patience, and you have run out? All that you need and all that you lack can be found in Jesus. When you serve Jesus, you serve a God of limitless supply. In the words of A. W. Tozer, "How completely satisfying to turn from our limitations to a God who has none."[4] In which area of your life do you need Christ to fill what you are lacking?

Reject: when Church is evil does

Quiet your heart and enjoy His presence…Ask Him to reveal Himself to you.

"For the law was given through Moses; grace and truth came through Jesus Christ. No one has ever seen God; the only-begotten Son, who is in the bosom of the Father, he has made Him known" (John 1:17–18).

The law given through Moses showed the Israelite people how they were to live, but it didn't give them the power to do it. When Jesus came, everything changed. Because of His willingness to not only take on human nature but also die in our place, we now have access to the grace we need to live life the way God desires. Jesus has not only made it possible for us to know God intimately; He offers us everything we need in order to live in such a way that we can remain close to God.

The progression of intimacy that we learned about in the opening talk is a reminder of how fortunate we are to live at a time when we have so much available to help us grow closer to God. True, "no one has ever seen God" (John 1:18), and we will always have questions for Him that remain unanswered, but Jesus steps into the gap and draws us closer, revealing what we need to know and giving us all we need not just to survive but to thrive.

Take some time to go to Him with your needs. Know that every detail of your life is of interest to the Lord. He wants to hear what you need, and He promises to give you grace upon grace.

---

4   Aiden Wilson Tozer, *The Knowledge of the Holy* (New Delhi: General Press, 2019), 59.

"Women's concern"
Catholic Chap 129-130

Day Three: John the Baptist's Testimony

Read John 1:19–34.

John the Baptist was sent to prepare the way for Jesus. The baptisms he performed were for repentance. This preparation was necessary because hearts needed to be cleansed of sin in order for the people to receive Jesus. Hearts full of sin would find it difficult to recognize the Messiah, as He wasn't who the people had expected. The people had been waiting for a Messiah who would bring political freedom and revolution. The freedom and peace that Jesus was to offer were within the human heart.

1. A. How did John the Baptist describe Jesus when He came toward him in John 1:29?

    B. What does Exodus 12:21–27 tell us about the significance of a lamb in the Jewish religion?

2. Why was it significant that Jesus was called the Lamb of God? In what ways did His life and mission reflect the role of a lamb in the Old Testament? For extra help, see Isaiah 53:6–11, 1 John 1:7, 1 Corinthians 5:7, and 2 Corinthians 5:21.

3. Think of the specific point in the Mass when we pray, "Lamb of God, You take away the sins of the world; have mercy on us." Why do you think the Church gives us these words to pray? How do they prepare us for what follows in the Mass?

Quiet your heart and enjoy His presence…Take a moment to contemplate Jesus as the Lamb of God.

"Lamb of God, who takes away the sins of the world, have mercy on us. Lamb of God, who takes away the sins of the world, have mercy on us. Lamb of God, who takes away the sins of the world, grant us peace."

How often do we mindlessly recite these words in Mass rather than picturing our sins being transferred to Jesus as He pays the ultimate price in our place? Can you even imagine—Jesus preferred to suffer and die rather than experience the suffering of your sins separating you from Him? Being separated from you was unendurable. May this truth help us to confess our sins with true sorrow for what our sin has cost Him.

"Dear God,

"My sins cause me to feel distant from You. I know You are not the one who has moved away. The truth is, my choices have not led me to good places. I've listened to the lies of the enemy and gone down paths that have led away from You. All too often I've listened to voices other than Yours, and the results have not been good. Forgive me for the many times I have blamed others, rationalized my behavior, and minimized my sin. I know You love me and created me to walk in freedom as Your beloved daughter. You see into the depths of my soul and know my thoughts, excuses, and intentions. So I am done hiding from You and instead confess that I desperately need You. Please forgive me for the times I have turned away from You. Please forgive me and make me clean again. Please give me the grace to turn back to You, time and time again. Amen."

Day Four: The First Disciples

Read John 1:35–42.

1. When Jesus saw two disciples (probably Andrew and John) following Him, He asked them, "What do you seek?" Jesus cares about each person and sees our wants, needs, and desires. He asks us the same question: What do *you* seek from Him? What do you hope to get out of this Bible study?

The disciples answered Jesus' question "What do you seek?" with the question "Where are you staying?" They wanted to know more about Jesus' identity. As they came to know Jesus better, it gave Andrew the confidence to invite Peter to come and meet Him. The circle of intimacy was widening.

John Baptist — "bird on head" symbol

2. This growth in intimacy set the stage for Jesus changing the name of Peter. The meaning of a person's name held great significance in the Jewish culture. It usually described the child's nature or personality or what the parents wanted their child to become as an adult. When God was about to do a great work or make a significant transformation in a person's life, He often changed that person's name. For example, He changed Abram's name to Abraham, Sarai's name to Sarah, and Jacob's to Israel. In John 1:42 Jesus changed Simon's name to Cephas, which is translated Peter in English. Simon means "a small rock," but Cephas[5] (or Peter) means "a huge stone." What was the significance of this particular name change? (See Matthew 16:18.)

3. Jesus is all about giving people a fresh start. He loves a good before-and-after transformation. His extreme makeovers change who we are; He changes our identities. There is often a stark contrast between who we were before Christ redeemed our lives and who we are after we let Him begin His transforming work in us. Scripture records many times when God signaled a change was coming by giving someone a new name.

   We have been called many names throughout our lives—some of them endearments, others, wounding barbs. When Jesus gives us a new name, He calls out our deepest identity. He looks at you and calls you "Daughter. Delight. Beloved. Chosen." As it says in Isaiah 62:4, "No more shall you be termed 'Forsaken,' nor…'Desolate,' but you shall be called 'My delight is in her.'"

   Do you see evidence of God doing His transforming work in your life? If so, can you describe your experience? If not, will you write a short prayer here, letting God know the area in your life that you would like to see transformed?

Quiet your heart and enjoy His presence…Take a moment to contemplate what it will be like in heaven when you learn your new title of nobility. Meditate on what it means to be a daughter of the King of kings.

Then prayerfully read Isaiah 43:1–4, reminding yourself of God's incredibly personal love for you:

---

5   "Cephas" is Simon's new name in Aramaic. "Peter" is Simon's new name in Greek.

But now thus says the LORD, he
Who created you, O Jacob,
He who formed you, O Israel:
Fear not, for I have redeemed you;
I have called you by name, you are mine.
When you pass through the waters I will be with you;
And through the rivers, they shall not overwhelm you;
When you walk through fire you shall not be burned,
And the flame shall not consume you.
For I am the Holy One of Israel, your Savior.
I give Egypt as your ransom,
Ethiopia and Seba in exchange for you.
Because you are precious in my eyes,
and honored, and I love you.

Day Five: The Calling of Nathanael

Read John 1:43–51.

1. When Jesus spoke of Nathanael, He said, "Here is a true Israelite. There is no duplicity in him" (John 1:47 NABRE). *Merriam-Webster's Collegiate Dictionary* defines *"duplicity"* as "contradictory doubleness of thought, speech, or action; especially: the belying of one's true intentions by deceptive words or action." A person who is duplicitous is disingenuous, saying one thing but thinking another. Why do you think the lack of duplicity made Nathanael appealing to Jesus? If Nathanael lacked duplicity, what might he have been like? What did he possess? Do you think lack of duplicity is an essential character trait for followers of Christ? If so, why?

2. John 1:51 ("Truly, truly, I say to you, you will see heaven opened, and the angels of God ascending and descending upon the Son of man") is alluding to Jacob's dream in Genesis. Read Genesis 28:11–19.

    A. What did Jacob rename the place where he slept?

B. In John 1:51, whom did Jesus say the angels of God would ascend and descend upon?

C. The title "the Son of man" is used frequently to refer to Jesus. When He places Himself at the center of this vision, what is He claiming? See also John 10:7–9 (NAB) and John 2:19–22, remembering that the Temple was the place in the Old Testament where God dwelled.

Quiet your heart and enjoy His presence…Take a moment to contemplate Jesus' greatness. Think about Him as the Creator. Think about Him as the gateway to heaven. Think about His power and ability to transform people and give them fresh starts.

Take another moment to contemplate Jesus' humility. Think about His sacrifice. Think about the fact that He dwells in your heart through the Holy Spirit. The greatness of the Godhead dwells in your soul. He loves you so much, and He longs for intimacy with you. He holds nothing back in order to win your heart.

Conclusion

We all long to be loved passionately. Deep in each of our hearts is a desire to be someone whom another counts as worth fighting for.

Erin Wood knows what it is to be worth fighting for and to be worth dying for. She and her husband, Brian, were traveling to visit family in Washington state two months before their first baby was due. An oncoming Chevy Blazer weaved wildly on the road, racing straight toward them. As the car approached, Brian braked hard and swerved to the right, ensuring that he would take the full force of the crash as the Blazer hit them. In doing so he sacrificed his life for the lives of his wife and unborn child. In the midst of her grief for her selfless husband, Erin was able to say, "He definitely saved us. He made that choice."[6]

Oh, to be loved that much!

---

6   Michael Inbar, "Husband Steers into Crash to Save Wife, Unborn Child," *Today* (September 13, 2010): https://www.today.com/news/husband-steers-crash-save-wife-unborn-child-wbna39146785.

We are. We just don't always recognize it. Our knight in shining armor comes to us clothed as a lamb. The Lamb of God came for the sole purpose of rescuing us. He was willing to endure any amount of suffering if it meant that we could be safe. He didn't complain as He suffered. Instead, He encouraged others as His own life ebbed away. Let that truth wrap around your heart.

My Resolution

"My Resolution" is your opportunity to write down one specific, personal application from this lesson. In James 1:22, we're told that we shouldn't just hear the Word of God; we are to "do what it says." So what qualities should be found in a good resolution? It should be **personal** (use the pronouns "I," "me," "my," "mine"), it should be **possible** (don't choose something so far-fetched that you'll just become discouraged), it should be **measurable** (a specific goal to achieve within a specific time period), and it should be **action oriented** (not just a spiritual thought).

In what specific way will I apply what I learned in this lesson?

Examples:

1. God has placed me within my extended family as a light in the darkness. It's hard to keep shining there. I'm going to be a light, showing God's love to a specific family member. I'll do this by writing a letter of encouragement, calling my loved one, doing some act of service, or sending a small gift to let him or her know that I am thinking of him or her.

2. Colossians 1:16 tells us that "All things were created through Him and *for Him*" (emphasis added). Each morning I will ask God to show me what His purpose is for my day. Which things on my to-do list matter the most to Him? I'll do those things first.

3. During Mass when I pray to the Lamb of God, I will pay attention to the meaning. I'll think about the fact that Jesus was willing to endure anything for me because He loves me so much.

My Resolution:

Catechism Clips

CCC 291 "In the beginning was the Word…and the Word was God…all things were made through him, and without him was not anything made that was made." The New Testament reveals that God created everything by the eternal Word, his beloved Son. In him "all things were created, in heaven and on earth…all things were created through him and for him. He is before all things, and in him all things hold together." The Church's faith likewise confesses the creative action of the Holy Spirit, the "giver of life," "the Creator Spirit" (*Veni, Creator Spiritus*), the "source of every good."

CCC 1996 Our justification comes from the grace of God. Grace is favor, the free and undeserved help that God gives us to respond to his call to become children of God, adoptive sons, partakers of the divine nature and of eternal life.

Verse Study

See appendix 3 for instructions on how to complete a verse study.

John 1:14

1. Verse:

2. Paraphrase:

3. Questions:

4. Cross-references:

5. Personal Application:

NOTES

Lesson 3

JESUS, OUR SOURCE OF FULFILLMENT

Introduction

While living in Germany, I frequently found myself at odds with the country's cultural norms. I did my best to figure out the rules and follow them, but it seemed that more often than not, I learned those rules by breaking them.

One night two weeks after Laeka, our second child, was born, I was out driving during rush hour. A friend of mine had done her laundry at my house and hadn't come back to pick up her clean clothes. I knew she was leaving early in the morning for a trip and had no car, and all her clothes were in my dryer. So I packed it all up to deliver it to her. I was still feeling weak from giving birth, two-year-old Amy needed to go to bed, Laeka was so tiny, and my husband, Leo, was out of town…but I put everyone in the car and set out.

Just as we were in the middle of a bridge, with traffic flying along as everyone drove home for the evening, my car sputtered to a stop. I looked down. The gas gauge was on empty. I was absolutely petrified! I summoned the courage to get out on the busy highway, praying people would see me even though it was dark. I hadn't put a hat on Laeka or shoes on Amy, and it was cold. I put them in the double stroller and began the long walk to the gas station. By the time I reached it, I was in tears and in pain. The attendants thought the whole situation was hysterical, laughing as I tried to explain my dilemma in broken German. I finally got the gas can and began the long trek back to my car, pushing the stroller with one hand and holding the gas can in the other. As I reached the top of the bridge, I saw blinking lights and police cars surrounding my car. *Oh, good!* I thought. *They've come to help me! Isn't God good? I'm so thankful!* This thought made me cry even more. When I reached the police officers, I began thanking them for stopping to help me. One put up his hand.

"We're not here to help you. We're here to give you a ticket. Didn't you know it's against the law to run out of gas?"

I learned a valuable lesson that day. Whether you are in a car, in a relationship, or just coasting through everyday life, you can't run on empty. When this happens we endanger not only ourselves but those around us as well.

Are you running on empty?

Does the gauge in your life point to E because your life is too busy, or the pressure of your responsibilities is too great, or your family is too demanding?

Does the gauge in your life point to E because your heart is full of misery and empty of hope?

Do you feel empty of happiness, joy, or satisfaction?

In our fast-paced culture, our days are full, but often, our souls can feel empty of peace and fulfilment. This was never God's intention. One of the messages Jesus came to bring us is, "I came that they may have life, and have it abundantly" (John 10:10).

Of the many lessons Jesus taught during His ministry on earth, this one really excites me. We don't need to wait until heaven to experience something of this fullness! Unfortunately we tend to try out all the less satisfying substitutes before giving the Miracle Worker a chance to fill us. Our Gospel reading for this week can serve as a reminder to us to go to the true source of fulfilment for all that we need.

Day One: The Wedding at Cana

Read John 2:1–12.

Jewish wedding feasts such as this one could be celebrated for an entire week or more. Hospitality was extremely important to the Jewish people. To run out of wine on such a grand occasion was mortifying. It wasn't as if the host could just run down the street and pick up some more bottles.

The wedding took place at a time when poverty, hard work, and the frustration of being under Roman occupation made life difficult. A weeklong celebration with family, friends, wine, and feasting would have been full of joy! Instead of going on a honeymoon, the newlywed couple stayed and partied with their loved ones.

The story of the Wedding at Cana is the first of the seven signs (or miracles) in John. We'll look at all seven as we move through the Gospel. Notice how each one of them reveals something important about Jesus.

1. A. In CCC 1613, what does the Church teach about the importance of Jesus' presence at the wedding celebration at Cana?

Jesus began His ministry at a celebration of the covenant of marriage. He has taken on flesh to win His own bride, the Church (you and me). How beautiful that our Savior inaugurated His plan of redemption where spousal love and a new family was formed and celebrated.

B. In *Humanae Vitae*, Pope Paul VI described the beauty of a sacramental marriage as free, total, faithful and fruitful. For the marriage to be free, it must begin with an act of the free will. For it to be total, it needs a particular kind of love. Pope Paul VI describes that love as "a love which is total—that very special form of personal friendship in which husband and wife generously share everything, allowing no unreasonable exceptions and not thinking solely of their own convenience. Whoever really loves his partner loves not only for what he receives, but loves that partner for the partner's own sake, content to be able to enrich the other with the gift of self."[7] Married love is to be faithful and exclusive, until death. Lastly, it is to be fruitful. "Marriage and conjugal love are by their nature ordained toward the procreation and education of children. Children are really the supreme gift of marriage and contribute in the highest degree to their parents' welfare."[8] Can you think of some examples of marriage where all four qualities have been present (free, total, faithful and fruitful)? What was the impact of that marriage on the lives of those around the couple?

---

7 Pope Paul VI; Humane Vitae; https://www.vatican.va/content/paul-vi/en/encyclicals/documents/hf_p-vi_enc_25071968_humanae-vitae.html; accessed April 25, 2022.

8 Pope Paul VI; *Humane Vitae*; https://www.vatican.va/content/paul-vi/en/encyclicals/documents/hf_p-vi_enc_25071968_humanae-vitae.html; accessed April 25, 2022.

C. A sacramental marriage should be free, total, faithful and fruitful. Ideally, this is the lived experience of all married couples. But when even one quality is missing, pain and brokenness results. We have a Bridegroom who always loves us perfectly. How did Jesus the Bridegroom display this kind of love (free, total, faithful and fruitful) in this miracle?

It would be easy to think Jesus had just started His ministry—didn't He need to get some serious work done? Yet He takes time to celebrate at this wedding. We see that Jesus takes time to celebrate not apart from His ministry but because the point of His life, our life, is to enter into all of our daily realities.

2. When Mary noticed that there was no more wine, what did she do? How can we apply this to our own lives? See also CCC 2618.

3. Jesus' words to His mother, "O woman…" can sound a little harsh to our ears. Actually, referring to someone as "woman" was not disrespectful at that time. In fact the word *"woman"* is packed with biblical meaning.[9] Jesus went on to say to Mary, "My hour has not yet come." He knew that when He began to perform miracles, a chain of events would be set in motion. What would be the final result? See John 11:45–53 and John 12:23–24.

Whenever Jesus used the phrase "my hour," He was referring to Calvary. Responding to His mother's request for a miracle hastened the beginning of the end—Jesus' Passion. Mary had some sense that for Jesus to begin his public ministry would mean He'd begin to confront the powers of evil and the hatred of those who would reject him.[10]

---

9 In Genesis 3:15, there was a prophecy about "the woman" who would battle the serpent with her male offspring. Then in Galatians 4:4, we see the word again, referring to Mary giving birth to Christ. At the foot of the cross, Jesus says to Mary, "Woman, behold your son!" Finally Revelation 12 refers to her again as the woman with child who was clothed with the sun, with the moon under her feet, crowned with twelve stars. When Jesus calls Mary "woman," He refers to her as the woman of Genesis, Revelation, and Galatians, and she will be the woman at calvary. *"Woman"* is not a derogatory term; it's establishing her as *the* woman of Scripture.

10 See Fulton J. Sheen, *Life of Christ* (New York: Doubleday, 1958), 89–90.

4. What did Mary tell the servants to do? What does her instruction to the servants say about her relationship with Jesus?

5. Many people mistakenly believe that Catholics are encouraged to *worship* Mary. It is important to recognize the difference between devotion to Mary and honoring her and worshipping her. What insight into this do we gain from CCC 971?

6. Why do you think Jesus decided to begin his public ministry at a wedding? Do you think this beginning makes his love more or less intimate? More or less obvious?

Quiet your heart and enjoy His presence...Welcome the Bridegroom.

There are actually two bridegrooms in this story. There is the one who we see most clearly—the groom who needed more wine for the party. But there is a second bridegroom—a hidden one—and that is Jesus.

Jesus' love at the wedding at Cana is free, total, faithful; it is personal, surprising, better than expected. His love can be described as spousal. Not only does Jesus cause a stupendous amount of wine to be made, but its quality is unheard of. Wine is a sign of the new covenant between God and man. Wine is a sign of messianic joy as well as wedding joy. When Jesus turns water into wine at the wedding at Cana, He comes to renew the "sounds of joy and gladness...the voices of the bride and bridegroom." No longer will God's people be "desolate" (John 14:18). Jesus has the intimate, tender, seeking love of the Divine Lover who comes to give himself to the Church. Mary represents the Church—the one whose response to the Lord is always complete, always whole-hearted. There is no one who "gets" Jesus quite like Mary does. This understanding of their intimacy explains why most paintings that depict the Miracle of the Wedding at Cana show Jesus and Mary as the visual focus rather than the bride and groom of Cana. Yet Mary doesn't jealously protect her unique relationship with Jesus. She invites the servants into her very unique obedience of faith. She urges the servants (us) to "Do whatever He tells you." Mary makes Jesus aware of the need; she knows that the problem is on his mind. She awaits him trustingly.

In this miracle Jesus reveals His heart. Where is yours? What is the miracle that Jesus wants to work in your heart? What is the wine with which Jesus wants to gladden your heart? Can you believe that He comes to you, seeking intimacy with you as gentle as a humble lover? Jesus has made his dwelling with you in intimacy and wishes you joy, the joy of his own person, his own presence. Can you entrust yourself to him? Are you willing to let him be close to you? In Isaiah 62:5, the Lord declares his joy in you is "as the bridegroom rejoices over the bride, so shall your God rejoice over you." He has chosen you as his beloved. He is completely preoccupied with you: "You have ravished my heart, my sister, my bride, you have ravished my heart with a glance of your eyes, with one jewel of your necklace" (Songs 4:9).

Day Two: The Cleansing of the Temple

Read John 2:13–25.

1. The Passover was a very important feast for the Jewish people. It was celebrated once a year to commemorate the exodus of the Jews from slavery in Egypt to freedom in the Promised Land. In Jesus' time, pilgrims traveled from all over Palestine to celebrate the Passover in Jerusalem, the location of the Temple.

   A. What important activity were they to take part in at the Temple during this feast? See Numbers 28:16–25.

   B. Why might this pose a challenge to people who had to travel long distances to reach Jerusalem?

   C. Based on these facts, why were merchants selling animals and changing money in the Temple?

2. Why did this make Jesus angry? See CCC 583 and 584.

3. In his book *Uprooting Anger*, author Robert D. Jones describes the following three criteria that mark righteous anger:

   • It reacts against actual sin.

   • It focuses on God and His concerns (not on me and my concerns).

   • It coexists with other godly qualities and expresses itself in godly ways.[11]

---

11 Robert D. Jones, *Uprooting Anger: Biblical Help for a Common Problem* (Phillipsburg, NJ: P&R, 2005), 34.

A. How did Jesus' anger in the Temple illustrate these three criteria?

B. When attacked personally, how did Jesus respond? See 1 Peter 2:23.

C. How can we apply these lessons to ourselves when we deal with anger?

Quiet your heart and enjoy His presence…Take a moment to contemplate the difference between righteous anger and ungodly anger.

Dear God,

It's so easy to deceive myself into thinking that all my anger is justified and therefore acceptable in Your eyes. It's hard to stop and take the time to check whether my motives are pure. You set the example of turning the other cheek. When people attacked You personally, You didn't retaliate. This is a hard example for me to follow. I'm so tempted to repay those who have hurt me. I can do this with my words (they can be deadly), by withdrawing, by raising my voice…I have many tactics. Help me to turn to You and leave judgment to You.

Help me to also recognize when I need to stand up and be righteously angry. It would be wrong for me not to stand up for the oppressed. There are times when it would be sinful for me to stay silent.

Help me to always respond in a way that is Christlike, whether I am standing up and speaking out or leaving judgment in Your hands.

Day Three: Jesus and Nicodemus

Read John 3:1–15.

Nicodemus was like so many of us. He was only able to take small, hesitant steps towards the Lord. Why? He hadn't understood the depths of God's love. He thought the Messiah was only coming to put the finishing touches on what had already been done throughout salvation history, when Christ's true mission was the complete renewal of the human spirit. This is still His mission; this is still His dream for every human heart.[12]

---

12 John Bartunek, *The Better Part: A Christ-Centered Resource for Personal Prayer* (Modesto, CA: Catholic Spiritual Direction, 2011), 817.

1. Place yourself in the middle of this story. Imagine what was running through Nicodemus' mind.

   A. What might have been some of his preconceived notions about Jesus, salvation, and the Holy Spirit?

   B. Why do you think he chose to approach Jesus at night?

2. When Jesus spoke of "being born of water and the Spirit" (John 3:5), what did He mean? Use the following Catechism references and Bible verses to support your answer.

   A. CCC 1215 and 1257

   B. Titus 3:5

   C. 1 Peter 3:21

3. In John 3:8, Jesus said, "The wind blows where it wills, and you hear the sound of it, but you do not know where it comes from or where it goes; so it is with every one who is born of the Spirit." We don't actually *see* the Holy Spirit enter hearts, but we can see the effects. Have you ever experienced the effect of the Holy Spirit's presence in your life? Do you have a before-and-after story—how you were before you encountered the indwelling Holy Spirit in a deeper way, and how you are now, afterward?

4. Nicodemus was well-versed in the Old Testament Scriptures. Describe how the following Old Testament passages should have served as "lightbulbs" to Nicodemus as he heard Jesus describing a rebirth of water and the Spirit in John 3:5.

A. Ezekiel 36:25–27

B. Isaiah 44:3

5. What Old Testament event was Jesus referring to in John 3:14? See Numbers 21:4–9. What New Testament event does this remind us of? What does the bite of the serpent represent in our own lives?

Quiet your heart and enjoy His presence…He wants to renew you from the inside out.

In John 3:10, Jesus said to Nicodemus, "Are you a teacher of Israel, and yet you do not understand this?" Jesus wasn't trying to insult Nicodemus with this question. His heart, always filled with compassion and love, wanted nothing more than to see Nicodemus be spiritually reborn. In the words of Saint Augustine:

> *Are we to suppose that the Lord deliberately meant to insult this master of the Jews? The Lord knew what he was doing; He wanted him to be born of the Spirit. Nobody can be born of the Spirit without being humble, because humility is what brings us to birth by the Spirit; because the Lord is close to those whose hearts are bruised (Psalm 33:19).[13]*

Jesus was preparing Nicodemus to receive a great spiritual gift: conversion. This is what He offers to each one of us. But the first step in receiving this is an act of humility: admitting that we do not know better than the Lord, and we need to be taught by Him. Ask Him to open your eyes and heart to His Truth, even if it contradicts something you thought you knew. Ask Him to blow away any confusion and doubt.

Day Four: God's Love for the World

Read John 3:16–21.

1. A. Why did God give His only begotten Son? See John 3:16.

---

13 Saint Augustine, *Homilies on the Gospel of John 1–40* (New York: New York City Press, 2009), 233.

B. What does God ask for in response to His gift of His Son? See John 3:16.

C. What gift are we promised if we respond as God desires? See John 3:16.

2. Is it God's desire to condemn people? See John 3:17 and 2 Peter 3:9.

3. What statement does Jesus make in John 3:19–20?

These verses explain what keeps some people away from faith and the rescue from sin that Jesus offers. It's because they are drawn to darkness; they love it more than the light. This is sobering. There is often a moral dimension to unbelief that is ignored. All too often people say it's unanswered questions, scandals in the Church, or a lack of proof of God's existence that blocks their faith. But the honest truth is that many of us love our sin and don't want to face it or give it up. We might think this only applies to notorious sin—the sorts of things that most people agree are wrong. But it also applies to the sin of wanting to be the lord of our own lives, of wanting to be the ones in charge, of refusing to give God the place of honor and authority that He deserves.

4. Is there a sin in your life that you are playing around with and not taking seriously? Are there certain habits that cause you to draw away from God and keep you from coming to the light because the closer you get to God, what is true comes to light? Can you confess them here and ask God to help you to have the grace to love light more than darkness?

Quiet your heart and enjoy His presence…"He who does what is true comes to the light" (John 3:21).

When we come to the light and expose our sins to God, we are always met with mercy. The only thing that blocks His mercy is our refusal to confess our sin, our tendency to hide in the darkness rather than approaching the One who loves us unconditionally. Does His love waver, depending on how you behave? Do you have to "clean up" to be loved by God? No. His love is not altered by anything we do or don't do.

Meditate on this verse: "While we were yet helpless, at the right time Christ died for the ungodly. Why, one will hardly die for a righteous man—though perhaps for a good man one will dare even to die. But God shows his love for us in that while we were yet sinners Christ died for us" (Romans 5:6–8). His love and pardon are sure. There is nothing beyond the reach of His mercy. But it's up to us to ask for forgiveness. This is the first step to being born anew.

Day Five: Jesus Above All

Read John 3:22–36.

1. Some of John the Baptist's disciples were feeling a little put out and bitter as they watched many people leaving their group to follow Jesus instead. John replied, "No one can receive anything except what is given him from heaven" (John 3:27). He was saying that God had called him to step back and fade into the background, and he was content to be there. John the Baptist shows a complete lack of envy and a genuine desire to live out God's will instead of seeking attention and fame. We can learn from his example.

   In what areas of your life do you struggle with discontent? Perhaps this discontent arises from your state of life (married, single, widowed), or your job or ministry. Do you slip into comparison mode, looking at ways God has gifted others and wishing you had those same gifts and opportunities? How can John the Baptist's example help you to grow in contentment? See also 1 Corinthians 12:4–11 and Jeremiah 29:11.

2. How is John the Baptist's humility summarized in John 3:30?

Being humble means seeing ourselves as God sees us. It does not mean that we perceive ourselves as worthless. God thinks we are worth dying for, and He delights in the uniqueness of each one of us. As we see ourselves through God's eyes, we realize that "we are more sinful and flawed in ourselves than we ever dared believe, yet at the very same time we are more loved and accepted than we ever dared hope."[14]

---

14 Tim Keller and Kathy Keller, *The Meaning of Marriage: Facing the Complexities of Commitment with the Wisdom of God* (New York: Penguin Books, 2011), 44.

His love for us is intensely personal. God does not absorb His followers into one bland corporate mass of Jesus clones. Our Father delights in all the variety He has designed into each individual. It is one of the paradoxes of our faith that as we surrender (decrease) and live to honor God and not ourselves, somehow in this process we become not less but *more*—more fully ourselves, more uniquely beautiful.

3.   A.   Read John 3:31–35. How are Jesus and His ministry described in this passage?

     B.   How is the fullness of the Spirit described in Isaiah 11:2? (Note: This verse is a prophecy about the Messiah.)

4.   A.   What does John 3:36 say we have to do in order to have eternal life?

     B.   The study notes in the Ignatius Catholic Study Bible give added insight into this verse:

> Faith is exercised when we trust in God and entrust ourselves to God. Because it involves both the assent of the mind and the consent of the will, it can never be a purely intellectual decision that exists independently of one's behavior (James 2:14–26). It is because faith and faithfulness are two sides of the same coin that the opposite of faith is not just unbelief, but disobedience (CCC 161).[15]

We will find it easier to trust in God and entrust ourselves to Him when we strengthen our intellect. The "assent of the mind" described in the study note is not necessarily describing a blind leap of faith. It can come as a result of taking the time to learn the "*why*" behind what we are to believe and what we are to do.

Is there an area of your spiritual life where you find it hard to believe or obey? Have you invested time and attention trying to understand the Church's teaching or a Biblical command in a deeper way?

---

15   Study note on John 3:36, Ignatius Catholic Study Bible: The Gospel of John, Second Catholic Edition RSV (San Francisco: Ignatius Press, 2003), 24.

Quiet your heart and enjoy His presence…Take a moment to contemplate John the Baptist's humility and focus on Christ.

> *"Lord, I want to be like John the Baptist—filled with a desire to see less of me and more of You in my heart. Help me to be filled by Your Spirit so that my own selfish desires will diminish. Help me to want to see Your will fulfilled in my life. I need You to give me this desire; I can't create it myself. The pull to have my own way is so strong! I also struggle with a deep desire to be loved by those around me. I want to lead people to love You, Lord, not me. Please help me do this so that You may receive all the glory.*
>
> *"I want my life to be characterized by faith and faithfulness. Help me to take an honest look at the areas of my spiritual life where I find it hard to obey You. Guide me to people who can teach me the "why" behind it all. Give me the tenacity to dig deeper into what You've taught rather than giving up because it's hard and contrary to what I like and desire. Purify my heart, God, so that I want what You want, when You want it, how You want it. Amen."*

Conclusion

No one knows us as well as Jesus does. He looks into our hearts and sees our empty places. He sees our struggles. He knows our longings, our unmet desires, our fears, our dreams, and our hopes. He longs for us to turn to Him so that we can experience His healing touch. That doesn't mean we will live lives free from trouble. But more and more, as we follow Mary's instructions in John 2:5, "Do whatever he tells you," His kingdom will reign in our hearts, and we will grow in trust as we learn through experience that His way is the best way.

As we let His will for us determine what we do, we will feel more and more the fulfillment He promises us. We'll realize that when we live according to our own wisdom and whims, our lives are a bit like the original wine served at the wedding at Cana—basic and ordinary, thirst quenching but nothing special. But when we do things God's way, our lives become like fine wine—balanced, aromatic, and satisfying. God's will may come packaged as suffering or difficult obedience, but in the end, it is always transforming. And this is what He most desires for us—a complete interior renewal. A new birth. A fresh start.

There will be moments on this journey of transformation when the process is painful. When John the Baptist said, "He must increase, but I must decrease," he wasn't talking about a wave of a magic wand suddenly making him humble. He was describing a road of self-sacrifice that most people avoid at all costs. But John the Baptist knew that God is never outdone in generosity. Whatever he would give up for God, God would return to him many times over.

We must keep that truth at the forefront of our minds, or else just when faith and obedience are required, we'll shrink back. But if we keep our eyes fixed on the fact that "God so loved the world that he gave his only-begotten Son" (John 3:16), which means God has held nothing back from us; if we remember that "it is not by measure that he gives the Spirit" (John 3:34), which means that God offers us an unlimited supply of power, wisdom, and grace for anything we face, we will find strength and help to do the next right thing in God's eyes, day by day and moment by moment.

My Resolution

In what specific way will I apply what I learned in this lesson?

Examples:

1. I have a tendency to ask all my friends for advice and sympathy before going to Christ. This week, I resolve to start my morning with prayer time, during which I will list all my worries and concerns, presenting them first to God. I'll ask for His insight and help with these issues.

2. "He must increase, but I must decrease" (John 3:30). In order to grow in this virtue, I will pray the Litany of Humility (see appendix 5) every morning.

My Resolution:

Catechism Clips

CCC 583 Like the prophets before him Jesus expressed the deepest respect for the Temple in Jerusalem. It was in the Temple that Joseph and Mary presented him forty days after his birth. At the age of twelve he decided to remain in the Temple to remind his parents that he must be about his Father's business. He went there every year during his hidden life at least for Passover. His public ministry itself was patterned by his pilgrimages to Jerusalem for the great Jewish feasts.

CCC 584 Jesus went up to the Temple as the privileged place of encounter with God. For him, the Temple was the dwelling of his Father, a house of prayer, and he was angered that its outer court had become a place of commerce. He drove merchants out of it because of jealous love for his Father: "You shall not make my Father's house a house of trade. His disciples remembered that it was written, 'Zeal for your house will consume me.'" After his Resurrection his apostles retained their reverence for the Temple.

CCC 971 "All generations will call me blessed": "The Church's devotion to the Blessed Virgin is intrinsic to Christian worship." The Church rightly honors "the Blessed Virgin with special devotion. From the most ancient times the Blessed Virgin has been honored with the title of 'Mother of God,' to whose protection the faithful fly in all their dangers and needs...This very special devotion...differs essentially from the adoration which is given to the incarnate Word and equally to the Father and the Holy Spirit, and greatly fosters this adoration." The liturgical feasts dedicated to the Mother of God and Marian prayer, such as the rosary, an "epitome of the whole Gospel," express this devotion to the Virgin Mary.

CCC 1215 This sacrament [Baptism] is also called "the washing of regeneration and renewal by the Holy Spirit," for it signifies and actually brings about the birth of water and the Spirit without which no one "can enter the kingdom of God."

CCC 1257 The Lord himself affirms that Baptism is necessary for salvation. He also commands his disciples to proclaim the Gospel to all nations and to baptize them. Baptism is necessary for salvation for those to whom the Gospel has been proclaimed and who have had the possibility of asking for this sacrament. The Church does not know of any means other than Baptism that assures entry into eternal beatitude; this is why she takes care not to neglect the mission she has received from the Lord to see that all who can be baptized are "reborn of water and the Spirit." God has bound salvation to the sacrament of Baptism, but he himself is not bound by his sacraments.

CCC 1613 On the threshold of his public life Jesus performs his first sign—at his mother's request—during a wedding feast. The Church attaches great importance to Jesus' presence at the wedding at Cana. She sees in it the confirmation of the goodness of marriage and the proclamation that thenceforth marriage will be an efficacious sign of Christ's presence.

CCC 2618 The Gospel reveals to us how Mary prays and intercedes in faith. At Cana, the mother of Jesus asks her son for the needs of a wedding feast; this is the sign of another feast—that of the wedding of the Lamb where he gives his body and blood at the request of the Church, his Bride. It is at the hour of the New Covenant, at the foot of the cross, that Mary is heard as the Woman, the new Eve, the true "Mother of all the living."

Verse Study

See appendix 3 for instructions on how to complete a verse study.

John 3:16

1. Verse:

2. Paraphrase:

3. Questions:

4. Cross-references:

5. Personal Application:

NOTES

- Gratitude!
- healing, trust & joy
- discernment
- patience
- wisdom, patience
- focus
- Jenny –
- Better Communication
- One Day/step @ time
- memory

Lesson 4

JESUS, THE LIVING WATER

Introduction

For years my neat-as-a-pin father has been asking me to kindly come and remove my letterman jacket, dolls, books, and other childhood possessions from his basement. Figuring I am dealing with more clutter than he is, I have been a little slow to comply. At my fortieth birthday party, my dad stood up to make a speech. I prepared for some words of encouragement or a compliment or two (it was, after all, my birthday), but when I saw him take a brightly colored notebook out of his jacket, I realized I was in for a surprise. The notebook was my high school diary (found in one of the basement boxes), and he opened it and began to read. After a few lines that were thankfully rather benign, he said, "I have a deal for you, Lisa. If you *promise* that you will come and take your boxes from the basement, I will give you this diary. If you don't, I will give it to Amy [my then-sixteen-year-old daughter]." You'd be amazed at how quickly I promised.

I didn't want Amy to read my diary because what it revealed was a younger me, desperate for a boyfriend. I longed for the validation, the prom date, to be someone's favorite. I wanted another person to fill up what was lacking in me and to love me unconditionally. Page after page documented the searches, the victories, and the heartaches.

We could chalk this up to normal high school longings. I think it reveals something more: a desire to be pursued and romanced and completed. I think most of us share this desire, and it lasts long past high school. So often we look for a man to fill us and validate who we are. But no man can do what God wants to do in the hearts of His precious daughters. He has left a part of our hearts accessible only to Him.

Our reading today starts with the story of a woman who had the longings I've just described, and she went from man to man in search of fulfillment and happiness. Considering the number of husbands she had, I think we can conclude that she wasn't very satisfied. She was broken and in need of healing. She had a thirst for true love that wasn't being quenched. Her search ended with an offer of living water—an offer that came from an unexpected source. It was an offer of refreshment, healing, and restoration, and it's available to you and me today. Are you thirsty?

Day One: A Divine Appointment

Some background information from the Old Testament is helpful in understanding this passage.

In the Old Testament book of 1 Kings, the kingdom of Israel split in half when King Solomon's son (King Rehoboam) took over the throne. Ten Israelite tribes remained together in the northern kingdom and retained the name Israel. Two tribes banded together in the southern kingdom. Their kingdom was called Judah. The northern tribes fell into idolatry, and so God allowed Assyria to conquer them, hoping that their suffering would draw them back to Him.

When Israel was taken over by the Assyrians, many of the Israelites were deported. In their place the Assyrians shipped in people from Babylon, Cuthah, Avva, Hamath, and Sepharvaim and settled them in the midst of the remaining Israelites. Eventually the two groups mingled and intermarried. That region of Israel was renamed Samaria. Samaria was the region of Israel that had previously been inhabited by the tribe of Ephraim.

The people whom the Assyrians resettled in Israel (from Babylon, Cuthah, Avva, Hamath, and Sepharvaim) brought with them their worship of pagan gods. God wasn't pleased with this, and He sent lions among them to kill them. Word of this reached the King of Assyria, who requested that one of the Israelite priests whom he had deported be sent back to instruct the Samaritans in the true worship of God. The people had blended and had mixed the worship of the God of Abraham with the worship of the pagan gods, called Baals.

1. A. Describe the Samaritan religion based on the background information given. (See also 2 Kings 17:33.)

B. Why do you think the Jews later avoided contact with the Samaritans?

With that background in mind, read John 4:1–8.

2. Drawing water at the well was a daily ritual for women during this time of history. It was a wonderful opportunity to chat with friends and catch up on current happenings. Women typically drew water during the cooler times of the day—early in the morning or in the evening. The Samaritan woman came alone to draw her water at noon: "It was about the sixth hour" (John 4:6).

3. Why do you think she came at this time of day?

A. Think about what rejection and broken relationships do to the heart of a woman. How do you think the Samaritan woman at the well felt about herself when she met Jesus? What kind of hurts might she have carried deep within?

B. Can you relate to the Samaritan woman? Have you ever avoided getting together with certain people because you felt you didn't measure up to them in terms of accomplishments, beauty, or wealth?

We may hold it together on the outside, but so many of us are walking around with deep hurt and hunger within: the high school girl who gives away her virginity hoping to guarantee love; the woman who hates herself so much that she eats to fill the void; the woman who throws up what she eats in order to find control and attain the "right" body; the divorced woman who wonders if she'll ever be loved again; the married woman whose marriage is not what she hoped it would be; the woman who whispers, "Is this all there is?"…

There are a lot of aching hearts looking for healing.

Quiet your heart and enjoy His presence…Take a moment to contemplate a specific hurt or insecurity within you.

indifferent
ignored
invisible
loved
hated
not as hard
accept

"Chosen"
Penn Cinurs
amazon Prime

Open that part of your heart to God and ask Him to bring healing and freedom there. That's why Jesus came. He came to bind up the brokenhearted and to proclaim freedom to the captives. He came for you. Thank Him for loving you that much and for caring about the little hurts and the enormous pains that you have experienced and are experiencing. Let Him wrap His arms around you. Rest there.

Day Two: The Living Water

Read John 4:7–15.

1. When Jesus speaks of "living water," what does He mean? See CCC 2652.

2. According to the Catholic Catechism, what are four wellsprings where Christ awaits so that He may enable us to drink of the Holy Spirit?

    A. The _____ of _____ (CCC 2653)

    B. The _____ of the _____ (CCC 2655)

    C. The _____ _____ (CCC 2656–2658), which are

       _____ , _____ , and _____

    D. _____ (CCC 2659)

    E. In which of these ways do you most feel the presence of the Holy Spirit?

3. Read John 4:13–14 and Jeremiah 2:13.

   A. What two evils did the people do in Jeremiah 2:13?

   B. Which "broken cisterns" do you tend to turn to when in need?

We can relate to the Israelites. We, too, struggle to turn to God first. Jesus offers us His Spirit—living water—which is the best source of comfort, guidance, and hope. Too often our response is, "Just a minute, Jesus! Let me try out some of my own solutions first. Let me see if my girlfriend has something to say to make me feel better. Let me have a glass of wine (or two, or three) and see if that doesn't take the edge off. Let me surf the internet for a while and find a little something to purchase that will perk me up. Let me grab that bunch of cookies and see if I feel satisfied."

Jesus says to us, "That cistern is empty. You won't find what you're looking for there."

Quiet your heart and enjoy His presence…Take a moment to contemplate the satisfaction that only Jesus can give. Read Psalm 63:1–5 as a prayer:

> *O God, you are my God, I seek you,*
> *my soul thirsts for you;*
> *my flesh faints for you,*
> *as in a dry and weary land where no water is*
> *So I have looked upon you in the sanctuary,*
> *beholding your power and glory.*
> *Because your merciful love is better than life,*
> *my lips will praise you.*
> *So I will bless you as long as I live;*
> *I will lift up my hands and call on your name.*
> *My soul is feasted as with marrow and fat,*
> *and my mouth praises you with joyful lips.*

Day Three: Tender Honesty

Read John 4:16–26.

1. When Jesus offered living water to the Samaritan woman, all sorts of thoughts probably ran through her head: *If He really knew me, He probably wouldn't be offering me this spiritual gift. He'd know that I'm not worth it. I'm so glad that none of the other women are around to tell Him about my past!* Then out of the blue, Jesus revealed that He knew all about her many relationships and had known from the beginning of their conversation. He was unlike anyone she'd ever met.

    A. Based on what you know of Jesus, what tone do you think He used when speaking to the Samaritan woman as recorded in verses 16–18?

    B. Why do you think Jesus brought attention to her sin? See 1 John 1:8–9.

Sin isn't always a spectacular event. In essence sin is estrangement from God. Often our relationship with God becomes estranged not because we do something terrible but simply because of neglect, because of drift. Think about a relationship in your life that has gone from closeness to "Christmas-card-exchange" status. Sometimes people just grow apart. They stop spending time together. They don't call as often. There is no intention to hurt the other person or cut off the relationship; the closeness and intimacy between you just wanes.

To experience the living water of the Holy Spirit, we need to experience a conversion of heart just as Nicodemus did. The first step in that conversion is reconciling with God. We begin by saying, "I have not loved You the way I should. I've ignored You. I admit You haven't felt real to me, and instead of doing all I can to grow closer to You, I've filled up my life with other things."

    C. The sacrament of Reconciliation leads us back to intimacy with God. What lesson does each of the following verses contain that can serve as encouragement when preparing for this sacrament?

    Ephesians 3:17–19

2 Corinthians 5:17–19

2. In John 4:20, the Samaritan woman said, "Our fathers worshiped on this mountain; and you say that in Jerusalem is the place where men ought to worship." How did Jesus describe the type of worship that God was looking for?

The Samaritan woman connected worship to a geographical place. But worshipping in spirit denotes internal worship—not just external. It's worshipping with our heart, mind, and soul, through the Holy Spirit. It's not about going to a particular place; it's about what is going on within us.

Worshipping in truth means we are worshipping who God really is—not a figment of our imagination. We need to take the time to learn what is true about God and what is true about the way that He wants to be worshipped. Our worship needs to be free from idolatry. This was an issue for the Samaritans, but we struggle with idolatry, too, whenever we give something in our lives the importance that is due only to God.

3. Jesus didn't reveal His identity as the Messiah to Nicodemus, the religious leader. He revealed Himself to the Samaritan woman, an outcast. In fact there are only three times when Jesus accepts the title "Messiah": here at the well in Samaria, when Peter declares it (Matthew 16:16), and at His trial (Mark 14:61–62). Why is this? What do you think it was about the Samaritan woman that compelled Jesus to reveal Himself to her?

Jesus was always aware of His limited time on earth and didn't want to prematurely ignite the passion and anger of the religious leaders. Claiming to be the Messiah would have riled them up. Perhaps He saw a spiritual hunger and an openness in her. She had looked for love in so many places with so many men. He saw her need and her shredded heart, together with her fragile faith, and it just ripped His holy heart open. He could not hold back from offering everything to this desperate, outcast daughter. He wanted her to know that she had a Savior—and He was standing in front of her.

wealth – self
pleasure – self
power – self
honor of self

- *Someone on my side*
- *want taught*

Quiet your heart and enjoy His presence…Jesus thirsts for you.

> *"I AM" begs for water from one of the most despised and broken women,*
> *who is no one, with no name, who is nothing in the eyes of society.*
> *Jesus reveals to her who she is and who she will become—*
> *a source of the waters of life of God—*
> *if she opens up her heart to him and receives his love.*
> *Misery and mercy meet in love.*[16]

No matter what you believe disqualifies you from God's love, the truth is, Jesus delights in you. He wants to hear all the details of your life—the worries, the joys, the dreams. Do you often keep Him waiting? Tell Him you are sorry for the times you've ignored Him and accept His loving embrace. Share with Him what is heavy on your heart right now. He is the best listener. Ask Him for the specific grace you need today. He will not pull away. He will always lean in, beckoning you closer.

Day Four: The Transformation

Read John 4:27–42.

1. A. Because she had encountered Jesus, the Samaritan woman was utterly transformed. Remember that this was a woman who so wanted to avoid contact with the other women of the community that she chose to collect her water at the hottest time of day. What did her encounter with Jesus cause her to do in John 4:27–29?

    B. The water jar that had seemed so essential when she arrived at the well was left behind. The Samaritan woman had discovered something (actually, someone) that mattered so much more. Think of your own time and the things that demand your attention. Are there any smaller things that could be set aside so you have more time to devote to matters of greater importance?

---

16 Jean Vanier, *Drawn into the Mystery of Jesus Through the Gospel of John* (Ottawa, Canada: Novalis, 2004), 98.

C. One could certainly argue that the Samaritan woman lacked training as an evangelist. But her honest and enthusiastic words resulted in many coming out of the city to meet Jesus. She had no theological training. She didn't know apologetics or the best way to defend the faith. But she could share her personal experience. She shared the change Jesus had made in her life. She had a before-and-after moment, and she could explain that. Think of your own life. What was it like before you encountered Jesus? Can you think of one word to describe what your life was like without Him and one word to describe the difference He has made? Record them here. This is all you need to be able to share your faith with others. You don't need a lot of words, just courage enough to share what you've experienced.

2. How did Jesus respond when the disciples offered Him food? Why did He respond this way? See John 4:32–34. How important is our response to Jesus? Does it matter to Him?

3. What harvest was Jesus speaking of in verse 35? See also Luke 10:2.

4. What are three ways Jesus encouraged His disciples in their work for Him in John 4:36?

Quiet your heart and enjoy His presence...Take a moment to contemplate the need in your loved ones' lives for Christ.

Can you remember what those days felt like before your faith really came alive? Can you remember feeling empty and unsettled inside? Did you find yourself filling up your life with all sorts of things, but nothing totally satisfied? Did you have fears of the future? Did you long for something more?

Is there anyone in your life who is still in that place? Do you have a friend who is all about the superficial, feels empty, lacks purpose? Is there someone you love who has lost all hope, sees no way anything will ever change, and is stuck in a rut of self-destructive habits?

It's so easy to look at someone and say, "Boy, does she ever need God in her life. I'll pray for her." And we may even pray, "God, bring people into her life who can tell her about You!" But we don't want to be the person. We don't want people to think we are weird. We don't want to offend. We don't know what to say. We conclude, "I'll just live out my faith through my actions, and that should be enough." Sometimes we think we're required to answer every question, never reveal a flaw, and have perfect communication skills. Since that seems impossible to achieve, we figure we'd better not try.

Which would be fine if the goal was our own comfort. But the Bible suggests that our comfort isn't God's main objective:

"Things that we have heard and known, that our fathers have told us. We will not hide them from their children, but tell to the coming generation" (Psalm 78:3–4).

"You received without pay, give without pay" (Matthew 10:8).

"See to it that no one fail to obtain the grace of God" (Hebrews 12:15).

What step could you take to share your before-and-after moment with someone you love?

Day Five: The Healing of an Official's Son

Read John 4:43–54.

In this passage, Jesus returned to Cana, the location of His first sign (turning water into wine). It was also in Cana that His second sign took place. The story involved an "official." A Roman-Jewish historian named Josephus used this term ("official") to describe the officers who worked for Herod Antipas, the Tetrarch of Galilee. This official would have been a man of influence and well-respected in Roman circles.

1. Do you think it would have been difficult for the royal official to approach Jesus for a healing? What would his coworkers and family have thought? What motivated his pursuit of Jesus?

2. How did Jesus heal the official's son? What was the official's reaction?

3. As with Jesus' first sign in Cana, this second sign represents a miracle that God wants to perform in the life of each of His children. Jesus healed the royal official's son. He wants to bring healing to us too. The first step for the royal official was realizing that he was out of options and needed to turn to Jesus for help. This is the first step for us too. In what specific area of your life would you like to see healing occur? Write a short prayer asking Jesus to touch you with His healing power.

Quiet your heart and enjoy His presence...Take a moment to contemplate Jesus as the Great Physician.

Think about His power. He spoke, and the world came into being. He touches, and healing occurs. Think of times in your life when He has healed and restored you in some way. Thank Him for His constant care and for His desire to touch with healing what is ailing and broken in our lives.

Conclusion

Have you ever been confronted by a friend regarding an area of your life that needs change? Her words may have been hard to receive. It takes a very special person to confront things in a manner that makes you feel more loved than criticized. I've always been amazed by the way the woman at the well received Jesus' words. He spoke directly to her area of greatest sin, and she responded by telling everyone how amazing He was. What was His delivery like? How did He look in her eyes? What compassion did He show her?

What do you think will really bring about the change within you that you long to see? I believe we are far more motivated by love for Jesus than we are by a set of rules or fear of punishment. A set of religious regulations, if not adhered to by a heart in love, can quickly feel like a weight around our ankles.

In the same way, your love can draw others to Jesus. You might mistakenly think that in order to be a significant person in someone's spiritual journey, you need to be full of knowledge. Nothing could be further from the truth. You need to be full of love. And you need to do whatever you can to be easy to love. When a person is drawn to you, you can, in turn, point them to Christ. You don't do that by knowing more than they do. You accomplish this by being transparent and admitting your flaws. You do it by pulling back the curtain, dropping the mask, and letting them see that you really need God and that He comes through for you. No one needs you to be perfect. But you will be much easier to love if you can be honest about your mistakes and failings.

There is simply no substitute for your physical presence in the life of your loved one. There's no substitute for time—time spent listening—and, when God gives you the nudge, time spent pointing to Him. It doesn't have to be with a big theological explanation. But if you never mention Him at all, people will have no idea *why* you are different.

I think there is nothing better than walking alongside a friend while she begins to open her heart to God. Stepping out and exploring spiritual matters is a huge exit from the comfort zone for most people. It's one thing to say to a friend, "You really should be over there. That's a good place to grow spiritually."

It's quite another to say, "Let's do this together. Would you go through a Bible study with me? I'd just love to have that time with you." Don't underestimate the power of your presence. It just might end up changing someone's life.

My Resolution

In what specific way will I apply what I learned in this lesson?

Examples:

1. Instead of ignoring Christ when life gets busy, I will commit to starting and ending my day in prayer. I want Christ to be the first and the last person I talk to each day this week.

2. I will commit to praying each day for a specific loved one to experience new spiritual life in Christ.

My Resolution:

Catechism Clips

CCC 2652 The Holy Spirit is the *living water* "welling up to eternal life" in the heart that prays. It is He who teaches us to accept it at its source: Christ. Indeed in the Christian life there are several wellsprings where Christ awaits us to enable us to drink of the Holy Spirit.

The Word Of God
CCC 2653 The Church "forcefully and specially exhorts all the Christian faithful…to learn "the surpassing knowledge of Jesus Christ" (Philippians 3:8) by frequent reading of the divine Scriptures…Let them remember, however, that prayer should accompany the reading of Sacred Scripture, so that a dialogue takes place between God and man. For "we speak to him when we pray; we listen to him when we read the divine oracles."

The Liturgy of the Church
CCC 2655 In the sacramental liturgy of the Church, the mission of Christ and of the Holy Spirit proclaims, makes present, and communicates the mystery of salvation, which is continued in the heart that prays. The spiritual writers sometimes compare the heart to an altar. Prayer internalizes and assimilates the liturgy during and after its celebration. Even when it is lived out "in secret," prayer is always prayer *of the Church*; it is a communion with the Holy Trinity.

The Theological Virtues
CCC 2656 One enters into prayer as one enters into liturgy: by the narrow gate of *faith*. Through the signs of his presence, it is the Face of the Lord that we seek and desire; it is his Word that we want to hear and keep.

CCC 2657 The Holy Spirit, who instructs us to celebrate the liturgy in expectation of Christ's return, teaches us to pray in *hope*. Conversely, the prayer of the Church and personal prayer nourish hope in us. The psalms especially, with their concrete and varied language, teach us to fix our hope in God: "I waited patiently for the lord; he inclined to me and heard my cry." As St. Paul prayed: "May the God of hope fill you with all joy and peace in believing, so that by the power of the Holy Spirit you may abound in hope."

CCC 2658 "Hope does not disappoint us, because God's *love* has been poured into our hearts by the Holy Spirit who has been given to us." Prayer, formed by the liturgical life, draws everything into the love by which we are loved in Christ and which enables us to respond to him by loving as he has loved us. Love is the source of prayer; whoever draws from it reaches the summit of prayer.

Today

CCC 2659 We learn to pray at certain moments by hearing the Word of the Lord and sharing in his Paschal mystery, but his Spirit is offered us at all times, in the events of each day, to make prayer spring up from us.

- Understand/accept election
- trust/healing
- Balance day/time
- Comfort
- Perseverence
- Peaceful heart
- Special intentions
- focus

Verse Study

See appendix 3 for instructions on how to complete a verse study.

John 4:14

1. Verse:

2. Paraphrase:

3. Questions:

4. Cross-references:

5. Personal Application:

# NOTES

Lesson 5: Connect Coffee Talk 2

JESUS, THE LIVING WATER

The accompanying talk can be viewed via DVD or digital download purchase or accessed online at walkingwithpurpose.com/videos.

Key Verses

"Whoever drinks of the water that I shall give him will never thirst; the water that I shall give him will become in him a spring of water welling up to eternal life" (John 4:14).

"And I will betroth you to me for ever; I will betroth you to me in righteousness and in justice, in steadfast love, and in mercy. I will betroth you to me in faithfulness; and you shall know the LORD" (Hosea 2:19-20 [RSVCE]).

"For freedom Christ has set us free; stand fast therefore, and do not submit again to a yoke of slavery" (Galatians 5:1).

"I led them with cords of human kindness, with ties of love. To them I was like one who lifts a little child to the cheek, and I bent down to feed them" (Hosea 11:4 [NIV]).

Jesus invites us to run to Him in our hour of need.

Jesus had a very personal, one-on-one connection with the Samaritan woman. He sought her out and found her and satisfied her deepest needs. He wants to do the same for each one of us.

Just as He did with the Samaritan woman, Jesus calls us to:

I. **Recognize Our False Gods**

    A. Identify our "empty cisterns." Where do we go to fill our longings?

    B. Conquer our cravings and redirect them to God.

II. **Invite Him into Our Struggle**

    A. Confess our attachments.

    B. Ask the Lord to dig out the web of roots that entangle us.

    C. Relinquish what feels good in the moment for what is best for eternity.

III. **Depend on His Strength to Persevere**

    A. Count on the Lord's strength as we write a new pattern into our life.

    B. Run to the Lord with *all* of our needs.

He is the only One who will quench the thirst inside us.

Questions for Discussion or Journaling

1. Which "broken cisterns" do you tend to turn to when in need? Is there a "well" you keep returning to that has run dry?

2. It's critical that we lean on the Lord's strength and not our own as we work to persevere in writing a new pattern into our lives. What are some practical things you can do to apply that truth to your current challenges?

3. In John 4:14, Jesus promised that "whoever drinks the water I give them will never thirst; the water I shall give them will become in them a spring of water welling up to eternal life." Have you ever experienced Jesus satisfying or refreshing you, despite your circumstances not being changed?

NOTES

Lesson 6

Jesus, the Authority

Introduction

Things I haven't felt like doing today:

1. Getting up early to pray

   My excuse: I'm very tired. I need sleep, or I will be crabby all day long.

2. Giving my child a good morning hug *before* launching into the morning litany ("Have you made your bed? Brushed your teeth? Put fruit in your lunch? Studied for your test? Found your other shoe?")

   My excuse: The bed is not made. The teeth are not brushed. There is nothing but junk in the lunch. The last test grade was bad. The shoe is *always* missing at the last minute. And I have about two seconds before I have to jump in the shower.

3. Exercising

   My excuse: I had the flu last week, and if I really concentrate, I think I feel a vestige of nausea.

4. Thanking my husband for the good things he does instead of noticing every little thing that he could do better

   My excuse: Life could be made easier for me (and I'd get so much more done) if everyone would just do things my way.

Excuses, excuses. If I give in to them, I'll get temporary relief, but I'll be forfeiting what I actually want most. What do I really want? I want to be a woman of character who is close to God and a blessing to her family. And if I want that desire to go from being something I hope for to being my reality, I'll need to humble myself before the Lord and ask Him to give me both the will and the strength to do the next right thing.

Don't we all want the fullness of life embodied in satisfaction, peace, and joy? We want to experience healing in those places within us that are broken. We want freedom from our bad habits and painful memories. These aren't new desires. They are as old as humankind. And we, like the generations before us, want those desires fulfilled in the way and with the timing that we prefer. We don't want to bow to a higher authority. Often times this is because we fear the unknown. Part of us prefers bondage to the familiar rather than the uncertainty that comes with a journey to freedom. All too often we cling to what cripples us.

Our readings for this week begin with the healing of a man who has been crippled for years. This is the third of Jesus' signs. When Jesus encounters him, He asks, "Do you want to get well?" He asks the same of us. How will we respond? Will we answer yes and then cooperate with His work in our lives, or will we sit in a rut, tired of the same old, same old but lacking the humility to acknowledge our desperate need for God's wisdom, power, and grace? Will we kick our excuses to the curb and do the hard work of submitting to God's authority in our lives, doing things His way?

He has plans for each one of us that He put together when we were still in our mothers' wombs.[17] They are plans to help us prosper, not to harm us;[18] plans to give us hope and a future. But until we get to the point where we recognize His authority in our lives and the superiority of His plan compared to our own, we'll be settling for less than His best. So no more excuses. Let's get walking.

Day One: The Pool of Bethzatha

Read John 5:1–6.

As soon as Jesus arrived in Jerusalem, He went to the pool of Bethzatha. Invalids surrounded this pool because they were waiting for the movement of the water. It was said that "an angel of the Lord went down at certain seasons into the pool, and

---

17 "Before I formed you in the womb I knew you, and before you were born I consecrated you" (Jeremiah 1:5). "For you formed my inward parts, you knitted me together in my mother's womb…You know me right well…Your eyes beheld my unformed substance; in your book were written, every one of them, the days that were formed for me, when as yet there was none of them" (Psalm 139:13, 14, 16).

18 "For I know the plans I have for you, says the Lord, plans for welfare and not for evil, to give you a future and a hope" (Jeremiah 29:11).

troubled the water; whoever stepped in first after the troubling of the water was healed of whatever disease he had."[19]

1. Imagine yourself in the midst of this scene. What does it smell like? What is the overall spirit among the people there? What thoughts might have been running through the mind of the paralyzed man as he lay by the pool? Many people were gathered there. Do you think it felt like a community?

2. Blind, lame, and paralyzed people sat around the pool in hopes of being the first into the water if it began to bubble. As Jesus looked at them, He saw more than their physical disabilities. He saw their interior sicknesses as well.

   A. In what ways are people today struggling with interior blindness, lameness, and paralysis?

   B. Where do you see evidence of blindness, lameness, or paralysis in your inner life?

3. Being spiritually lame can also be described as being lukewarm. We're neither hot nor cold—neither spiritually on fire nor completely without interest. Jesus spoke to a lukewarm people in Revelation 3:15–19.

   A. What do you learn about these people from verse 17?

   B. What were they encouraged to do in verses 18 and 19?

   C. What verse from this reading indicates that Jesus takes spiritual lameness, or being lukewarm, very seriously?

---

19 Ignatius Catholic Study Bible: New Testament, Second Catholic Edition RSV (San Francisco: Ignatius Press, 2010), 171.

Quiet your heart and enjoy His presence...Jesus came for you.

Luke 4:18 reveals what Jesus came to do: "The Spirit of the Lord is upon me, because he has anointed me to preach good news to the poor. He has sent me to proclaim release to the captives and recovering of sight to the blind, to set at liberty those who are oppressed."

Ask Him to lift from your eyes any blindness that is preventing you from seeing His work in your life. Ask for the grace to see the many times He intersects your life to bring joy, protection, and comfort. Thank Him for these countless graces.

Day Two: Do You Want to Be Healed?

Read John 5:1–9.

1. A. What did Jesus ask the paralyzed man in verse 6?

    B. Why do you think He asked this question?

Physical weakness, emotional pain, spiritual inertia, fear of what it might cost us, and depression can all rob us of the willpower to do our part to bring change. Jesus wanted to know that the man was ready to leave the familiar discomfort of his paralysis and take the risk of going on a journey of healing.

    C. What was the paralyzed man's answer? Write his response in your own words.

2. A. How did Jesus invite the man to make an act of faith and cooperate in his own healing? See John 5:8.

B. Jesus knows we are crippled. He knows the extent of our brokenness, both internal and external. He will never ask us to reach beyond our ability, but He will ask us to reach our limit. Then He will extend His loving hand and meet us there. What paralyzes you and keeps you from reaching for Christ's hand? What specific things are holding you back from taking the first steps toward healing?

C. What do the following verses teach us about how we can cooperate in our own healing?

Mark 1:35

Philippians 4:4–7

Philippians 4:8–9

Quiet your heart and enjoy His presence…Take a moment to contemplate your own spiritual blindness, lameness, or paralysis.

Jesus asks you, "Do you want to be well? Do you want to be whole? Do you want to experience the abundant life I have planned for you?"

Talk with Him about your desire for healing as well as what you are afraid of. If you want to see change, ask Him to intersect your life, bringing transformation. If you are afraid of what that change might entail, pray for the desire to do whatever it takes to live your life according to His plan. Take a moment to prayerfully imagine what life would be like on the other side of his healing action. Sometimes we have been hurting for so long and so deeply that it will take a healing work of God for us to even want to do things His way. He understands.

Day Three: Healing on the Sabbath

Read John 5:9–18.

1. A. Why were the Jews upset that the man had picked up his pallet and was walking with it?

    B. See Jeremiah 17:21–22. What was the purpose of this Sabbath law?

    C. What did Jesus consider the purpose of the Sabbath day? See CCC 2173.

The Jewish authorities were so busy finding fault with others that they completely missed the miracle in their midst. Yet before we are too hard on them, we need to wonder, Have we ever done the same thing? What thoughts run through our heads when we're sitting behind a mother with badly behaving children at Mass? Do we judge her or recognize that it's a miracle that she is there? With our loved ones, are we more apt to criticize the way they are doing things, or do we appreciate little miracles in their willingness to help? Do we criticize our pastor, or do we recognize that his fidelity to the priesthood is a miracle of God?

2. What insights do the following verses give us about judging others?

    Matthew 7:1–5

    1 Samuel 16:7

    Ephesians 4:32

3. Think of a person whom you tend to judge. What is something specific you can do to offer that person mercy instead of judgment? Could you practice curiosity, asking questions and gaining information before making assumptions? Could you practice empathy, taking time to look at things from his or her perspective? Could you make note of your own thoughts and emotions? Are you feeling nervous, insecure, or upset? Could your feelings be clouding your judgment?

4. A. John 5:18 reveals an additional reason, besides breaking the Sabbath, for why the Jews wanted to kill Jesus. What was it?

   B. In what way were the Jews doing the very thing they were accusing Jesus of? See James 4:12.

Quiet your heart and enjoy His presence…Take a moment to contemplate the little miracles that God performs every day in your life.

Thank Him for three specific things that you may not have noticed in the past few days. Ask Him to open your eyes to see circumstances and people as He does.

Slow me down, Lord. It's hard for me to see people as You do when I am rushing past them. It's hard for me to take the time to think about their hurts or their intentions and far easier for me to make a quick judgment. I ask for Your eyes so that I can see the good in people. Free me from a critical spirit.

Day Four: The Right to Judge

Read John 5:18–29.

1. Why did the Jews want to kill Jesus? (See John 5:18.)

2. A. We established during day three that it's not our job to judge others. Who *has* been given the right to judge others? See John 5:22, 26, and 27.

B. Why does He have the right to judge? See CCC 679.

3. A. The Last Judgment is described in John 5:28–29 and CCC 1038. Describe the two different types of resurrection.

   B. Do we get another chance after death to choose Christ? See CCC 1021 and Hebrews 9:27.

4. How do these verses reveal Jesus' heart as He contemplates judgment day?

   John 3:17

   2 Peter 3:9

5. "For the gate is narrow and the way is hard, that leads to life, and those who find it are few" (Matthew 7:14). But this gate is wide enough for every person to pass through. According to CCC 679, whose choice determines whether we make it through the gate?

Quiet your heart and enjoy His presence...Take a moment to contemplate the following truth: God is God, and I am not.

Say it out loud: God is the judge; I am not. As my Creator, God gets to decide what is required of me to spend eternity with Him. Does He stand over me with fire in His eyes, waiting to catch me messing up? No.

God, my Creator, chose to stoop down, gently wipe the dirt off my face, and pay the price for my sin. He gives me a choice. Do I want to do it my way or His way? Do I want to receive what is due me according to my works (which will fall short of what He requires), or do I want to receive what is not my due but is a gift of grace? God offers me eternal life, but not based on my own merits. He offers me this gift because of the merits of His Son.

Oh, Spirit of love, come fill my heart! All I can offer You is empty hands, but I ask You to fill them with Yourself. I give You my heart and ask You to reside there.

Day Five: The Testimony to Jesus

Read John 5:30–47.

1. Jewish law required two or three witnesses for a claim in court (Deuteronomy 19:15). In John 5:30–47, Jesus wasn't in a court of law. Nevertheless His authority was being questioned by the Jews. There were many witnesses who testified to Jesus' authority; thus He had more than the number required by law. What different witnesses does He mention in these verses?

2. Jesus' words to the Jews are direct. Why was He speaking so strongly to them? What was He trying to accomplish? See John 5:34.

3. A. What did Jesus say was one reason the Jews refused to believe in Him? See John 5:44.

   B. One of the things that hold people back from believing in Jesus is the same thing described in John 5:44. All too often it matters more to us what other people think of us than what God thinks. Is there anyone in your life whose opinion matters greatly to you and, as a result, causes you to hold back from fully surrendering to God? Or do you find yourself editing your words around him or her, not sharing authentically about your faith in God? What are you afraid you will lose if you are more honest? Could it be that in holding back, you are preventing this person from seeing an authentic witness of the difference Christ can make in someone's life?

Quiet your heart and enjoy His presence…Take a moment to contemplate Jesus' authority and His love.

God, as the Creator and sustainer of all, could command our obedience from a "distant heaven." Yet for all his power, He is not distant but near. Jesus chooses to walk with us, even to carry us, and to offer Himself as food for the journey back to our Father. The things that keep us from trusting Him (our excuses) are only preventing us from walking in the path of His blessings and His healing love.

Lord, help me to see Your will so clearly and compellingly that all my excuses fall by the wayside. As I lean on Your grace, help me to obey You with my whole heart.

Conclusion

Isn't it hard to want what God wants? When I stop to listen to the Lord and lay my plans before Him, sometimes I find that He calls me to a steeper path than I would have otherwise chosen. Other times He commands rest when I am wrestling with not doing enough. Whether He asks more or less of me, His plans are always better than mine are. Sometimes I need the reminder that God is God, and I am not. I need to remember that when God laid out the plan for the *best* way to live on earth and the *only* way to spend eternity with Him, He wasn't just making little suggestions. He was offering me a lifeline.

One thing I know: *I want to be well.* I long to live a fulfilling, healthy life of wholeness and purpose. Over the years I have learned that the key to experiencing that kind of life is listening attentively to Jesus in prayer and walking the road of obedience to His will. The following quote from Saint Thérèse of Lisieux is a beautiful example of this degree of abandonment. I pray my heart would become more like hers. Can you join me in that prayer that God would do the same work in us that He did in her? Remember Luke 1:37, "For with God, nothing will be impossible." Saint Thérèse writes:

> I desire neither suffering nor death, yet I love both; but it is love alone which attracts me. I have no other compass. My heart is full of the will of Jesus. Ah, if my soul weren't already filled with His will, if it had to be filled by the feelings of joy and sadness which follow each other so quickly, it would be a tide of very bitter sorrow. But these alternatives do nothing but brush across my soul. I always remain in a profound peace, which nothing can trouble. If the Lord offered me the choice, I would not choose anything; I want nothing but what He wants. It is what He does that I love. I acknowledge that it took me a long time to bring myself to this degree of abandonment. Now I have reached it, for the Lord took me and put me there.[20]

---

20   d'Elbee, *I Believe in Love*, 86.

It encourages me that Saint Thérèse admitted that it took her a long time to get to that degree of interior surrender. I'm not there yet, but I want to be. I'm so grateful that God sees our desires and knows who we *want* to be. As we begin the process of spiritual healing and growth in obedience, God knows that the road ahead can be overwhelming and scary. He wants to walk with us, right by our side, throughout the journey. He isn't like a drill sergeant who screams at us to get up and get going. He gently asks us if we want to be well, and then He leads us by the hand and by the heart. His yoke is easy, and His burden is light.

My Resolution

In what specific way will I apply what I learned in this lesson?

Examples:

1. I will identify an area of my life where I have been reluctant to obey God. I will list my excuses and examine how they prevent me from walking in faith and receiving the blessings of obedience. I will write a response to each excuse. If I can't think of one, I will ask for input from someone I trust. Here is an example: *God wants me to stop gossiping. My excuse: I feel more interesting to others when I do. My response: While gossiping may interest others, it ultimately leads them to see me as untrustworthy. Gossip also hurts others and hurts God. My resolution: I will acknowledge my weakness before God and ask for His grace to resist the temptation to gossip this week.*

2. I will begin each day with this reminder: God is God, and I am not. When things don't go my way, I'll say it again. When God allows suffering to intersect my day, I'll say it again. When I want my way instead of God's way, I'll say it again.

My Resolution:

Catechism Clips

CCC 679 Christ is Lord of eternal life. Full right to pass definitive judgment on the works and hearts of men belongs to him as redeemer of the world. He "acquired" this right by his cross. The Father has given "all judgment to the Son." Yet the Son did not come to judge, but to save and to give the life he has in himself. By rejecting grace in this life, one already judges oneself, receives according to one's works, and can even condemn oneself for all eternity by rejecting the Spirit of love.

CCC 1021 Death puts an end to human life as the time open to either accepting or rejecting the divine grace manifested in Christ. The New Testament speaks of judgment primarily in its aspect of the final encounter with Christ in his second coming, but also repeatedly affirms that each will be rewarded immediately after death in accordance with his works and faith. The parable of the poor man Lazarus and the words of Christ on the cross to the good thief, as well as other New Testament texts, speak of a final destiny of the soul—a destiny which can be different for some and for others.

CCC 1038 The resurrection of all the dead, "of both the just and the unjust," will precede the Last Judgment. This will be "the hour when all who are in the tombs will hear [the Son of man's] voice and come forth, those who have done good, to the resurrection of life, and those who have done evil, to the resurrection of judgment." Then Christ will come "in his glory, and all the angels with him...Before him will be gathered all the nations, and he will separate them one from another as a shepherd separates the sheep from the goats, and he will place the sheep at his right hand, but the goats at the left...And they will go away into eternal punishment but the righteous into eternal life."

CCC 2173 The Gospel reports many incidents when Jesus was accused of violating the Sabbath law. But Jesus never fails to respect the holiness of this day. He gives this law its authentic and authoritative interpretation: "The Sabbath was made for man, not man for the Sabbath." With compassion, Christ declares the Sabbath for doing good rather than harm, for saving life rather than killing. The Sabbath is the day of the Lord of mercies and a day to honor God. "The Son of Man is lord even of the Sabbath."

Verse Study

See appendix 3 for instructions on how to complete a verse study.

John 5:23

1. Verse:

2. Paraphrase:

3. Questions:

4. Cross-references:

5. Personal Application:

NOTES

Lesson 7

JESUS, THE EUCHARIST

Introduction

True confessions:

After singing a solo during a church service while in high school, I told my mom that it really bothered me that no one had clapped at the end of it. No matter how much she patiently explained that my comment indicated I was missing the point of why I was singing, I continued to think that a little round of applause would have been appropriate.

Years later I sat in Mass, confounded by two things I was observing. One, I couldn't figure out why all parents weren't using the nursery for their little ones. A friend of mine explained that she wanted her daughter, from the start, to be there for the Eucharist, even if she couldn't receive it. *What is she talking about?* I wondered. *How can anyone pay attention to anything while taking care of a squirming one-year-old?* Two, I couldn't fathom how my husband could arrive at Mass lacking peace and leave as a refreshed, different person. All I seemed to notice was a homily that wandered and failed to inspire me.

In each of these situations, I was coming to church with my focus on myself. Did I feel appreciated? Did I like the music? Did the homily inspire me? I'd come and go, never recognizing that Jesus was present in an incredible way in the Eucharist. I pined for inspiring words from a speaker and music that excited me, not knowing that Jesus was there, waiting to fill, satisfy, and strengthen me. I didn't yet grasp that the Creator of the universe desired intimacy with His children enough to "make Himself into bread, a little host, in order to descend onto our lips and into our hearts, to bridge all distance between Himself and us."[21]

---

21   d'Elbee, *I Believe in Love*, 86.

As I write, I'm at the end of a long Saturday. It's been filled with needs and demands, so many of which have required the patient and careful attention of the wife and mother of the house. That's me. I keep waiting for Alice, the beloved housekeeper from *The Brady Bunch*, to come through the door, but as of right now, I seem to be alone. I'm halfway through the weekend, feeling, once again, that what I have to offer is not enough. My family's needs go beyond my resources. Clothes still need to be washed, an aching heart needs to be listened to, refreshments for the youth group need to be prepared...But first thing tomorrow, I am going to Mass. I can't wait. Whether or not the words of the homily inspire, I know that Christ will meet me there and quiet my heart with His presence, and if I let Him, He'll enter my heart and smooth a balm over my worries, disappointments, and unrest. He'll fill me with grace so that I have what I need to be the woman God is asking me to be. To think that I might have settled for a little applause when love, peace, fulfillment, and grace were being offered.

I spent many years attending Mass before I learned these truths. It was John 6 that pierced my heart and awakened me to the gift of the Eucharist. May these words offer us all a strong awakening: the Eucharist is real. It's incredibly important to God that we grasp the transforming power of Christ Himself, present in the Eucharist.

Day One: Feeding the Five Thousand

Read John 6:1–15.

He provides.

The multiplication of the loaves and the fishes was the fourth of Jesus' signs. When we read of His signs in John's Gospel, the signs also indicate a miracle that Jesus wants to perform in our lives too. Jesus can take our "fishes and loaves" and turn them into something much more.

1. The people who came to hear Jesus teach were hungry. It seemed impossible to feed them all; there simply wasn't enough food. In what area of your life do your resources feel slim? Time? Money? Wisdom? Patience? Love?

2. A. What did the boy risk when he handed over all of his barley loaves and fishes?

B. What character traits do you see in his act?

C. In what ways can we feel tempted to keep some or all of our barley loaves and fishes to ourselves instead of handing them over to Christ?

D. When we give over all we have and still feel inadequate, how can the following verses encourage us?

Philippians 4:19

2 Corinthians 9:8

Matthew 19:26

3. What does the miracle of the multiplication of the loaves prefigure? See CCC 1335.

Quiet your heart and enjoy His presence…Take a moment to think about what it might have felt like to sit on the grassy hill, hungry. "I'm so hungry…but His words speak straight to my heart…! If I leave, I'll have to walk so far to find food. Can I stand to stay just a while longer?" How would you have felt as the baskets were passed and person after person received enough to eat?

Lord, satisfy me! Please come and fill in the gaps where my efforts are not enough. I try so hard to be self-sufficient, forgetting that You are delighted when I turn to You first. You provide superabundance when I unclench my fists, give You what I have, and wait for You to act. You can multiply whatever I have to offer.

"Now to him who by the power at work within us is able to do far more abundantly than all that we ask or think, to him be glory in the Church and in Christ Jesus to all generations, forever and ever. Amen" (Ephesians 3:20–21).

Day Two: Jesus Walks on the Water

Read John 6:16–21.

He calms.

1. A. Why did the disciples get into the boat and start across the sea? See Matthew 14:22.

   B. What does this tell you about how God trains us?

2. It certainly appeared to the disciples that things were out of control. It was the fourth watch of the night (between 3:00 and 6:00 a.m.); the sea was rising, strong winds were blowing, and they were being battered by the waves. What was Jesus doing during this time? See Matthew 14:23–24.

3. A. Is there an area of your life that feels out of control? Can you relate to the disciples' exhaustion and fear?

   B. What is Jesus doing right now? See Hebrews 7:25 and Romans 8:34.

   C. What light does James 1:2–4 shed on your difficulties?

4. A. What words did Jesus speak to the disciples in John 6:20?

B. The second part of Jesus' sentence wouldn't have much meaning without the first part. The reason why He could tell the disciples not to be afraid was because He was with them. Does Jesus ask the same of us today? Does He ask us to face our threats alone?

C. He is by our side. And this makes all the difference. Note the following fears and the way in which the related verse reveals how God's presence can help us keep moving forward, even when we're scared.

"I'm afraid I'll be attacked if I am vulnerable."
Deuteronomy 3:22

"I'm afraid I'll be rejected, abandoned and alone."
Isaiah 41:10

"I'm afraid of death."
Psalm 23:4

"I'm afraid that I won't know what to say."
Matthew 10:19–20

Quiet your heart and enjoy His presence…Take a moment to contemplate the different perspectives that you and God have on your life.

You see the here and now. He sees with a wide camera lens; He sees the future and what is possible if you rely on Him.

Corrie ten Boom, a Dutch watchmaker who became a hero during WWII for hiding Jews in her home and resisting the Nazis, knew the fear of death. When she discussed this fear with her wise father, he asked her a question:

"Corrie," he began gently, "when you and I go to Amsterdam—when do I give you your ticket?"

I sniffed a few times, considering this.

"Why, just before we get on the train."

"Exactly. And our wise Father in heaven knows when we're going to need things, too. Don't run out ahead of Him, Corrie. When the time comes that some of us will have to die, you will look into your heart and find the strength you need—just in time."[22]

The strength always comes when we need it if we turn to the Lord. At the hour when we will face death, and at the countless other times when we desperately need Him, without fail, He will always be there, giving us exactly what we need.

"It is the Lord who goes before you; he will be with you, he will not fail you or forsake you; do not fear or be dismayed" (Deuteronomy 31:8).

Day Three: The Bread from Heaven

Read John 6:22–51.

He is the bread of life.

1. What similarities do you see between the message Jesus was communicating to the Jews in John 6:27 and His message to the Samaritan woman in John 4:13–14?

2. Read the following study notes on John 6:35–39, then answer the questions.

   Interpretations of this sermon often take one of two positions in Christian circles. Some think of the discourse as an extensive invitation to faith, so that eating the bread of life is seen as a metaphor for believing in Jesus. Others interpret the discourse along sacramental lines, so that eating the bread of life means partaking of the Eucharist. Both of these views are true and can be correlated with a natural and symmetrical division of the sermon into two parts.

   (1) *Invitation to Faith* (6:35–47). The first half of the discourse opens with the statement, "I am the bread of life" (6:35). This is followed by a string of

---

22 Corrie Ten Boom, *The Hiding Place* (Grand Rapids, MI: Baker, 2006), 44.

invitations to come to Jesus and believe in Him for salvation. The metaphorical import of Jesus' teaching is so obvious that it stands out in the response of the Jews, who ask Him not why He calls Himself bread but how He can claim to have descended from heaven (6:42).

(2) *Invitation to the Eucharist* (6:48–58). The second half of the discourse likewise opens with the statement, "I am the bread of life" (6:48). This is followed by a string of invitations to eat the flesh of Jesus and drink His blood. Here the literal import of Jesus' teaching is so obvious that it, too, stands out in the response of the Jews, who ask how it is possible to consume His flesh (6:52). In the end these two halves of the sermon work in tandem, since without faith we can neither be united with Christ nor recognize His presence in the Eucharist. If eating is believing in 6:35–47, then believing leads to eating in 6:48–58 (CCC 161, 1381).[23]

A. What are the two invitations made in this passage?

B. Why do we need to respond to both invitations?

C. When asked, "What must we do to be doing the works of God?" what did Jesus reply?

D. What does it mean to "believe"? See James 2:14–16.

3. In today's reading, John 6:22–51, which verses show Jesus' desire to see all people accept His offer of life-giving bread?

---

23 Ignatius Catholic Study Bible, RSV, 174.

Quiet your heart and enjoy His presence...Take a moment to contemplate the fact that Jesus waits every day to satisfy the longings of your heart.

Jesus, the bread of life, is the only One who can truly fill us. As we saw in John 1:16, "And from his fullness have we all received grace upon grace." In his book Interior Freedom, *Father Jacques Philippe explains how to receive His grace: "Like the manna that fed the Hebrew people in the desert, grace can't be stockpiled. We can't build up reserves of grace but only receive it moment by moment, as part of the 'daily bread' we pray for in the Our Father."*[24]

This means that we need to go to God moment by moment, every single day. As you look to your day ahead, what have you filled it with? Remember that even if you check everything off your to-do list, you won't feel satisfied unless you connect with Christ. Take a deep breath and ask God to calm your heart. Ask Him to fill you with His presence.

Day Four: The Real Presence

Read John 6:52–59.

The readings today and tomorrow contain strong biblical defense of the real presence of Christ in the Eucharist. When someone asks us why we believe the host and the wine really become the body and blood of Jesus, let's not say, "I don't know. I guess I've just always believed it." Instead we can memorize key verses in these passages so that we are able to reference the direct teaching of Jesus in the Scriptures. It is important for us to know *why* we believe so that we can help others find real fulfillment in Christ.

1. A. How many times does Jesus refer to eating His flesh and drinking His blood in John 6:53–56?

    B. What did Jesus say we will lack if we don't eat His flesh or drink His blood? See John 6:53.

    C. What three things did Jesus say will happen if we eat His flesh and drink His blood?

---

24 Father Jacques Philippe, *Interior Freedom* (New York: Scepter, 2007), 88.

2. Was Jesus speaking literally and sacramentally or metaphorically? See CCC 1374.

3. Why were the followers of Christ resistant to the idea of consuming His blood? See Leviticus 17:10–12, paying special attention to verse 11.

Clearly Jesus' words were radical. They pushed the Jewish people far beyond their comfort zones. Drinking blood?! Eating flesh?! Sounds like cannibalism! Without recognizing Jesus' authority, it would be difficult to trust these new teachings. Yes, there is life in the blood, as the Bible teaches in Leviticus 17:11. But the blood that Jesus is offering isn't the natural blood of animals that the Jewish people were prohibited from drinking. He is offering a sharing in His supernatural life and in His divine nature. His blood is offered as atonement for our sins.

4. What is the principal benefit of receiving Christ in the Eucharist? See CCC 1391.

Quiet your heart and enjoy His presence…Take a moment to contemplate this magnificent invitation: The Creator of the universe offers you intimate union with Him.

If you struggle to believe this, ask Jesus to increase your faith so that you can believe in truths you cannot see. Ask God to help you to make regular Mass attendance a priority and a reality in your life. Thank Him for loving you so much that He makes Himself available to fill you every day. "The steadfast love of the Lord never ceases; his mercies never come to an end; they are new every morning; great is your faithfulness" (Lamentations 3:22–23).

Day Five: The Words of Eternal Life

Read John 6:60–71.

1. When Jesus told His followers that the bread of life was actually His flesh, which they were to eat, how did many of them react? How did Jesus respond to them? See also CCC 1336.

2. A. When Jesus asked, "Will you also go away?" how did Peter respond?

    B. Do you think Peter understood everything Jesus had just explained in the bread of life discourse? Why or why not? What virtue was revealed in his response?

Believing in Christ's real presence in the Eucharist requires faith, but it's not a leap of faith without any biblical backing. As we learn in these passages, we need to take Jesus at His word even though we can't "prove" what He says is true. But we trust who He is, and we trust what He says about Himself. If Jesus truly is who He claims to be, is it not possible for Him to give Himself under the appearance of Bread? We are called to believe in something we cannot see with human eyes but, rather, with the eyes of the heart.

    C. Have you taken this leap of faith? Do you believe enough in Christ's words to say, "I believe; help my unbelief" (Mark 9:24)? If you do believe, how often do you receive Christ in the Eucharist? How would you describe your experience when you do?

3. Summarize John 6:52–69 in your own words. Write it as if you are explaining this passage to someone who does not believe in the real presence of Christ in the Eucharist.

Quiet your heart and enjoy His presence…Take a moment to contemplate the intimacy Christ offers you in the Eucharist. Pray the following prayer, written by Saint Teresa of Calcutta:

O God, we believe You are here. We adore You and love You with our whole heart and soul because You are most worthy of all our love. We desire to love You as the Blessed do in Heaven…Flood our souls with Your spirit and life. Penetrate and possess our whole being utterly, that our lives may only be a radiance of Yours. Shine through us, and be so in us, that every soul we come in contact with may feel Your presence in our soul: Let them look up and see no longer us, but only Jesus! [25]

---

25 Mike Aquilina and Regis J. Flaherty, *The How-To Book of Catholic Devotions* (Huntington, IN: Our Sunday Visitor, 2000), 171.

Conclusion

Jesus provides. Jesus calms. In the story of the loaves and fishes, we saw Him take a young boy's offerings and turn them into enough to feed a multitude. When Jesus walked on the water and calmed the sea, we saw His power to create peace in the midst of chaos. When Jesus taught that He was going to offer His own body as the bread of life, He promised future provision that would provide complete satisfaction.

But in each one of those instances, the people encountering Him had a choice. He didn't force any of them to believe in or receive Him. The same is true today, and unfortunately, many reject what He offers. What results is lack of peace and confusion.

Pope Benedict XVI described the remedy for this: "In a world where there is so much noise, so much bewilderment, there is a need for silent adoration of Jesus concealed in the Host."[26] Noise and bewilderment are what results when we stop looking to God for an explanation of who we are and why we're here.

Pope Benedict challenges us to step out of the noise and bewilderment of our world and choose to take part in the "silent adoration of Jesus concealed in the Host." But He is assuredly there, holding everything together.

He comes to us in the Eucharist to give us what we need: connection with Him, his own life in us. When we take the time for adoration, He enters into the busyness of our lives and calms our anxious and troubled hearts. Let's throw open the doors of our souls and invite the Christ of the Eucharist to dwell within us.

My Resolution

In what specific way will I apply what I learned in this lesson?

Examples:

1. Whenever I pray the Our Father, I say, "Give us this day our *daily* bread." Lord, I want to receive You in the intimacy of the Eucharist as often as I can. I will go to daily Mass more often this week than I usually do.

---

[26] Pope Benedict XVI, *Sacramentum Caritatis*, Post-Synodal Apostolic Exhortation, February 22, 2007.

2. I'll make an appointment this week to meet Jesus in adoration. I'll put it on my calendar and protect it as much as I would a doctor's appointment. Jesus is the Great Physician, offering healing in places no one else can reach.

My Resolution:

Catechism Clips

CCC 1335 The miracles of the multiplication of the loaves, when the Lord says the blessing, breaks and distributes the loaves through his disciples to feed the multitude, prefigur[ing] the superabundance of this unique bread of his Eucharist.

CCC 1336 The first announcement of the Eucharist divided the disciples, just as the announcement of the Passion scandalized them: "This is a hard saying; who can listen to it?" The Eucharist and the Cross are stumbling blocks. It is the same mystery, and it never ceases to be an occasion of division. "Will you also go away?": the Lord's question echoes through the ages as a loving invitation to discover that only he has "the words of eternal life" and that to receive in faith the gift of his Eucharist is to receive the Lord himself.

CCC 1374 In the most blessed sacrament of the Eucharist "the body and blood, together with the soul and divinity, of our Lord Jesus Christ and, therefore, the whole Christ is truly, really, and substantially contained." "This presence is called 'real'—by which is not intended to exclude the other types of presence as if they could not be 'real' too, but because it is presence in the fullest sense: that is to say, it is a substantial presence by which Christ, God and man, makes himself wholly and entirely present."

CCC 1391 Holy Communion augments our union with Christ. The principal fruit of receiving Christ in the Eucharist in Holy Communion is an intimate union with Jesus Christ. Indeed, the Lord said: "He who eats my flesh and drinks my blood abides in me, and I in him" (John 6:56). Life in Christ has its foundation in the Eucharistic banquet: "As the living Father sent me, and I live because of the Father, so he who eats me will live because of me" (John 6:57).

Verse Study

See appendix 3 for instructions on how to complete a verse study.

John 6:56

1. Verse:

2. Paraphrase:

3. Questions:

4. Cross-references:

5. Personal Application:

NOTES

Lesson 8

JESUS, OUR MODEL OF FIDELITY

Introduction

There are days when I just wake up on the wrong side of the bed. Things irritate me that I would normally brush off. My prayer time seems more a duty than a joy. I may check "prayer" off my list, but I haven't really connected my heart to God's in an intimate way. I can go through half my day before taking the time to really analyze why I'm so grumpy. If I dig deeper, there is usually something I need to confess. Sometimes it's as simple as confessing my lack of gratitude; other times it's more than that.

I was having one of those days this week. I was going through the grocery store, thinking about how hard it is to run my errands with little children in tow. "No, Cap'n Crunch doesn't count as breakfast. Neither do doughnuts." "No, we aren't getting those toys [which are being featured in the canned vegetable aisle—why are they there?!]." "No, we aren't buying the candy that's enticing you as we wait in line to pay. No, we aren't buying a helium balloon either!"

When I went to check out, I was greeted by Anastasia. We are about the same age. She is so sweet and is always so genuinely interested in my children and me. She speaks patiently to the man with Down syndrome who helps bag the groceries. She could be rolling her eyes as I come through with my three noisy, small children. Instead she oozes kindness and patience.

That day I just had to ask her why she was always so joyful. As it turned out, her happiness comes from God. She chooses to see the good in life. She is so filled up with the Holy Spirit that it spills over into the lives of others.

This gave me a reality check and caused me to pause, open my heart to the Lord, and remember to count my blessings.

Sometimes life brings us major difficulties. And sometimes it's the little frustrations that just get the better of us. Jesus was under pressure throughout John 7, yet He remained balanced, pleasant, and composed. In the big and in the small occurrences, Jesus serves as an example of how we should respond when life doesn't go smoothly, when people don't support us as we'd like, and when roadblocks keep us from moving forward. His grace is sufficient for us (see 2 Corinthians 12:9).

Day One: The Unbelief of Jesus' Brethren

Read John 7:1–9.

1. Why did the Jews seek to kill Jesus? See CCC 574.

2. The feast being discussed in this passage is the Feast of Tabernacles, also called the Feast of Booths. This feast commemorated the years when the Israelites wandered in the wilderness, waiting to enter the Promised Land. The people lived in tents or shelters, also called tabernacles. It was an old-fashioned camping trip! The feast also celebrated the completion of the Temple and the harvesting of crops. This was a favorite festival of the Jewish people and one that was always filled with joy. Families gathered and focused on God's blessings (Leviticus 23:33–43 and Deuteronomy 16:13–16).

    Two liturgical ceremonies were a part of this feast: the Water Pouring Ceremony and the Festival of Lights. Both ceremonies commemorated specific Old Testament events. What were they?

    Water Pouring Ceremony (Numbers 20:2–11)

    Festival of Lights (Exodus 13:21–22 and 33:10)

3. A. What do you think Jesus meant by the words "My time has not yet come, but your time is always here"? Note: When Jesus refers to His "time" in this passage, He means "opportune time" and refers to the hour of His Passion.

   B. Jesus was obedient to God's timetable. What kind of changes, if any, do you need to make in terms of how you spend your time so as to align your will with God's will for you?

Quiet your heart and enjoy His presence...Take a moment to contemplate how the urgent things of the day tend to crowd out the truly important.

How often do we leave undone the things that ought to be done and instead do the things that don't matter in the long run? As you look ahead to your schedule for the day, ask God to show you how He wants you to be using your time. Note which things you are doing that have eternal value and which are temporal. Remember, there is always enough time to do God's will and to be faithful to what He is asking. But often we have to say no to good things in order to say yes to what is best.

Day Two: Jesus at the Feast of Tabernacles

Read John 7:10–24.

1. Which miracle was Jesus speaking of in John 7:21 when He said, "I did one deed, and you all marvel at it"? What aspect of this miracle made the Jews so angry that they wanted to see Him killed? (See John 5:1–9.)

2. How would you summarize Jesus' response to their criticism, found in John 7:21–24?

3. What did Jesus have to say about knowing whether His teaching was from God? (See John 7:17.) What does this say about the hearts of the Jews persecuting Jesus?

Read the following commentary from *The Better Part*:

> Jesus reveals the prerequisite for understanding his doctrine: "If anyone is prepared to do his [the Father's] will, he will know whether my teaching is from God or whether my doctrine is my own…"
>
> The disposition of our will determines our capacity to recognize the truth. A heart free from inordinate attachments to selfish desires will be docile to God's action and inspirations. That docility will give the Holy Spirit room to work, enlightening and strengthening the soul. A heart that has idolized something, however, whether it be money, pleasure, position, power, popularity, or success of any kind—or even just comfort and ease—that heart is not free to respond to God's action; it is chained to its idol. The wind of the Holy Spirit blows, but the idolatrous soul is tied to the shore and makes no progress towards the light. Often God has to send a storm to break the moorings and detach that soul from its idol. Only then can grace begin to work.[27]

4. Can you identify anything that your heart is currently longing for (such as money, pleasure, position, power, popularity, success, or comfort and ease)? How does this longing get in the way of recognizing God's action and inspiration in your life?

5. When have you experienced a storm in your life that freed you from something you were idolizing? Did this storm feel good, feel like God's plan at first?

Quiet your heart and enjoy His presence…Take a moment to contemplate the statement, "The disposition of our will determines our capacity to recognize the truth."

Ask God to reveal to you the true disposition of your will. Have you taken up certain commitments or beliefs (political, psychological, scientific, social) that condition how you respond to Jesus? To Church teaching? Does God need to measure up to you? Fit in with your stances? Do you have a stance that predetermines what you'll see or how you'll respond? Are there spiritual matters that cause you to doubt?

---

27   Bartunek, *The Better Part*, 862.

If a difficult teaching proved to be truly from God, would you hesitate to respond with obedience? Is the real issue doubt, or do you resist changing your life?

Day Three: Is This the Christ?

Read John 7:25–36.

1. Why did the people conclude that Jesus was not the Christ (the long-awaited Messiah)? See John 7:27, 41–42.

2. The people of Jerusalem made a decision about Jesus based on incomplete knowledge. In doing so, they failed to recognize their Savior in their midst. In what ways do people today make the same mistake? How can this be avoided?

3. What "hour" is referred to in John 7:30? See CCC 730.

4. What does Jesus mean by the words, "I shall be with you a little longer, and then I go to him who sent me; you will seek me and you will not find me; where I am you cannot come" (John 7:33–34)?

Quiet your heart and enjoy His presence…Take a moment to contemplate the kinds of thoughts that occupy your mind every day.

How often is your focus superficial? How much time do you spend thinking and praying about things that have eternal value? Excessive busyness, noise, worry, and materialism can put obstacles in the way of spiritual contemplation. Which of these get in the way of taking the time to go deeper spiritually? Ask God to help you to correct a faulty focus. Shift your eyes and heart to Him. Ask Him for the grace to see your day through His eyes, recognizing and acting on the things that He deems most important.

Day Four: Rivers of Living Water

Read John 7:37–39.

Place yourself in the midst of this scene. The Jews had been enjoying the weeklong Feast of Tabernacles. They'd caught up with family and friends who had travelled to Jerusalem for the festivities. They had reminisced about the days when their ancestors wandered in the wilderness, living as nomads. At one point, they would recall, the Israelites were so frustrated by the lack of housing and water that they had threatened to stone Moses, saying, "Why have you made us come up out of Egypt, to bring us to this evil place?... There is no water to drink" (Numbers 20:5).

Each day of the feast, the Jews had watched the priest perform the Water Pouring Ceremony:

> The priest would go to the Pool of Siloam, fill two golden pitchers with water, and walk back to the Temple. Pilgrims who lined the streets along his route shouted, "We will draw water from the well of salvation with joy." The people would then sing psalms as the priest went into the Temple and up to the altar. When he actually poured the water, which symbolized God's salvation from Egypt and a deeply satisfied life, a great shout would arise from those assembled.[28]

Can you picture it? Our passage opens with the Jewish people gathered together on the final day of the feast. In their midst, Jesus rises and says, "If anyone thirsts, let him come to me and drink!" It's as if He is saying, "Are you looking for a deeply satisfied life? I'm the source! Your ancestors received water miraculously to sustain them. I'm offering you something even better! Are you still thirsty? Come to me!"

Although Jesus didn't want to travel up to Jerusalem to the feast with His brethren (John 7:8), He was not going to miss the opportunity to attend the feast so as to stand up at the crucial moment and, in essence, say, "This celebration is all about me! Don't miss what it's all about!"

1. When Jesus spoke of coming to Him to drink (John 7:37) and rivers of living water flowing out from us (John 7:38), what was He talking about? (See John 7:39.)

---

28   Anne Graham Lotz, *Just Give Me Jesus* (Nashville, TN: W. Publishing Group, 2000), 154.

2. God, in His infinite wisdom, allowed many events that took place in the Old Testament to serve as types, foreshadowing, or "prefigurations of what he accomplished in the fullness of time in the person of his incarnate Son" (CCC 128). "The New Testament has to be read in the light of the Old. Early Christian catechesis made constant use of the Old Testament. As an old saying put it, the New Testament lies hidden in the Old and the Old Testament is unveiled in the New" (CCC 129).

   A. Who was the rock in the Old Testament miracle of water pouring out from the rock (Numbers 20:10–13)? See also 1 Corinthians 10:3–4.

   B. In what way does the miracle of water pouring from the rock in the wilderness prefigure what God accomplished through Christ?

3. In the Old Testament, God miraculously allowed a solid rock to pour forth refreshing water. When Jesus came, He was pressed, crushed, and crucified. From Him flowed our salvation and the gift of the Holy Spirit.

   When *we* are pressed or afflicted in some way, what typically flows from us? It has been said that the true sign of the Holy Spirit's presence in a person is the way in which he or she is a blessing to others. The Holy Spirit isn't meant to just dwell in us so that we can contain Him. He's meant to flow from a person. "Out of his heart shall flow rivers of living water" (John 7:38). Jesus pours His Holy Spirit into our hearts, and likewise, He wants the Spirit to flow out of our hearts and into the lives of others.

   In what area of your life do you find you are most often pressed, aggravated, or persecuted? Think of a specific circumstance or person who frustrates you. When your buttons are pushed, what flows out—the Holy Spirit, or anger and agitation? What gift of the Holy Spirit do you need in facing the same circumstance or person? Ask for that gift. Prayerfully imagine responding to the same circumstances or person with this new grace.

Quiet your heart and enjoy His presence…Take a moment to contemplate all the gifts given to you by the Holy Spirit.

When He takes up residence in our souls, the Holy Spirit brings the fullness of His love, joy, peace, patience, kindness, goodness, faithfulness, gentleness, and self-control. Which of these fruits of the Holy Spirit do you most need today? Ask Him to fill you with that fruit so that grace and goodness flow out of you into the lives of others.

Day Five: Division Among the People

Read John 7:40–53.

1. In verse 43, it's clear that Jesus divided the people. He still divides people; just mention His name at a party and note the reactions. When did you last find yourself defending Christ, either publicly or by your witness? How do you stand up for Him when you are outnumbered?

2. Most of Jesus' supporters were uneducated people. Nicodemus was the exception. He stood up for Jesus despite peers who encouraged him to denounce Him. Look back to Jesus' conversation with Nicodemus in John 3:1–15. In what ways did that conversation relate to what Jesus taught at the Feast of Tabernacles? How do you think these lessons helped Nicodemus to take a stand for Christ?

3. Jesus lived and ministered amid constant pressure. People continually questioned, challenged, and persecuted Him. In the midst of all the pressure, why did Jesus continue to give to others?

4. God has a plan for your day and for your life. How can trusting in His plan help you be a blessing in spite of the pressures you face?

Quiet your heart and enjoy His presence…Take a moment to contemplate the day ahead.

Ask God, "What's Your plan for my day?" not, "Here's my plan; please bless it." Be open throughout the day for divine interruptions—things that weren't on your calendar but are appointments made by God for you. Ask God for the eyes to see His divine interruptions as opportunities to love others, even when it's inconvenient.

Conclusion

It's hard to live life under pressure. We can be weighed down by financial pressure, worries about the future, not knowing how to fix a marriage, having too much to do in too little time, feeling like time is running out to have children…Pressure is real. Over time we can feel worn down and overwhelmed.

When the fire of life heats up and it feels like our feet are too close to the flames, we have a choice. Will we let our human tendencies have their way? Will we endure hardships but do so with hearts full of resentment? Will we shake our fists at God, demanding that He explain Himself and make life easier? Or will we remember that we are beloved? Will we see the pressure as one of the ways in which God gathers us to His chest, holding us close? When we feel we can barely keep trudging on, yet we reach out and grab hold of His hand, we are experiencing true dependence on God: We open ourselves to be strengthened by His power and might.

The Holy Spirit fills us with all we need to continue on our journeys, no matter how difficult they may be. We need to draw on the love, joy, peace, strength, and patience that are within us because of the Holy Spirit's presence.

We will face all sorts of problems each day. But He is near us—He has "made his dwelling among us," in our very details (John 1:14). If we use our troubles as means to draw close to God and be filled with His strength, He will make sure that we get through and that we are stronger, more peaceful, and more loving women as a result.

My Resolution

In what specific way will I apply what I learned in this lesson?

Examples:

1. The excessive noise and busyness of my life get in the way of taking the time to know God more deeply. When I am alone in the car this week, I will turn off my phone and the radio. I'll take that time to talk to God, imagining Him there in the

passenger's seat—God, who is always present, waiting to help me with whatever is on my heart.

2. I want the Holy Spirit to flow from me into the lives of others. When I am pressed this week, I want the Holy Spirit's sweetness to flow out, rather than my own frustration. Each time something "pokes" me or makes me angry, I will say a quick, silent prayer ("Come, Holy Spirit! Help!") and choose to respond with grace.

My Resolution:

Catechism Clips

CCC 128 The Church, as early as apostolic times, and then constantly in her Tradition, has illuminated the unity of the divine plan in the two Testaments through typology, which discerns in God's works of the Old Covenant prefigurations of what he accomplished in the fullness of time in the person of his incarnate Son.

CCC 129 Christians therefore read the Old Testament in the light of Christ crucified and risen. Such typological reading discloses the inexhaustible content of the Old Testament; but it must not make us forget that the Old Testament retains its own intrinsic value as Revelation reaffirmed by our Lord himself. Besides, the New Testament has to be read in the light of the Old. Early Christian catechesis made constant use of the Old Testament. As an old saying put it, the New Testament lies hidden in the Old and the Old Testament is unveiled in the New.

CCC 574 From the beginning of Jesus' public ministry, certain Pharisees and partisans of Herod together with priests and scribes agreed together to destroy him. Because of certain of his acts—expelling demons, forgiving sins, healing on the Sabbath day, his novel interpretation of the precepts of the Law regarding purity, and his familiarity with tax collectors and public sinners—some ill-intentioned persons suspected Jesus of demonic possession. He is accused of blasphemy and false prophecy, religious crimes which the Law punished with death by stoning.

CCC 730 At last Jesus' hour arrives: he commends his spirit into the Father's hands at the very moment when by his death he conquers death, so that, "raised from the dead by the glory of the Father," he might immediately give the Holy Spirit by "breathing" on his disciples.

Verse Study

See appendix 3 for instructions on how to complete a verse study.

John 7:38

1. Verse:

2. Paraphrase:

3. Questions:

4. Cross-references:

5. Personal Application:

 NOTES

Lesson 9

JESUS, THE LIGHT OF THE WORLD

Introduction

How often do self-defeating thoughts run through your mind? Thoughts like:

If he doesn't love me, I must be unlovable.

If I don't meet everyone's expectations, then I'm a failure.

I have got to lose weight…I hate my body.

My finances are a mess and so am I.

I'm not enough.

I'm too much.

I'm inferior to other people.

I'm hopeless.

I have to be perfect.

These thoughts, which so many of us have, lead down a dark path. And if we have a rare moment when the voices are quiet and we feel OK about ourselves, we're afraid it's not going to last.

Jesus came to show us another way to live. He came to shed the light of His Truth into our hearts so that we'll clearly see who He is, who we are, and what our purpose is. He came to shed light on our identity so that we will root our sense of self in Him. Because He is unchanging and His love for us never wavers, seeing ourselves through His eyes anchors us. Jesus also came to shed light on why we are here and where we are heading. Without His divine light, we can't figure out the answers to those critical questions.

When we leave God out of the picture in our search for identity, purpose, and truth, we remain in darkness and confusion. You would think that everyone would be repelled by this confusion, because we all want to feel settled and secure. But this confusion is dressed up in our culture to look trendy and appealing. The word *"authenticity"* is a current buzzword, and while it can be used to describe a rejection of unattainable perfectionism (this is good), the contemporary understanding of the word "means to present what would traditionally be considered a fault or a sin as a badge of honor."[29] When we buy into this type of authenticity, we find we have company—plenty of people to commiserate with us as we dance in the darkness. But in the quiet moments when we've put our phones down and are alone with ourselves, we feel empty and untethered.

We hate to admit that we are wrong, but sometimes, our darkness is caused by our sin. When this is the case, His light can cause us to want to hide. We don't want our faults illuminated. But if we invite Christ's light to reveal what is broken within us, we'll have taken the first step to healing.

There are other times we feel we're in darkness because of our circumstances. We point outside ourselves to the things that have robbed us of hope. It's a temptation to blame God or to be angry with Him in the midst of those trials. It can be hard to welcome His light when we are in such pain, and we often turn inward instead of turning to Him. But if we will let Him work out His purpose in our lives, especially during the dark times, His light will drive away the darkness in our hearts.

There is an alternative to living in confusion and darkness. It begins when we acknowledge that we need Christ's light to guide us and help us see clearly. Let's pray that His light will shine in our hearts this week and always.

Day One: Jesus at the Mount of Olives

Read John 8:1–11.

Imagine the fear and panic that must have gripped the woman caught in adultery as she was thrust through the crowd and made to stand in front of Jesus. Her disheveled appearance contrasted with the smug expressions of those who had caught her. What thoughts were running through her mind? *Will He condemn me? What will it feel like to have stone after stone tearing at my skin? I don't want to die! What will happen to my children? What was I thinking? How could I have been so stupid? I'm so ashamed. I feel dirty. Who can help me?*

---

29 Noelle Mering, *Awake, Not Woke* (Gastonia, NC: Tan Books, 2021), 101.

1. A. The scribes (the men who copied and taught the Holy Scriptures) and Pharisees wanted to trap Jesus. What two options did they give Him, and how would either response have entrapped Him? (See also John 18:31.)

   B. How did Jesus evade the trap entirely? Do His words excuse her sin?

2. As the Pharisees and scribes thought about their own sins, they put down their stones, one by one, and walked away. We, too, are called to put down our stones of judgement and criticism. Jesus calls us to recognize that not only are we unworthy to judge, but we lack the insight to grasp the full picture. If we knew the whole story of another person's life, we'd probably be more merciful. Perhaps people don't seem to deserve our kindness; then again, do we deserve the mercy that Jesus offers us? Think of someone whom you have condemned, criticized, or judged. In what concrete way can you show mercy to that person, even if he or she is undeserving? Can you do this out of love for Christ, even if you lack esteem for the person?

3. What two qualities of Jesus does John 1:14 show us? In what way do we see those qualities in Jesus in John 8:1–11?

Quiet your heart and enjoy His presence…Take a moment to contemplate Jesus' love for this woman, even in the midst of her shame and guilt.

Jesus didn't turn away from the woman; instead He extended a hand of mercy. In His compassion Jesus finds the woman a way out. Jesus is merciful. Jesus forgives. Sometimes we are so aware of our guilt that we are overwhelmed with shame. We feel naked before Him in our sinfulness, and so we turn away. Jesus holds out His hand to us and calls us back. He offers us grace and encourages us to begin again.

God knows what we have done. Hebrews 4:13 (NAB) says, "No creature is concealed from him, but everything is naked and exposed to the eyes of him to whom we must render an account." Nothing is hidden from His eyes. But He is not repelled by us when we are at our worst. He asks us not to turn away, because He is not looking at us with disgust but, rather, with love. He sees into the depths of our hearts; He sees our hurts and disappointments and all the things that led up to our poor choices. He always offers us another chance. He covers our nakedness with His robe of righteousness. He clothes us with His compassion and mercy. He leads us back to purity and wholeness.

In prayer, claim His promise from 2 Corinthians 5:17: "Therefore if anyone is in Christ, he is a new creation; the old has passed away, behold, the new has come."

Day Two: The Light of the World

Read John 8:12–20 and the following commentary from *The Better Part*:

One of the most exciting rituals associated with [the Feast of Tabernacles] took place at night in the second court of the Temple where the Treasury was. This courtyard was surrounded by porticoes that housed thirteen large alms-boxes, where pilgrims and worshippers could make the various offerings that Temple worship required. During the festival, a kind of grandstand was erected all around the porticoes, which could hold huge numbers of spectators. In the center of the courtyard, four gigantic candelabras were erected. When the full darkness of night had descended and the galleries were full, the candelabras were lit, creating a blaze so bright that, ancient sources record, the light spread to all the streets and courtyards throughout the city. (The Temple was located on a higher level than the rest of the city, so light there would be visible from afar.) This firelight commemorated the pillar of fire that God used to guide Israel through the desert every night during their forty-year sojourn from Egypt into the Promised Land. Throughout the night, Israel's holiest and wisest teachers would perform ceremonies of worship that included singing of psalms and dancing in praise and thanksgiving to God, whom the Scriptures repeatedly referred to as the light of his Chosen People. The faithful pilgrims would join in the celebration and enjoy the dramatic ceremony until the sun came up.

The setting gives Christ's words, "I am the light of the world," spectacular eloquence. With this experience fresh in the minds of His rapt listeners, speaking in the very courtyard where the ceremony of light had taken place, Jesus proclaims that He is the light of the world. Just as the pillar of fire had led the people of Israel into the Promised Land, and just as the great candelabras illuminated the holy city of Jerusalem, Jesus Himself, His person and His teachings, is the pillar of saving fire that shines throughout the entire world, leading whoever believes in Him to the fullness of life itself. [30]

1.   A.   We can choose to dwell in darkness or to dwell in Jesus' light. How do the following verses from 1 John chapters 1 and 2 suggest that we stay in Jesus' light?

   1 John 1:9

   1 John 2:3

   1 John 2:6

   1 John 2:10

   1 John 2:15

   1 John 2:24

   1 John 2:28

   B.   Choose one of the verses from part A and explain in your own words why applying it would be a source of hope and light during a time of personal darkness.

   For example, 1 John 2:24 says that we are to make sure what we have heard remains in us. If we've taken the time to study Scripture, then we'll have heard many lessons that talk about God's love for us. We can recall those truths during seasons of darkness when we are tempted to think God has abandoned us. It's

---

30   Bartunek, *The Better Part*, 874–5.

also helpful to keep a prayer journal. This is a way of recording times of trial and answers to prayer. When life seems dark, rereading a journal that lists answered prayers serves as a reminder that God listens, cares, and acts.

2. Jesus, the Light of the World, gives meaning and direction to our lives. He sheds light on who we are and what our purpose is. But Jesus is a gentleman. He won't shine His light into our hearts unless we invite Him in. Write a prayer to Him in the space that follows, inviting Him to shine His light into your heart. Ask Him to help you to see your need for Him and any sins that need to be confessed. Ask Him to light your path, giving you guidance.

    Dear Jesus,

Quiet your heart and enjoy His presence…Take a moment to contemplate any time you have experienced spiritual darkness as a result of your own poor choices.

"Man's tendency is to hide from his sin, seeking refuge in the darkness. There he indulges in self-pity, denial, self-righteousness, blaming, and hatred. But [Jesus is] the Light of the world, and [His] illumination decimates the darkness. Come close to [Him] and let [His] light envelop you, driving out darkness and permeating you with Peace."[31]

Day Three: I Am

Read John 8:21–30.

Arguing, debating, discussing—how much time did Jesus spend trying to convince hard-hearted people of the truth concerning Him? In this passage we see Jesus explaining that the decision they would make about Him would be a matter of life and death.

1. In verse 24, Jesus said, "For you will die in your sins unless you believe that I am he." What is meant by the phrase "I am"?

---

31 Sarah Young, *Jesus Calling: Enjoying Peace in His Presence* (Nashville, TN: Thomas Nelson, 2004), 147.

Use the following verses and CCC 211 to find the answer.

Exodus 3:13–15

John 8:58

CCC 211

What else must we know and believe about God, according to Isaiah 43:10–11 and Acts 4:12?

2. Jesus' words didn't convince all His listeners of His identity. Which future event would confirm Jesus' divinity? (See Matthew 27:45–54 and John 8:28.)

3. What did Jesus claim to do in John 8:29? How can we apply this to our own lives? See CCC 1693 and 2825; John 15:5. Be sure to mention *how* we are to do this.

Quiet your heart and enjoy His presence…Take a moment to contemplate the fact that what we believe about Jesus determines our eternal destiny.

We either "die in our sins" or we die with our sins forgiven. God gives us this choice. Meditate on Deuteronomy 30:19–20: "I have set before you life and death, the blessing and the curse. Choose life then, that you and your descendants may live, by loving the Lord your God, heeding his voice, and holding fast to him. For that will mean life for you." What is your choice? Life or death?

Day Four: True Freedom

Read John 8:31–38.

"You will know the truth, and the truth will make you free" (John 8:32).

"Freedom consists not in doing what we like, but in having the right to do what we ought."[32]

Freedom—isn't that what we all long for? We often think of freedom as the ability to do whatever we want to, but so often, that false freedom leads to sinful habits that actually keep us in bondage. We need to not only know what is true; we need to believe it so deeply that it affects how we live. The kind of freedom that Jesus is talking about comes from knowing God's Truth—all that He has revealed about Himself—and how we can remain in an intimate relationship with Him who is our true worth and our purpose. What a difference it would make if we not only knew the truth but lived accordingly.

1. Where is truth found? How can we pursue it in our lives? See John 17:17, Ephesians 4:21, 1 John 5:8, and CCC 2466.

2. According to Romans 1:25 and 2 Timothy 4:3–4, what do many people pursue instead of God's Truth?

3. Through His death and Resurrection, Jesus has delivered us "from the dominion of darkness" (Colossians 1:13) and has brought us into the light of His Truth. But remaining in this truth is a battle, and Satan loves nothing more than keeping people in the dark. What do you learn from Ephesians 6:12–18 regarding this battle?

4. A. Think about an area of your life in which you would like to experience a newfound freedom from a particular sin, fear, habit, or addiction. How do you justify this behavior? What are your thoughts that lead you down the path of temptation?

---

32 "Homily of His Holiness John Paul II," Oriole Park at Camden Yards, Baltimore (October 8, 1995): https://www.vatican.va/content/john-paul-ii/en/homilies/1995/documents/hf_jp-ii_hom_19951008_baltimore.html.

B. What are some sources of God's Truth that you can turn to to learn more about His perspective on that area of your life?

C. Which "piece of armor" mentioned in Ephesians 6:12–18 can you employ to help battle this temptation?

Quiet your heart and enjoy His presence…Take a moment to contemplate the freedom Christ offers you.

Dear Lord,

I long to live in the freedom that You offer me! Help me to drink deeply of Your truth so that I recognize the lies that justify my wrong behavior. May Your truth transform me. Help me to have the self-discipline to read Scripture and apply it. I don't want to be a woman who surrounds herself with flatterers. I want to be a strong, godly woman who welcomes Your light, even when it's pointing out things that need to change. Give me a teachable spirit; free me from pride, which keeps me from admitting my need. I don't have it all together. I need You. Help me to acknowledge the areas in my life where I'm weak, Lord, and give me the desire to pursue Your truth and the courage to change with Your grace.

Day Five: Jesus and Abraham

Read John 8:39–59.

1. The Jewish people in this passage were walking in darkness. They falsely believed that their religion was acceptable to God because they were sons of Abraham. We don't become children of God because our parents are Christians, because of our nationality, or because of church attendance. What do the following verses say we must do in order to have God as our Father?

John 8:42

John 8:47

John 1:12

1 John 3:10

2. Although the Jews claimed that their father was Abraham (John 8:39), who did Jesus say was their father? How was their father described?

3. The devil has been spinning lies since the beginning of time (CCC 391, 392). He crafts a message and hopes we'll believe him. If we do, we'll step out of God's light and into the darkness of discouragement and confusion. One of the devil's favorite deceptions is to question God's love for us. He tells us that our worth depends on what we look like, what we do, and what we own. Which of his lies cause you to question your God-given value?

True freedom comes from living as a beloved daughter of God. We combat the devil's lies by filling our minds with God's Truth. We need to check what we're reading and watching. Does what we consume promote and reinforce the world's values and voices? Does this lead to emptiness and pursuit of the superficial? Are we nourishing ourselves on Scripture and God's promises? This is not to say that we can't enjoy a good novel or entertainment, but we need to recognize that if we feed on garbage, it's going to impact our ability to believe God's word regarding our lovability.

Quiet your heart and enjoy His presence…Take a moment to contemplate the truth that God is crazy about you.

He knew that the devil would whisper lies to you, telling you that only those who have it together are acceptable to God, that what you look like matters more than inner character, that you'll never amount to much…The devil will feed you all sorts of negative thoughts. So God made sure that you'd have strength to counter those lies by meditating on His Word in Scripture.

What's the truth?

God has known you from the beginning: "You formed my inward parts, you knitted me together in my mother's womb…You know me right well; my frame was not hidden from you, when I was being made in secret, intricately wrought in the depths of the earth. Your eyes beheld my uniformed substance; in your book were written, every one of them, the days that were formed for me when as yet there was none of them" (Psalm 139:13, 15–16).

Nothing will separate you from God's love: "Who shall separate us from the love of Christ? Shall tribulation, or distress, or persecution, or famine, or nakedness, or peril, or sword?...Neither death, nor life, nor angels, nor principalities, nor things present, nor things to come, nor powers, nor height, nor depth, nor anything else in all creation, will be able to separate us from the love of God in Christ Jesus our Lord" (Romans 8:35, 38–39).

God has a plan for your life—a plan for blessing: "For I know the plans I have for you, says the Lord, plans for your welfare and not for evil, to give you a future and a hope. Then you will call upon me and come and pray to me, and I will hear you. You will seek me and find me; when you seek me with all your heart" (Jeremiah 29:11–13).

Conclusion

One of the reasons we so desperately need Christ's light to shine in our lives is that God has a unique path for each one of us to follow. When we were still in the womb, God was planning specific works for us to do, life purposes that would bring us the greatest fulfillment and satisfaction. "For we are his workmanship, created in Christ Jesus for good works, which God prepared beforehand, that we should walk in them" (Ephesians 2:10). As we read in Jeremiah 29:11–13, those plans and purposes are meant to bless us if we choose to participate in them.

Because each of those paths is so personal, we aren't going to discover God's individual plan for us by looking at what the rest of the world is doing. This path will be revealed when the light of Christ shines in our hearts, and His light shines brightest when we are in close communion with Him. As we give Him the place of highest priority in our lives by starting our day with prayer, talking to Him throughout the day, filling our minds with His Truth through Scripture reading, availing ourselves of the sacraments, and applying what we learn from the Catechism, we'll grow closer to Him. As our hearts are filled with His presence, His light will shine within us. The Light of the World will dispel the darkness and make us into candles for our world.

My Resolution

In what specific way will I apply what I learned in this lesson?

Examples:

1. I want Christ's light to shine in the dark places of my heart, the places where sin hides. Although it's unpleasant to look so honestly at myself, I will take time each day to ask God to shine His light on my heart, revealing things I need to confess. I'll sit in silence for a few minutes following my prayer and allow Him to speak to my heart.

2. After identifying lies that often play in my mind, I'll take the time to find a Bible verse that reveals God's Truth on the matter. I will write that Scripture verse on an index card and carry it with me. When the lie pops into my head, I'll read the verse, replacing the lie with God's Truth.

My Resolution:

Catechism Clips

CCC 211 The divine name, "I Am" or "He is," expresses God's faithfulness: despite the faithlessness of men's sin and the punishment it deserves, he keeps "steadfast love for thousands." By going so far as to give up his own Son for us, God reveals that he is "rich in mercy." By giving his life to free us from sin, Jesus reveals that he himself bears the divine name: "When you have lifted up the Son of man, then you will realize that 'I AM.'"

CCC 391 Behind the disobedient choice of our first parents lurks a seductive voice, opposed to God, which makes them fall into death out of envy. Scripture and the Church's Tradition see in this being a fallen angel, called "Satan" or the "devil." The Church teaches that Satan was at first a good angel, made by God: "The devil and the other demons were indeed created naturally good by God, but they became evil by their own doing."

CCC 392 Scripture speaks of a sin of these angels. This "fall" consists in the free choice of these created spirits, who radically and irrevocably *rejected* God and his reign. We find a reflection of that rebellion in the tempter's words to our first parents: "You will be like God." The devil "has sinned from the beginning"; he is "a liar and the father of lies."

CCC 1693 Christ Jesus always did what was pleasing to the Father, and always lived in perfect communion with him. Likewise Christ's disciples are invited to live in the sight of the Father "who sees in secret," in order to become "perfect as your heavenly Father is perfect."

CCC 2466 In Jesus Christ, the whole of God's truth has been made manifest. "Full of grace and truth," he came as the "light of the world," he is the Truth. "Whoever believes in me may not remain in darkness." The disciple of Jesus continues in his word so as to know "the truth [that] will make you free" and that sanctifies. To follow Jesus is to live in "the Spirit of truth," whom the Father sends in his name and who leads "into all the truth." To his disciples Jesus teaches the unconditional love of truth: "Let what you say be simply 'Yes or No.'"

CCC 2825 "Although he was a Son, [Jesus] learned obedience through what he suffered." How much more reason have we sinful creatures to learn obedience—we who in him have become children of adoption. We ask our Father to unite our will to his Son's in order to fulfill his will, his plan of salvation for the life of the world. We are radically incapable of this, but united with Jesus and with the power of his Holy Spirit, we can surrender our will to him and decide to choose what his Son has always chosen: to do what is pleasing to the Father.

Verse Study

See appendix 3 for instructions on how to complete a verse study.

John 8:36

1. Verse:

2. Paraphrase:

3. Questions:

4. Cross-references:

5. Personal Application:

Lesson 10: Connect Coffee Talk 3

JESUS, THE LIGHT OF THE WORLD

The accompanying talk can be viewed via DVD or digital download purchase or accessed online at walkingwithpurpose.com/videos.

Key Verses

"Those who are led by the Spirit of God are sons [and daughters!] of God. For you did not receive the spirit of slavery to fall back into fear, but you have received the spirit of sonship. When we cry, 'Abba! Father!' it is the Spirit himself bearing witness with our spirit that we are children of God, and if children, then heirs, heirs of God and fellow heirs with Christ, provided we suffer with him in order that we may also be glorified with him" (Romans 8:14–17).

"Am I now seeking the favor of men, or of God? Or am I trying to please men? If I were still pleasing men, I should not be a servant of Christ" (Galatians 1:10).

"God will supply every need of yours according to his riches in glory in Christ Jesus" (Philippians 4:19).

"Fear not, for I am with you, be not dismayed, for I am your God; I will strengthen you, I will help you, I will uphold you with my victorious right hand" (Isaiah 41:10).

Jesus invites us to follow Him—to walk in His light—and to experience the true freedom He desires for us.

I. **Freedom from the Pain of the Past**

    A. Pray that our pain will be redeemed.

       Ask God to teach us everything He has for us in this painful circumstance.

"Endurance is not just the ability to bear a hard thing, but to turn it into glory" (William Barclay).

Jesus can turn our pain into glory. We only need to ask.

B. Ask God for the grace to forgive.

II. Freedom from the Pressure of the Present

A. Examine our burdens and prayerfully ask, "Has God asked me to carry these?" Distinguish between our busyness and God's business.

B. God cares what we do with our time and why we do it.

C. God wants us to give our time to things of lasting value.

III. Freedom from the Fear of the Future

A. God promises the strength and grace to get us through our difficulties—not our wild imaginings.

B. Consider worry a call to prayer.

C. Keep our eyes on the quality of our eternity.

Can we trust in God's love for us? Do we know for certain that He will only allow what is best for us in the long run?

Questions for Discussion or Journaling

1. In philosopher Steve Grundman's "Competing Christian Visions of the Person," we are introduced to two different ways of looking at God. One vision sees God as a master and causes us to respond like slaves. The other sees God as a father and draws us to behave as daughters. The slave asks, "What do I have to do?" The daughter asks, "How can I be happy? What's the right way to do this, Dad? Tell me the right way to live." Which approach most describes you? Do you see God's instructions as an external restraint or as an aid to freedom?

2. In order to experience freedom from the pain of the past, we need to offer the gift of forgiveness to those who have hurt us. Is there someone you need to forgive, or do you need to forgive yourself?

3. We take a big step forward in being freed from the pressure of the present when we examine the burdens we are carrying and discern whether we are carrying them because God has asked us to or because we are trying to please people in our lives. Are you carrying an impossible load? Could it be that you are doing some things out of a sense of obligation to people rather than obedience to God?

 NOTES

Lesson 11

JESUS, THE CONSOLER AND SHEPHERD

Introduction

I didn't feel like I had asked too big a favor of God. I figured that with all the power in the world at His disposal, He could grant me my one request.

I had spent the summer dealing with the ups and downs of early pregnancy. Intense nausea made it difficult to take care of my six children, and memories of two previous miscarriages fed me a steady stream of worst-case scenarios. I struggled with worry that I'd lose the baby, worry that I'd have the baby but something would go wrong, worry that I wouldn't have enough to give, that there wouldn't be enough of me to go around. I also worried what people would think. "Another pregnancy? Do these people not have a TV? Isn't there something else they can do with their time? There's no way she can be a good mother to all those children. Someone must be getting lost in the shuffle."

The weeks progressed, and "the peace of God, which passes all understanding" (Philippians 4:7) was settling in my heart. I came to a place of acceptance in the event that this baby would have special needs. I even began to think it would be a blessing to our family, teaching us things that we wouldn't otherwise learn and bringing us joy that we wouldn't otherwise experience. My oldest daughter gave me an immense gift when she told me that she was thrilled our family would grow, believing that having many siblings was the best way to keep from being self-absorbed and allow her to develop a heart of service instead. It was week eleven. I was almost to that golden week twelve, when fears of miscarriage normally abate.

But God's plan wasn't for this pregnancy to go to term. An ultrasound confirmed that the baby was dying. The heartbeat was so very slow; it was only a matter of time before I would miscarry. I was sent home to wait.

My heart was breaking, but I promised God that I would see His providence in this loss and learn the lessons He had for me in it. My one request was that I not lose the baby at home and specifically not on Wednesday night. Wednesday night was William's birthday party. William is in the middle, and I was determined that he get some much-deserved attention. I wanted to be there and give him his special moment of celebration. The next morning was little Bobby's first day of preschool. I wanted to be there for that milestone too.

The days went by, and it looked like God was following my plan. All the children arrived at the party, and my yard was filled with seventh-grade boys playing laser tag. I ran inside to get the camera, and contractions began. The timing couldn't have been worse. I asked that the pain not be too great, but it was. At one point I hyperventilated from fear that I wouldn't be able to stand it. I asked my husband to get me a paper bag to help with my breathing. He ran upstairs to our room carrying a large Williams-Sonoma shopping bag. Not helpful.

In the days that followed, I tried to make sense of it all. Why hadn't God answered my prayers as I'd hoped? I asked Him lots of difficult questions. "Why?" was certainly one of them.

People suffer in far worse ways than I have described. But someone told me once that suffering is suffering. That rings true for me. Regardless of suffering's intensity, we long to make sense of things—to have answers to our questions.

Our questions aren't new ones; the people who lived during Jesus' time asked them too. How did He respond then? Let's find out...

Day One: Healing of the Blind Man

Read John 9:1–12.

As we read at the end of John chapter 8, Jesus barely escaped being killed (John 8:59) after He had rightly claimed He was God. It wouldn't be surprising if He felt a need to take a break. Most people would feel justified in spending the next day recuperating. Instead, Jesus was walking the streets with His disciples, always ready to teach, heal, and give. His eyes were drawn to a suffering blind man. The disciples noticed the man too. Their response was different from Jesus' however. They talked about the blind man as if he wasn't even there, as if he was the subject of a theological debate instead of a person with feelings and a desire for love and respect.

1. A. What was the disciples' question as they observed the blind man? Explain how their question reflected their belief regarding the relationship between sin and sickness. See Job 31:3, Psalm 107:17, and Tobit 3:3.

    B. In order to understand those Old Testament passages, it's important to clarify the difference between consequences resulting from a parent's sin and judgment for a parent's sin. It is true that the consequences of a parent's sin can be felt in subsequent generations. We see this in cases of alcoholism; in sexual, physical, and emotional abuse; and in disbelief in God, to name a few. Deuteronomy 5:9 states that negative consequences are felt even down to the third and fourth generations. But experiencing the consequence of a parent's or grandparent's sin is not the same as being punished for it. What does Ezekiel 18:20 say regarding this issue?

2. A. Why did Jesus say the man had been born blind?

    B. Saint Paul experienced much suffering, and he wrote of it in 2 Corinthians 12:8–10. After reading his words, explain how weakness or suffering is an opportunity to display the work of God. See also CCC 1508.

When tragedy occurs, lives that otherwise go unnoticed are suddenly on everyone's radar. When we are suffering, people's eyes are on us. This is when we have the opportunity to prove the promises of God. Is He truly sufficient to meet all our needs? Does He really provide for us? When the world comes crashing down, is He enough? Observers of our suffering might be asking these questions. When we are able to endure because of the difference He makes, we are displaying the works of God.

3. A. Jesus could have performed this miracle of healing the blind man with a word. Instead He chose to use clay and spittle. What other times did Jesus use physical matter to perform a miracle?

    John 2:7–11

John 6:8–13

Mark 14:22–25

B. The use of physical matter in the healing process anticipates the sacraments (see CCC 1084). We see the material objects (water, oil, wine, bread) and know that an unseen spiritual reality is taking place. Which of the sacraments comes to mind when we consider how Jesus asked the man to wash in the pool of Siloam?

4. In John 9:8–12, it appeared that the blind man didn't know enough about Jesus to lead anyone to Him. He could only say that he had been changed. Do you ever feel inadequate to share about your faith with another person? Be encouraged by the example of the formerly blind man. Sharing how you have been changed can be the strongest possible witness. List in the space that follows some of the ways in which you have been transformed from the inside out since following Christ.

Quiet your heart and enjoy His presence…We do not suffer alone—Jesus is there to console and strengthen us.

"But we have this treasure in earthen vessels, to show that the transcendent power belongs to God and not to us. We are afflicted in every way but not crushed; perplexed but not driven to despair; persecuted but not forsaken; struck down but not destroyed" (2 Corinthians 4:7–9).

"Dear Lord,

"When I am suffering, help me to draw on Your limitless power. You can sustain me through the most horrible circumstances. When I am weakest, You are strongest, because then I rely upon you. Instead of fighting against my circumstances and being crippled by bitterness and anger, help me to accept suffering and to rely on Your strength. May it transform me into Your likeness.

"If You choose to remove my suffering, I will be glad for the relief. But if You choose to allow it to remain, I pray that my very life would be the miracle—that people would see that I am still standing, and that it's all because of You. Amen."

Day Two: Investigating the Healing

Read John 9:13–41.

1. A. What were the various reactions to the formerly blind man's healing? Share the reaction of the Pharisees, the crowd of people, and his parents. See John 9:13–23.

    B. How do you think the parents of the formerly blind man would have felt about their son's spiritual boldness in the face of the Pharisees' opposition to Jesus?

    C. What do your parents think about the spiritual change in you? Is it difficult for you to express your faith within your family?

    D. We are called to respect and honor our parents. As adults, however, we are not called to obey them. How should we reconcile faith and family when the two collide? How can we be effective lights for Christ in our family without being offensive? (See 1 Peter 3:15.)

2. Describe the progression of the formerly blind man's witness for Christ using the following verses as a guide.

    John 9:11–12

    John 9:17

John 9:31–33

3. The formerly blind man's reward for standing up for Jesus was to be thrown out of the synagogue, alienated, and cut off from his community (John 9:34). Jesus sought him out and offered him comfort. Jesus consistently draws close to those who suffer. Summarize the encouragement found in the following verses.

Psalm 34:19 (NAB)

Psalm 18:17 (NAB)

Psalm 23:4(NAB)

4. The Pharisees claimed to see but were spiritually blind. List three things that they consistently didn't see. See CCC 588.

Quiet your heart and enjoy His presence…He draws near you in your suffering.

After He heard that the formerly blind man was cast out of the synagogue, Jesus went looking for him. He sought him out, especially because the man had been abandoned by his parents and excommunicated by the religious officials. In the face of such pain, Jesus does not offer a "fix." Rather, He offers Himself. He reveals himself to the formerly blind man. The man is so open to seeing—his faith is so entire—that he leans forward into Jesus' question, "Do you believe in the Son of man?" with entrustment: "Who is he that I may believe in him?" The formerly blind man realizes that he is looking upon God. The man understands that Jesus is divine and worships Him. What consoles the man for the abandonment of his parents and the ostracism from the Temple is intimacy with Christ.

When we suffer, we have the opportunity to encounter Jesus in a deeper way. Do we trust that He pursues us into our suffering, seeking us there? We can experience the peace He offers that passes all understanding, and we "may share his sufferings" (Philippians 3:10). Not only is Jesus with us in our suffering, but we are somehow with Him in His. When we experience a taste of what He suffered for us and recognize His sacrificial love in that suffering, we grow in intimacy with Him. It brings a deeper sense of awe regarding His steadfastness, His compassion, His patience, and His humility.

As Romans 8:28 tells us, "We know that in everything God works for good with those who love him, who are called according to his purpose." When we suffer, we are promised that good will come from it. Often we don't see that good thing occurring. We have to have faith that God is fulfilling that promise, but it may be that we need to wait until heaven to see exactly how He fulfills it. But we always can experience the good of being drawn closer to Christ. Suffering presses us close to the chest of Christ, and He holds us tightly as we pass through difficult times. In that intimate embrace, we come to know our Savior in a more personal way. That is the true gift. That is the treasure. "I count everything as loss because of the surpassing worth of knowing Christ Jesus my Lord" (Philippians 3:8).

Day Three: The Good Shepherd

Read John 10:1–21.

The imagery of sheep and a shepherd perfectly describes our relationship to Jesus. We are a lot like sheep. God seems to really love sheep throughout Scripture, despite the fact that they don't always make the best decisions. Sheep will eat grass in one area until there is nothing left, but they won't think to look for green grass somewhere else. A sheep will die of starvation if the shepherd doesn't lead him to fresh pasture. Sheep are helpless; if they fall over onto their backs, they can't get up. They need a shepherd to place them on their feet again. They are also defenseless. If they come face-to-face with a wolf, they'll simply freeze. They are prone to wander. Even if they are in the midst of a lush pasture, they'll wander to sparse ground and starve unless the shepherd brings them back.

Like sheep, how often do we feed on things that aren't good for us, wander away from God, and fall on our backs time and time again? Yet our Good Shepherd doesn't get tired of us; He continues to love us. Our vulnerability allows Him to show his tenderness, practicality, and provision. He draws us back to Him, offering shelter, love, protection, and guidance.

1. Using the story of a shepherd and his sheep, how did Jesus contrast the way He and the religious leaders treated the Jewish people? See John 10:1–2.

2. The Good Shepherd calls out His sheep by name. This is a mark of intimacy, familiarity, and trust. In the Bible a person's name has great significance. It signifies a person's character—what is unique about him or her. When Jesus calls us by name, it's a very personal call, one based upon His deep, thorough knowledge of who we are in the depths of our being. He knows us and considers us precious. What do the following verses mean to you in light of that truth?

    Isaiah 43:1

    Isaiah 49:1

    Isaiah 49:16

3. A. Jesus' third "I Am" is found in John 10:7–9. In chapter 6, we were introduced to Jesus as the Bread of Life, who makes sure we will never go hungry. In chapter 8, He is presented as the Light of the World, who dispels the darkness in our lives. What is Jesus' title in John 10:7–9?

    B. What do we experience if we receive Jesus in this way? In other words, how is that title associated with us?

4. A. Jesus' fourth "I Am" is found in John 10:11–14. Which title is He given here?

    B. What did Jesus say a Good Shepherd does?

        John 10:11

        John 10:14

John 10:16

John 10:17–21

Quiet your heart and enjoy His presence…Take a moment to contemplate Jesus' statements, "I am the gate," and "I am the Good Shepherd."

In the ancient Middle East, a shepherd would actually lie down across the opening of the sheepfold; he would be the door. He would be the protection at night. A wolf would have to fight him before reaching the sheep. If the sheep started to wander at night, they'd first encounter the shepherd.

Think about how this applies to your own life. Before heartache can ever touch your life, it has to go through God's hands. He measures your strength before it occurs. You may feel that you can't endure it, but He promises that with His help, you can. He is your protector. He will not let you be tempted or tried beyond what you can bear. Whatever you are going to experience in your future, He will have known it first.

Psalm 23 is a beautiful reflection of Jesus, our Divine Shepherd. Old Testament King David wrote it, reflecting back on his early years as a shepherd. He wrote, "The Lord is my shepherd, I shall not want; he makes me lie down in green pastures. He leads me beside still waters; he restores my soul. He leads me in paths of righteousness for his name's sake" (Psalm 23:1–3).

Verse 4 of Psalm 23 makes a change—David begins to write his words as a prayer, not just speaking about the Lord but speaking to Him. Make these words your own…

> *Even though I walk through the valley of the shadow of death,*
> *I fear no evil;*
> *For you are with me;*
> *Your rod and your staff,*
> *They comfort me.*
> *You prepare a table before me in the presence of my enemies;*
> *You anoint my head with oil,*
> *My cup overflows.*
> *Surely goodness and mercy shall follow me all the days of my life;*
> *And I shall dwell in the house of the Lord for ever. (Psalm 23:4–6)*

Day Four: The Feast of Dedication

Read John 10:22–28.

The Feast of Dedication was also called Hanukkah. This feast celebrated the deliverance of the Israelites from the Syrian oppression chronicled in 1 and 2 Maccabees. Specifically it celebrated the work of Judas Maccabeus in the cleansing and rededication (the consecration) of the Temple.

1. The Jews gathered around Jesus and asked Him to tell them whether He claimed to be the Messiah. Jesus replied that He had already told them and had done miracles to prove the truth of His words. Why did Jesus say they still didn't believe?

2. According to John 10:27, what must a person do to be considered one of Jesus' sheep?

3. Many people wonder how to hear God's voice. He speaks to us in many ways. He speaks to us and guides us through Scripture, through other people, through our circumstances, through the sacraments, and by guiding our thoughts. What insights do the following passages give regarding hearing from God?

    Psalm 25:8–9, 12

    Proverbs 2:6–9

    Proverbs 11:14

    Exodus 14:14

    John 16:13

4. According to John 10:28 and Romans 8:38–39, what can snatch us from God's loving hands?

Quiet your heart and enjoy His presence…Take a moment to contemplate Proverbs 3:5–6: "Trust in the Lord with all your heart, and do not rely on your own insight. In all your ways acknowledge him, and he will make straight your paths."

Only complete trust in Him will allow us to experience the protection, guidance, and security that Jesus offers us. In what area of your life are you feeling insecure? Can you trust God? Even when your own understanding suggests that you should take control, can you loosen your grip and ask God to take care of your needs?

Day Five: Rejected by the Jews

Read John 10:29–42.

1. Why were the Jews so scandalized when Jesus said, "I and the Father are one"?

2. Summarize Jesus' answer to the Jews found in John 10:34–36. His quote is from Psalm 82:6, which is a prayer to God that asks Him to punish the shepherds of Israel who were corrupt.

3. In John 10:36, Jesus claimed that He was consecrated by the Father, which means that He was "sanctified" or "set apart as holy." At which two solemn moments did the Father designate Jesus as "His beloved Son"? See CCC 444.

4. Name other ways in which Jesus was revealed as the Son of God.

   John 1:19–34

John 2:13–22

John 10:37–38

CCC 548

Quiet your heart and enjoy His presence…Take a moment to contemplate all the evidence that was set before the Jews; yet they still rejected Jesus as the Son of God.

Do you see the evidence that is around you? Does the creativity, intricacy, and grandeur of creation point you to the Creator? Have you seen changes in your personality and character and in the lives of people around you when God has been given the priority He deserves? Have you experienced answers to prayer? Allow all this evidence to strengthen your faith.

Conclusion

The Hebrew name for God, Yahweh, means "the God of grace; the God who is dependable; the faithful One; the God who is constant and in whom there is no change; the One who can be counted on to keep all His promises." We can count on Him, as our Good Shepherd, to protect, guide, comfort, and redeem us.

Our Good Shepherd is also the Lamb of God. He offers us redemption and His indwelling presence because of His sacrifice as the Lamb. He is the gateway to heaven. He is the door to salvation. He is the Good Shepherd. He is the Lamb of God. He is everything. He is all we need. He is more than enough.

If you've ever wished for someone to defend you…
If you've ever longed for someone to gently lead you…
If you've ever wanted to be protected by someone strong…
then fall into the loving arms of Jesus, the Good Shepherd.

If you lack direction, He will guide you.
If you are empty, He will fill you.
If you are weak, He will sustain you.
If you are facing a challenge, He will be with you to meet it.

If you are experiencing an unfulfilled longing, He will satisfy it.

Your Good Shepherd looks deep within your heart, beyond your actions and appearance, and sees what you need. He asks you to hear His voice and follow Him. He'll lead you to green pastures, where you can find rest for your soul.

My Resolution

In what specific way will I apply what I learned in this lesson?

Examples:

1. In my current suffering, I recognize others are watching my response. I have the opportunity to bring glory to God. I will ask God to enter my suffering and show me his face, giving me greater faith. I will look for the lessons I am learning through my difficulties and express that to people who want to know how I am doing.

2. In order to grow in my understanding of how I am loved personally by my Good Shepherd, Jesus, I will read the following Scriptures this week, inserting my name wherever I see the words *our*, *they*, and *them*: John 10:10, John 10:28, and 1 Peter 2:24–25.

My Resolution:

Catechism Clips

CCC 444 The Gospels report that at two solemn moments, the Baptism and the Transfiguration of Christ, the voice of the Father designates Jesus his "beloved Son." Jesus calls himself the "only Son of God," and by this title affirms his eternal pre-existence. He asks for faith in "the name of the only Son of God." In the centurion's exclamation before the crucified Christ, "Truly this man was the Son of God," that Christian confession is already heard. Only in the Paschal mystery can the believer give the title "Son of God" its full meaning.

CCC 548 The signs worked by Jesus attest that the Father has sent him. They invite belief in him. To those who turn to him in faith, he grants what they ask. So miracles strengthen faith in the One who does his Father's works; they bear witness that he is the

Son of God. But his miracles can also be occasions for "offence"; they are not intended to satisfy people's curiosity or desire for magic. Despite his evident miracles some people reject Jesus; he is even accused of acting by the power of demons.

CCC 588 Jesus scandalized the Pharisees by eating with tax collectors and sinners as familiarly as with themselves. Against those among them "who trusted in themselves that they were righteous and despised others," Jesus affirmed: "I have not come to call the righteous, but sinners to repentance." He went further by proclaiming before the Pharisees that, since sin is universal, those who pretend not to need salvation are blind to themselves.

CCC 1084 "Seated at the right hand of the Father" and pouring out the Holy Spirit on his Body which is the Church, Christ now acts through the sacraments he instituted to communicate his grace. The sacraments are perceptible signs (words and actions) accessible to our human nature. By the action of Christ and the power of the Holy Spirit they make present efficaciously the grace that they signify.

CCC 1508 The Holy Spirit gives to some a special charism of healing so as to make manifest the power of the grace of the risen Lord. But even the most intense prayers do not always obtain the healing of all illnesses. Thus St. Paul must learn from the Lord that "my grace is sufficient for you, for my power is made perfect in weakness," and that the sufferings to be endured can mean that "in my flesh I complete what is lacking in Christ's afflictions for the sake of his Body, that is, the Church.

Verse Study

See appendix 3 for instructions on how to complete a verse study.

John 10:4

1. Verse:

2. Paraphrase:

3. Questions:

4. Cross-references:

5. Personal Application:

 NOTES

Lesson 12

Jesus, the Resurrection and the Life

Introduction

There are a lot of truths about suffering that make sense…on paper. But when the police call in the middle of the night or your marriage fails or the medical report bears crushing news, these truths often lack comfort. You call out to God in hopes that He will make it all better or at least let you know why you are experiencing this pain. And you wait.

As you wait, well-meaning friends give advice. All too often this advice stings, or it makes you want to shout, "I already know these things! I know the truths, but they aren't comforting me. And what I need is comfort. I need something to soften this blow—something to lift this immense weight off my shoulders."

What you really need is Jesus Himself. If only He would explain. If only He'd come down and lift the weight. If only He'd take the pain. If only He'd make it all better. You may wonder where He is in the midst of your suffering.

Where is He? He is with you in the desolate place. No set of circumstances can separate you from the lover of your soul. The reason for suffering may be shrouded in mystery today. It may always be unclear why God allowed pain to come into your life. But if you will continue to trust Him, with time you will find that His presence is enough to get you through. You will come out the other end. You will still be standing. You will have endured beyond what you would have thought was possible, because the Lord held you together.

It isn't hard to relate to Mary and Martha in our reading this week. They understood loss, grief, heartbreak, and the confusion that accompanies the mystery of God's purposes. They didn't suffer because of their own mistakes. Mary was the one who chose the better part—who sat at Jesus' feet and soaked up His every word (Luke 10:42). She made the right choices, but tragedy still visited her door.

Day One: The Death of Lazarus

Read John 11:1–16.

1. Name three things in this passage that indicate Jesus' love for Mary, Martha, and Lazarus. Cite which verses illustrate His love.

2. "Now Jesus loved Martha and her sister and Lazarus. So when he heard that he was ill, he stayed two days longer" (John 11:5–6). It's easy to imagine that this purposeful wait was confusing to the disciples. If Jesus loved Lazarus so much, wouldn't He run to his side to help him before he died? Or why didn't Jesus just heal Lazarus with a word from afar, as He had done with the Roman official's son in John 4? Is it possible that Jesus made a miscalculation or a mistake by choosing to wait to help Lazarus?

3. What does the fact that Jesus waited longer before responding mean? How does Jesus show true love?

4. Have you ever prayed for something that didn't happen right away or at all? Did the waiting in any way bring glory to God?

5. Explain what Jesus meant by the words, "If anyone walks in the day, he does not stumble, because he sees the light of this world. But if anyone walks in the night, he stumbles, because the light is not in him" (John 11:9–10). Then apply these words to your own life.

As long as we are making decisions that are in keeping with God's will, we are safe. The safest place to be is in the center of God's will. Stonewall Jackson, a Confederate general during the Civil War, had this to say to one of his captains: "Captain, my religious belief teaches me to feel as safe in battle as in bed. God has fixed the time for my death. I do not concern myself about that, but to be always ready, no matter when it may overtake me. Captain, that is the way all men should live, and then all would be equally brave."[33] It's safer for us to be in a place of danger, if it's God's will, than in a seemingly safe place out of God's will.

6. We are so often tempted to measure God's love for us by the circumstances in which we find ourselves. What should the measure be?

Quiet your heart and enjoy His presence…Take a moment to contemplate the way in which God's divine love is that of a Father for His beloved child.

"God's love for His own is not a pampering love; it is a perfecting love. The fact that God loves us and we love Him is no guarantee that we will be sheltered from the problems and pains of life. After all, the Father loves His Son, and yet the Father permitted His beloved Son to drink the cup of sorrow and experience the shame and pain of the cross. We must never think that love and suffering are incompatible. Certainly they unite in Jesus Christ."[34]

Day Two: The Resurrection and the Life

Read John 11:17–27.

1. Mary and Martha had enjoyed a close relationship with Jesus. They shared an intimacy with Him that not many people did during His days on earth. Read Luke 10:38–42 for added insight into their friendship.

   A. What do you observe about Mary's relationship to Jesus from this passage? What does her behavior show us?

   B. In John 11:20, Mary and Martha responded differently to Jesus' arrival. How did they each respond? What might Mary have been feeling at this time?

---

33 John Selby, *Stonewall Jackson as Military Commander* (New York: Barnes and Noble Books, 2000), 25.

34 Warren Wiersbe, *The Wiersbe Bible Commentary: New Testament* (Colorado Springs: David C. Cook, 2007), 268.

2. In verses 21 and 32, Martha and Mary expressed a sentiment that echoes through the ages: "If you had been here, my brother would not have died." *If only!* It's easy to relate to the sentiment. It plagues us all when we are suffering and grieving. Death isn't the only thing that can cause us grief. Any change brings loss. We can experience the death of a dream, a marriage, a friendship, or our trust in a person. We can grieve when we move to a new area, when our children leave home and we are empty nesters, and when we experience the constraints and fears of financial hardship. Have you ever expressed an if-only to God when experiencing death, grief, or loss? Share your story.

3. Do you think Martha avoided the if-only trap? (See John 11:22.) In what way could she serve as an example for us when we grieve?

When we grieve, there is a period of time when it is necessary that our focus be on what we have lost. Stifling our feelings and refusing to look at them takes us to a place of unhealthy denial. This is not God's desire for us. But the time comes when our focus needs to shift, and we need to move toward healing. Otherwise we stay in the state of deep grief indefinitely, closing off our hearts and shutting down inwardly.

Martha showed faith in the midst of her grief by shifting her focus to what God could do. She said, "Even now I know that whatever you ask from God, God will give you." She left room in her grief for a miracle. If we will look for them, miracles will follow our grief. God promises to bring good out of our most terrible circumstances (Romans 8:28). He promises to do something in and through us when we experience suffering. But we must open our hearts to this possibility, or else bitterness or a spirit of resignation can take root in our hearts.

4. A. According to John 11:22, whom did Martha see as the one who could grant her request? In other words whom did she see as the source of life?

B. Jesus' reply in John 11:25 indicates who He wants her to believe is the source of life. Who is it? See also CCC 994.

C. Jesus didn't just state that He was the Resurrection and the Life. He asked Martha if she believed it. He asks us the same question. Do you believe that Jesus is the Resurrection and the Life? Do you believe He is the key not only to life after death but also to abundant life here on earth?

Quiet your heart and enjoy His presence...Take a moment to contemplate Martha's and Mary's responses to Jesus' late arrival.

They didn't hold back. They told Him just what they were feeling. Jesus invites us to follow their example. We have permission to tell God every if-only that we have stored up. We can pour out our hearts to Him. Hold nothing back. Are you angry with God in your grief? Tell Him. He already knows. He can handle your emotions. What He can't bear is when you hold back your heart from Him. Give Him what He most desires: honest dialogue. Let it out. He will not love you less.

Day Three: Jesus Weeps

Read John 11:28–37.

1. Imagine Mary's emotions as she went to meet Jesus. What did she need? What did Jesus give her? Can you apply this to the way we should respond to those who grieve?

2. Is grief a sin or a failure of faith? See Isaiah 53:3, Isaiah 63:8–9, and Romans 12:15.

3. When we read Revelation 21:4, what hope do we find in the midst of our grief and loss?

4. A. How did Jesus respond to Mary's grief?

B. In John 11:33, the Greek words translated as *"deeply moved"* or *"troubled in spirit"* mean "to be moved with anger." Why do you think Jesus responded this way?

It appears that Jesus was angry at the temporary victory that the devil experiences on earth. Death and grief were never supposed to be a part of our lives. This was not "plan A." In the Garden of Eden, man enjoyed God's presence, and there was no death. When sin entered the world, so did its consequences. Jesus experienced anger at the way in which evil destroys and hurts His loved ones. In the words of philosopher Francis Schaeffer:

> [Jesus] was furious; and he could be furious at the abnormality of death without being furious with Himself as God. This is tremendous in the context of the twentieth century. When I look at evil—the cruelty which is abnormal to that which God made—my reaction should be the same. I am able not only to cry over the evil, but I can be angry at the evil, as long as I am careful that egoism does not enter into my reaction. I have a basis to fight the thing which is abnormal to what God originally made. The Christian should be in the front line, fighting the results of man's cruelty, for we know that it is not what God has made. We are able to be angry at the results of man's cruelty [and the abnormal world resulting from sin] without being angry at God or being angry at what is normal.[35]

Quiet your heart and enjoy His presence…Take a moment to contemplate Jesus' presence in the midst of your suffering.

He is a fully personal God. He is your Savior, whose heart, hands, feet, and head bled for you. His heart aches over your pain. He weeps with you. He holds you as you cry. You may not see Him, but He is there.

Day Four: Lazarus Raised to Life

Read John 11:38–44.

1. When did the Jewish people believe that bodily decay begins? (See CCC 627.) In what condition would Lazarus' body be four days after death in a hot climate

---

35 Francis A. Schaeffer, *"He Is There and He Is Not Silent," in The Complete Works of Francis A. Schaeffer* (Westchester, IL: Crossway Books, 1982), I:301–2.

without embalming? How do you think Martha felt when Jesus told her to take away the stone that covered the tomb?

2. A. Many of the rabbis of Jesus' day believed that "the soul hovered near the body for three days but after that there was no hope of resuscitation."[36] Imagine being with Mary and Martha at the tomb. How hopeful did the situation seem?

B. Is there any situation in your life that appears hopeless?

C. How do the following verses help us when we are lacking hope?

1 Timothy 1:1

Ephesians 1:18

1 Peter 1:3–4

3. Why did Jesus pray? See CCC 2604.

4. What do you think Lazarus was experiencing? Jesus had just raised him from the dead. Might the words of Psalm 86:12–13 been on his mind and in his heart? Share your thoughts in the space that follows.

---

36 Ray, *St. John's Gospel*, 227.

5. Lazarus came out with his hands and feet still tied in burial cloths. He had experienced a rebirth, but the wrappings still kept him bound. Even when we have experienced spiritual rebirth, we can still be bound. What burial clothes need to be removed from you so that you can experience new life in Christ? Is there a bad habit, an unconfessed sin, a root of bitterness, or someone you need to forgive that is holding you back? Do you feel helpless in the face of habitual sin, longtime negative patterns? Are you bound by the slavery of perfectionism, equating worth with performance? Are you tied up by other people's expectations?

Quiet your heart and enjoy His presence…Take a moment to contemplate Jesus' words in John 11:41: "Father, I thank you that you have heard me."

His prayer was filled with confidence that God was always listening and ready to come to His aid. When we turn to God in prayer, He wants us to speak candidly with Him, as we would a friend. There is nothing weighing on our hearts that does not interest Him.

Once we pour out our requests, God is thrilled when we express our confidence in His sure and faithful response to our prayers. We can thank God for the answer He has set in motion, even when we can't see evidence of the results. No doubt, even though you've brought God your needs, the worries and concerns will continue to come to mind. When they do, stop and thank Him again for the answer He has already set in motion. Continuing to present the same request over and over can actually feed our fear. Thanking God for what He is doing at this very moment feeds our faith. Remember that prayer you begged God about? Prayerfully read Psalm 91:14–16, receiving these words from God, as spoken directly to you:

Because he cleaves to me in love, I will deliver him;

I will protect him, because he knows my name.

When he calls to me, I will answer him;

I will be with him in trouble,

I will rescue him and honor him.

With long life I will satisfy him,

And show him my salvation. (Psalm 91:14–16)

Day Five: The Plot to Put Jesus to Death

Read John 11:45–57.

1. How did the chief priests and the Pharisees react to the raising of Lazarus? What was the direct result of this miracle?

2. One might argue that at least the chief priests and Pharisees were concerned about the safety of their people and peace in their land. What do CCC 1753 and 1761 say about using immoral means to bring about an ultimate good?

3. What is the significance of Caiaphas' words in John 11:50–52?

4. In what sense do the events of this passage fulfil the prophecy of Psalm 86:14?

Quiet your heart and enjoy His presence…Take a moment to contemplate Caiaphas' words.

God was able to take the hate-filled words coming out of a man's mouth and make them a prophecy of His gift of salvation. God can take the most horrible circumstances and bring good from them. Even when it seems that evil is triumphing, God is still in control. Is there a circumstance in your life in which it appears that the devil is winning? Take heart! No circumstance is out of God's reach. If we will trust Him, even in times of darkness, when evil seems to have the upper hand, we will one day see the glory of God. It will be worth it. Keep holding on.

Conclusion

What circumstance in your life feels hopeless? Do you feel helpless to fix what is broken? Oh, beloved daughter of God, Jesus sees. Far from being distant from you in your trial, He has His eyes ever on you. Perhaps you have prayed, but His answer is delayed. Remember Mary and Martha's lesson: A delayed answer is not a refusal. God is at work. He wants to do more than just give a quick fix. He wants to bring glory to your situation. His purposes and His ways are so much bigger, so much better, than what you can imagine.

When Lazarus stepped out of the tomb, he was alive, but he was still wrapped in burial cloths. In what way do you feel bound? Do you wear burial cloths of expectations, perfectionism, or shame? Tight burial cloths keep us in a dark tomb, and it's hard to see a way of escape. Beloved one, God wants to set you free. He wants to unwrap your burial cloths, peel away each layer, and apply the balm of His unconditional love. He wants to release you to new life.

Dear God,

Please roll away the stone that stands between me and the abundant life You offer. Perhaps that stone is unbelief. If so, Jesus, please help me to see that You can do anything! Perhaps that stone is unconfessed sin. If so, Holy Spirit, please reveal to me what I need to confess, and give me the courage to be honest and real as I seek reconciliation. Perhaps that stone is a habit, something that gives me temporary comfort even while it hurts me. If so, almighty Father, fill me with the same resurrection power that raised Jesus from the dead, so that I can take the steps necessary to break free. Whatever my stone, please remove it. Lord, the one You love is sick. There is no physician like You. Come, Lord Jesus, come.

"But from there you will seek the Lord your God, and you will find him, if you search after him with all your heart and with all your soul" (Deuteronomy 4:29).

My Resolution

In what specific way will I apply what I learned in this lesson?

Examples:

1. Before Martha could see the glory of God, she had to obey. Jesus told her to roll away the stone. It was a step of faith, and she must have been afraid of what she would find. Obedience to God's will can be scary. This week I will identify an area of my life where I am afraid to obey. I'll ask God for faith like Martha's so that I can take the first step of obedience. I'll take the step, not looking ahead, not worrying about how I'll persevere the next day and the day after that. Instead I'll remember that God's strength and grace are sufficient for the day.

2. Someone I love is bound up in burial cloths. I will do what Lazarus' friends did for him. While I can't give her new life, I can help to unwrap the burial cloths. So many of the messages she hears each day keep her in that place of bondage. I'll counter those words by speaking words of truth and comfort into her life, telling her of God's unconditional love, reminding her of God's desire for her to experience a joyful and peace-filled life. I'll write her a letter or take her out for a cup of coffee to encourage her and show her that she's not alone.

My Resolution:

Catechism Clips

CCC 627 Christ's death was a real death in that it put an end to his earthly human existence. But because of the union which the person of the Son retained with his body, his was not a mortal corpse like others, for "it was not possible for death to hold him" and therefore "divine power preserved Christ's body from corruption." Both of these statements can be said of Christ: "He was cut off out of the land of the living (Acts 2:26–27)," and "My flesh will dwell in hope. For you will not abandon my soul to Hades, nor let your Holy One see corruption (Psalm 16:9, 10)." Jesus' Resurrection "on the third day" was the sign of this, also *because bodily decay was held to begin on the fourth day after death.* [emphasis added.]

CCC 994 But there is more. Jesus links faith in the resurrection to his own person: "I am the Resurrection and the life." It is Jesus himself who on the last day will raise up those who have believed in him, who have eaten his body and drunk his blood. Already now in this present life he gives a sign and pledge of this by restoring some of the dead to life, announcing thereby his own Resurrection, though it was to be of another order. He speaks of this unique event as the "sign of Jonah," the sign of the Temple: he announces that he will be put to death but rise thereafter on the third day.

CCC 1753 A good intention (for example, that of helping one's neighbor) does not make behavior that is intrinsically disordered, such as lying and calumny, good or just. The end does not justify the means. Thus the condemnation of an innocent person cannot be justified as a legitimate means of saving the nation. On the other hand, an added bad intention (such as vainglory) makes an act evil that, in and of itself, can be good (such as almsgiving).

CCC 1761 There are concrete acts that it is always wrong to choose, because their choice entails a disorder of the will, i.e., a moral evil. One may not do evil so that good may result from it.

CCC 2604 The second prayer, before the raising of Lazarus, is recorded by St. John. Thanksgiving precedes the event: "Father, I thank you for having heard me," which implies that the Father always hears his petitions. Jesus immediately adds: "I know that you always hear me," which implies that Jesus, on his part, constantly made such petitions. Jesus' prayer, characterized by thanksgiving, reveals to us how to ask: before the gift is given, Jesus commits himself to the One who in giving gives himself. The Giver is more precious than the gift; he is the "treasure"; in him abides his Son's heart; the gift is given "as well."

TRUST
NOT EXPECTATIONS

Verse Study

See appendix 3 for instructions on how to complete a verse study.

John 11:40

1. Verse:

2. Paraphrase:

3. Questions:

4. Cross-references:

5. Personal Application:

NOTES

Lesson 13

JESUS, THE KING

Introduction

How differently would you live if you knew that this was the last week of your life? Wouldn't every gesture, every interaction, every phone call take on new significance? What would you say to your loved ones? What would you do differently?

The events of John 12 took place six days before the Passover. Jesus' hour had come. A countdown had begun, and He wanted each moment to matter. He knew that He was to be the Passover Lamb, which meant that He had only a few days left to spend with His loved ones. His death was imminent.

While Jesus had typically quietly slipped away after His other miracles, He remained in Bethany after the raising of Lazarus. He knew that this miracle would ignite anger and fear in the hearts of the religious leaders. As the Sanhedrin[37] plotted His death, Jesus remained.

He was a king who had given up His throne in heaven and was now preparing for His greatest battle. He knew this would be a battle He would fight alone. How painful it must have been to look into the eyes of the people He was preparing to die for, knowing that they would be the ones clamoring for His crucifixion.

As we study Jesus' interactions and words this week, let's remember that in the back of His mind ran this perpetual thought: *I am preparing to die for you.*

---

37   The Sanhedrin was the supreme court of the Jews. While the raising of Lazarus upset all the religious leaders, it was especially maddening to the Sadducees, who didn't believe in the resurrection of the dead or eternal life. The raising of Lazarus made their lack of belief seem foolish.

Day One: Mary of Bethany

Read John 12:1–11.

The cost of the pure nard can be calculated this way: A Roman denarius is roughly equivalent to a day's wage.[38] If an average wage in today's currency was $100 a day, the cost of Mary's perfume would be $30,000. Perfume was often used as a financial investment due to size, easy transportability, and storage. It was in great demand and easily negotiated in the marketplace. This spikenard perfume may have represented Mary's life savings. The word used to describe the nard, "pure," is from the Greek word *pistis*, which is the word for "faith."[39]

1. What do you own that is worth almost a year's salary? What thoughts run through your mind as you imagine giving it all to Jesus? Do you think Mary had any of these same thoughts?

2. What is most important to us isn't necessarily money. We deeply value our marriages, our children, our time, our dreams, and our reputations. Think of something that is precious to you. What would it mean for you to pour this out at Jesus' feet?

3. Mary made an extravagant gesture of love to Jesus. As she did this, Judas sneered and mocked her sacrifice. When you think of giving your all to Jesus, do you worry what people will think? Whose approval are you afraid you will lose? How do the following verses encourage you to seek God's approval more than anyone else's? See Galatians 1:10 and John 12:42–43.

4. A. What do we learn about Judas Iscariot in John 12:4–6?

---

38 Matthew 20:2.
39 Ray, *St. John's Gospel*, 239.

B. In John 12:8, was Jesus saying that we don't need to take care of the poor? See Luke 11:41–42 and 12:33–34, Matthew 25:40, and CCC 2449.

Quiet your heart and enjoy His presence…Take a moment to contemplate what it would mean to sacrifice everything for Jesus.

It's a daunting thought. We imagine pouring out everything for Christ, and quickly our hearts catch. If I give everything to Christ, will I have anything left? Will there be enough left over to meet the needs of my family? Will I pour out everything and then have nothing? In John 12:3 we hear that "the house was filled with the fragrance of the ointment." Because we know of the association between the word for perfume and faith, perhaps John is telling us that the house (the Church) was filled with the beauty of Mary's faith and love. We long to be women who would imitate her gesture, but it isn't easy to offer Jesus what is most precious to us.

What holds each one of us back is unique. But I wonder if for many of us, if we were able to drill down to the depths of our hearts, we would find fear. 1 John 4:18 says that "perfect love drives out fear." The perfect love St. John is talking about in this verse does not find its source in us. It is a divine love that drives out fear. We can't muster this up. It's a gift that is infused into us, that seeps into our souls, the more time we spend with Jesus and the more we are able to experience His love.

Jesus loves you so much, my friend. He knows that what you are holding so close is very precious to you. He doesn't want you to pour it at His feet in order to control or manipulate you. He just knows the freedom that comes through surrender.

For many of us, the starting point is asking for the desire to surrender. Jesus meets us in this place. When we say, "Lord, I want to surrender to you, but you'll have to give me the desire for it and the ability to do it," He answers that prayer. He understands our reluctance. Sometimes "help me to desire it" is all we can offer the Lord. But be assured, He meets us where we are. Thanks be to God, His love is patient and kind (1 Corinthians 13:4).

Day Two: Jesus' Entry into Jerusalem

Read John 12:12–19.

We learned in John 12:9 that when the great crowd of Jews heard that Jesus had raised Lazarus from the dead, they came to Him in Bethany. When Jesus entered Jerusalem for the Passover feast, He was accompanied by the crowd from Bethany and was met by many of the pilgrims in Jerusalem who had heard that Jesus was approaching. What motivated them to come out in such droves to see Him? Here was a man whom the powerful religious leaders wanted to kill, and yet Jesus was brave enough to enter Jerusalem in broad daylight. Who was He? What was about to happen? Excitement filled the air. All wanted a glimpse of this courageous miracle worker. His name was on everyone's lips.

1. Read the following Old Testament passages and explain how they were fulfilled in the triumphal entry.

    Psalm 118:25–26

    Zechariah 9:9

2. For a king to ride on a donkey was a sign of peace and humility. In what way do the words *"peace"* and *"humility"* aptly describe the kingship of Jesus? See Ephesians 2:14, Philippians 4:7, and Philippians 2:5–8.

Jesus continues to relate to people in a spirit of humility. He doesn't charge into our lives, insisting that we give Him a throne in our hearts. Instead He issues an invitation. He offers His Lordship, which gives us the guidance, peace, and place of safety that our hearts need and desire. He is a gentleman. He doesn't force His way into our hearts.

3. A. At what point in the Mass do we say the words found in John 12:13 and Revelation 4:8? Why do you think it is significant that we say these words at this particular point in the Mass? See also CCC 1090.

B. The word *hosanna* means "God saves." Explain the significance of the crowd speaking this word to Jesus as He entered Jerusalem on Palm Sunday and of our own speaking of this word during Mass.

4. In John 12:16, St. John reflected, "His disciples did not understand this at first; but when Jesus was glorified, then they remembered." Has this ever been your experience? Can you think of a time when something didn't make sense in the midst of the circumstance, but later, you could see how God's hand had been in it, and you understood what had seemed confusing before?

Quiet your heart and enjoy His presence…Take a moment to contemplate the triumphal entry from the perspective of a Pharisee, written by Father John Bartunek, LC, in The Better Part. *Imagine you are there, seeing what the Pharisee sees. How will you respond?*

That was the day I started to believe in Jesus. Up until then I was convinced that He deserved to be silenced. But I was standing on the city walls when He came to Jerusalem, and I watched the crowds behind and before Him surge together like two great tides colliding. As He approached, I could see His face. The look He gave them wasn't the look of a power-hungry and self-absorbed demagogue. It was calm, glad, and—well, it sounds rather anticlimactic, but I think the best word to describe it is—good. His countenance irradiated goodness. The irrepressible ebullience of that immense mass of humanity would have made any normal man drunk with their adoration. But not Jesus. And for some reason, I recognized immediately why He was riding on the donkey. I had just been meditating on the prophecy of Zechariah that described how the Messiah would enter into His reign just this way. I had a kind of intuitive flash as I watched Him make His way slowly and gently through the forest of palm branches and the din of cheers. I seemed to see that this was the first swell of something entirely new, of a Kingdom that would surpass all of our small and antiquated expectations. And then—you may not believe me, but I promise you, it's true—then, just before He passed through the gate, He looked up, and His eyes met mine. His gaze gripped me and shone right through me as sunlight shines through glass; I couldn't resist it, but I didn't want to do so. It was just for a split second. And with that look He said to me, "Yes it is so"—just as if He had known everything I had been thinking while I watched His triumphal entry! And He had known it.

He knew it all, because in His mercy and love He had been inspiring those thoughts. From that day forward, I believed.[40]

Day Three: The Arrival of the Greeks

Read John 12:20–26.

1. Why did the arrival of the Greeks (in verses 20–21) prompt Jesus to say, "The hour has come for the Son of man to be glorified"? See John 1:29, 4:42, and 1 John 2:2.

2. A. How were Jesus' words in John 12:24 a description of what would happen through His death and Resurrection?

   B. There is a lesson for us in John 12:24: Blessing comes from brokenness. Can you think of an example from your own life when you have experienced this?

3. A. What do you think Jesus meant when He said, "He who hates his life in this world will keep it for eternal life" (John 12:25)? Does this mean that our earthly lives don't have value? Does He give us permission to live any way we feel like living?

   B. In speaking these words, does Jesus give us permission for self-destructive tendencies?

Quiet your heart and enjoy His presence…Take a moment to contemplate what a self-sacrificing King we serve.

When you are going through trials—little ones or big ones—deaths of a sort, and experiences of brokenness, it's important to remember that Jesus understands suffering from experience. Jesus entered

---

40   Bartunek, *The Better Part*, 918–9.

into what appeared to be meaningless suffering. He is not indifferent to what you are enduring. He sees all the little and big deaths that you experience. And He stands ready to bring new life in those places that feel desolate.

The prophet Jeremiah wrote of that process of transformation: "This word came to Jeremiah from the Lord: Arise and go down to the potter's house; there you will hear my word. I [Jeremiah] went down to the potter's house and there he was, working at the wheel. And the vessel he was making of clay was spoiled in the potter's hand, and he reworked it into another vessel, as it seemed good to the potter to do…can I not do with you as this potter has done? says the Lord. Behold, like the clay in the potter's hand, so are you in my hand" (Jeremiah 18:1–6).

These are the verses that get me through hardship. In difficult times I don't want to experience what I am going through. I want to escape. But these verses stop me before I numb out and remind me that I have a choice. I can offer myself to God as clay to a potter. I can say to Him, "In this particular set of undesired circumstances, I give you permission to shape me—to mold me—to transform me, because I want to experience a better eternity. I want to become the woman you created me to be. And if a death of sorts is required for new life to be born in me, I accept it. I say yes. I say, Jesus, I trust in you."

When the potter sees a bubble or a defect in the pot, he has to press the clay back onto the wheel and reshape the pot. But all the while, he is making it into something of great beauty. So here is the question: Can we trust God that when He asks us to experience something that is hard, He promises to use it to mold us into vessels that are filled with His Spirit? May we never forget—He can turn brokenness into blessing and beauty.

For further insight into the way in which suffering can be transformative, see appendix 6, "You, Take Russia!" by Father John Riccardo.

Day Four: Jesus Speaks About His Death

Read John 12:27–36.

1. A. Why was Jesus troubled in verse 27?

    B. What did Jesus request of His Father in John 12:28?

C. In what way can God's name be glorified when one of His children is suffering? Give an example of a time you have seen this occur.

2. What other times did the Father speak to Jesus audibly from heaven? See Matthew 3:17 and 17:5. What was the purpose of the Father speaking audibly?

3. A. When did Jesus defeat the ruler of this world, Satan? See Hebrews 2:14–15 and CCC 2853.

   B. When will Jesus destroy the ruler of this world (Satan)? See Revelation 20:10.

It is important to recognize that the Catholic Church teaches that Satan is real. CCC 2851 states, "Evil is not an abstraction, but refers to a person, Satan, the Evil One, the angel who opposes God. The devil…is the one who 'throws himself across' God's plan and his work of salvation accomplished in Christ." We are to avoid both the extreme of obsessive interest in Satan and disbelief in him. C. S. Lewis says it well in *The Screwtape Letters*: "There are two equal and opposite errors into which our race can fall about the devils. One is to disbelieve in their existence. The other is to believe, and to feel an excessive and unhealthy interest in them. They themselves are equally pleased by both errors and hail a materialist or a magician with the same delight."[41]

4. Satan has been defeated, but he has not been destroyed yet. He knows his destination and is determined to drag as many people along with him as he possibly can. He seeks to destroy God's children by tempting them to turn away from God (the light) and toward him (the darkness) through their beliefs and actions. But we are not to be discouraged or frightened by this. We can have hope and confidence in the face of such attacks. Read 1 John 4:4, Ephesians 1:18–20, and 1 Corinthians 10:13, and then explain how this is possible for us.

---

41   C. S. Lewis, *The Screwtape Letters* (New York: HarperOne, 2001), ix.

Quiet your heart and enjoy His presence…Take a moment to contemplate the ways in which God communicates with you.

Does God speak to you through the Scriptures? Has He ever offered you guidance through the wise counsel of a godly friend? Do you sense His direction when you quiet your heart in prayer? Think of an area of your life where you repeatedly experience temptation. As you think of this specific temptation, ask God to show you "the way of escape" that He promises to provide. Ask Him for an awareness throughout your day of the indwelling Holy Spirit, who stands at the ready to prove to you His power—a power far stronger than the pull of any sinful habit. The King of the Universe is on your side and is fighting for you! He has defeated your enemy.

Day Five: The Unbelief of the People

Read John 12:37–50.

1. "Though he had done so many signs before them, yet they did not believe in him" (John 12:37). What were some of the reasons the Jewish people did not believe in Jesus despite having seen Him perform astounding miracles?

   John 12:38–40, which quotes the prophet Isaiah, seems to be saying that God decided to blind their eyes and harden their hearts, as if they had no choice but to reject Jesus. It sounds as if God forced this reaction. It is essential to recognize that God, in His justice, allowed their eyes to be blinded and hearts to be hardened *as a result* or *as a consequence* of their disbelief. When Isaiah spoke these words, it was after he had preached to the Israelites for years and they hadn't repented. The message of the Bible from Genesis to Revelation is of God's plan to redeem all of humanity and to offer them a way back to Him: "[He] is forbearing toward you, not wishing that any should perish, but that all should reach repentance" (2 Peter 3:9).

2. We were created to worship; everyone worships something. Do I love ("worship") something that causes me to be blind or hard of heart toward spiritual values? In your experience, what are some things that people choose to worship, leading to the spiritual condition of blindness and hardness of heart?

3. When you read Jesus' words in John 12:44–47, what tone do you imagine him having? Pleading? Mourning? Let the meaning of His words in verse 47 penetrate your heart. He did not come to judge. He came to redeem. He came to bring mercy. He came to forgive. He came to build a bridge between you and your heavenly Father. Are we known by our mercy, humility, and love or by our judgment, criticism, and superiority?

Quiet your heart and enjoy His presence…Take a moment to contemplate our King entering Jerusalem on a donkey.

Notice His humility, His tenderness, and the peace that emanates from Him. But don't draw the conclusion that He lacks strength. He has the power to overcome death, defeat the enemy, and speak the world into existence. This power is never misused: "He will not break a bruised reed or quench a smoldering wick" (Matthew 12:20). He knows our struggles, weaknesses, and heartaches. He sees beyond the behavior to the person in pain. He loves us too much to leave us in harmful patterns of sinful behavior, so He restores us with gentleness.

Dear Lord,
Thank You for dealing with me mercifully. Sometimes I think that all I deserve is judgment. Yet You always forgive me mercifully. Help me to share that same mercy with others. When I see people making bad choices, it's so tempting to criticize and judge. Help me to remember that I don't see the whole picture in another person's life. Change me so that people feel love from me instead of judgment. Help me to remember that mercy triumphs over judgment.

Conclusion

What a contrast we see between the people who wouldn't believe in Jesus despite His miracles and Mary, who poured out her life savings from her alabaster jar over her King's feet. When Mary poured out her love through this extravagant act of worship, the fragrance filled the whole house. This is always the result of sacrifice made for Jesus. Will you follow Mary's example? Will you bow before your King and break your alabaster jar at His feet? If you will, the fragrance of your sacrifice will permeate the lives of those around you. The cost will be high. The sacrifice may be painful. But how can we hold anything back from the One who poured out everything for us?

In the early light of creation's dawn, the Father held His Alabaster Jar. It gleamed with the beauty of the Morning Star and was scented with the fragrance of the Rose of Sharon. It was His most precious possession. As His omniscient eyes looked down the years that stretched out before Him into generations and centuries and ages and millennia, He knew...

The Father slipped into the darkness of the world He had made and loved. The hands that held the Jar with such tender, eternal love, relaxed and opened as He placed the Jar ever so gently on the small manger bed of hay. During the years that followed, the beauty and the glory of the Jar were shared and admired by those who had eyes to see.

And then, with hands that were trembling yet certain, the Father once again picked up His Alabaster Jar. And on a hill so far away from His celestial home—a hill that was cold, barren, and bleak, swarming with an angry mob that was unruly and obscene—the Father smashed His Alabaster Jar on a rugged, wooden cross. As the contents of flesh and blood were poured out and the fragrance of His love permeated human history forever, our tears were on His face.[42]

My Resolution

In what specific way will I apply what I learned in this lesson?

Examples:

1. My alabaster jar is my time. I want to break it at Jesus' feet. I will do this by giving up something I love (perhaps sleep, a tennis match, a TV program, social media, checking my email first thing in the morning) in order to give Him that time, to be spent in prayer. Instead of rushing through my Bible study lesson, I'll take time to connect with Jesus first. I will make Him King over my time.

2. I recognize in myself the tendency to be critical and to judge. Each time I begin to think negatively about a person this week, I'll stop and pray for him or her. I'll remind myself that I don't know the full story of what that person is going through, the pain that's been endured, or the person's current heartache.

My Resolution:

---

42   Anne Graham Lotz, *My Heart's Cry* (Nashville, TN: W Publishing Group, 2002), 42.

Catechism Clips

CCC 1090 In the earthly liturgy we share in a foretaste of that heavenly liturgy which is celebrated in the Holy City of Jerusalem toward which we journey as pilgrims, where Christ is sitting at the right hand of God, Minister of the sanctuary and of the true tabernacle. With all the warriors of the heavenly army we sing a hymn of glory to the Lord; venerating the memory of the saints, we hope for some part and fellowship with them; we eagerly await the Savior, our Lord Jesus Christ, until he, our life, shall appear and we too will appear with him in glory.

CCC 2449 Beginning with the Old Testament, all kinds of juridical measures (the jubilee year of forgiveness of debts, prohibition of loans at interest and the keeping of collateral, the obligation to tithe, the daily payment of the day-laborer, the right to glean vines and fields) answer the exhortation of Deuteronomy: "For the poor will never cease out of the land; therefore I command you, 'You shall open wide your hand to your brother, to the needy and to the poor in the land.' Jesus makes these words his own: "The poor you always have with you, but you do not always have me." In so doing he does not soften the vehemence of former oracles against "buying the poor for silver and the needy for a pair of sandals…" but invites us to recognize his own presence in the poor who are his brethren:

> When her mother reproached her for caring for the poor and the sick at home, St. Rose of Lima said to her, "When we serve the poor and the sick, we serve Jesus. We must not fail to help our neighbors, because in them we serve Jesus."

CCC 2851 In this petition, evil is not an abstraction, but refers to a person, Satan, the Evil One, the angel who opposes God. The devil (*diabolos*) is the one who "throws himself across" God's plan and his work of salvation accomplished in Christ.

CCC 2853 Victory over the "prince of this world" was won once for all at the hour when Jesus freely gave himself up to death to give us his life. This is the judgment of this world, and the prince of this world is "cast out."

Verse Study

See appendix 3 for instructions on how to complete a verse study.

John 12:24

1. Verse:

2. Phrase:

3. Questions:

4. Cross-references:

5. Personal Application:

NOTES

Lesson 14: Connect Coffee Talk 4

JESUS, THE KING

The accompanying talk can be viewed via DVD or digital download purchase or accessed online at walkingwithpurpose.com/videos.

Key Verses

"Unless a grain of wheat falls into the earth and dies, it remains alone; but if it dies, it bears much fruit. He who loves his life loses it, and he who hates his life in this world will keep it for eternal life" (John 12:24–25).

"Now my soul is troubled. And what shall I say? 'Father, save me from this hour'? No, for this purpose I have come to this hour. Father, glorify your name!" (John 12:27–28).

"Trust in the Lord with all your heart, and do not rely on your own insight. In all your ways acknowledge him, and he will make straight your paths" (Proverbs 3:5–6).

"Mercy triumphs over judgment" (James 2:13).

"I can do all things in him who strengthens me" (Philippians 4:13).

"Apart from me you can do nothing" (John 15:5).

Jesus invites us to break our alabaster jars at His feet and become women of spiritual abandon.

I. **Build on the Foundation of God's Love**

    A. Abandon is the impulse that arises from a heart that is full of confidence in the Father's love and protection.

    Like the little child who sleeps in her father's arms, we can be that secure in God's love for us.

B. Our trust in God gives us the freedom to live life courageously.

II. Delve into God's Mercy

God waits for us to turn to Him and then delights in forgiving us. There is no sin that is beyond His mercy.

III. Pray in a Way That Builds Trust in God

Hold *nothing* back from Christ. There is no safer place than in the center of His will. That is where we will find our destiny and our joy.

The following prayers help to realign the heart each day:

Prayer for Perfect Resignation: My God, I do not know what must come to me today. But I am certain that nothing can happen to me that You have not foreseen, decreed, and ordained from all eternity. That is sufficient for me. I adore Your steadfast and eternal plans for my life, to which I submit with all my heart. I desire, I accept the all, and I unite my sacrifice to that of Jesus Christ, my divine Savior. I ask, in His name and through His infinite merits, patience in my trials and perfect and entire submission to all that comes to me by Your good pleasure. Amen.[43]

Prayer for Attaining Holy Abandonment: O my God, when will it please You to give me the grace of remaining habitually in that union of my will with Your adorable will, and in which, without our saying anything, all is said, and in which we do everything by letting You act. In this perfect union of wills we perform immense tasks because we work more in conformity with Your good pleasure; and yet we are dispensed from all toil because we place the care of everything in Your hands and think of nothing but reposing completely in You—a delightful state which even in the absence of all feelings of faith gives the soul an interior and altogether spiritual relish. Let me say then unceasingly through the habitual disposition of my heart, "Fiat! Yes, my God, yes, everything You please. May Your holy desires be fulfilled in everything. I give up my own which are blind, perverse, and corrupted by that miserable self-love which is the mortal enemy of Your grace and pure love, of Your glory and my own sanctification."[44]

---

43 Michael Harter, *Hearts on Fire: Praying with Jesuits* (St. Louis: Institute of Jesuit Sources, 1993), 64.

44 Jean-Pierre de Caussade, SJ, in Harter, *Hearts on Fire*, 65.

Questions for Discussion or Journaling

1. What area of your life or which person whom you love do you most want to control?

2. John 12:24–25 says, "Unless a grain of wheat falls into the earth and dies, it remains alone; but if it dies, it bears much fruit. He who loves his life loses it, and he who hates his life in this world will keep it for eternal life." Can you think of an example from your own life when something you treasured died, but seeds and fruitfulness resulted? Is there something in your life that you need to allow to fall to the ground and die?

3. Does your fear of losing your reputation with others (perhaps those who might say, "Why this waste?" Matthew 26:8) hold you back from giving your all to Jesus?

NOTES

Lesson 15

JESUS, THE SERVANT

Introduction

In John chapter 12, Jesus entered Jerusalem on a donkey, hailed as the King, the Messiah, and the hope of Israel. The disciples were now gathered in the upper room in Jerusalem. The mood had changed. The palm branches were gone, and the party was over. There was a solemnity in the room, a spirit of expectancy, an intensity of emotion.

This is the night when Jesus was betrayed. He only had a few hours left with His precious friends. What would He say? The next five chapters of John (13 through 17) contain Jesus' final instructions to His disciples—His last will and testament. In these chapters Jesus taught what He most wanted us to hear.

His first lesson wasn't taught with words. Jesus rose from the table and washed His disciples' feet. Washing feet was an unpleasant job typically reserved for servants. The streets of those days weren't just used by people, and they weren't paved. Animal waste mixed with dirt and became caked on everyone's sandal-clad feet as they went about their day. Foot washing was a disgusting, menial job but necessary if you didn't want your dinner party ruined by nasty smells. When Jesus bent down to wash His disciples' feet, He showed us sacrificial love in action.

Jesus' action wasn't performed begrudgingly. He *willingly* bent down and washed the dirt from His disciples' feet. Today He longs to bend down and wash the dirt within us. In the words of Saint John Paul II, "Do not be afraid! Throw open the doors to Christ!" Lay aside your pride, your self-sufficiency, your attempts to clean yourself up, your fear of letting Him see the real you. Give Him full access to your heart and experience the peace that comes from His cleansing. Nothing will please Him more. He won't recoil from anything He sees in you. Our need draws Him to us.

Day One: The Hour Had Come

Read John 13:1–4.

Jesus and His disciples were celebrating the Passover, one of the most significant feasts in the Jewish calendar. This feast of remembrance brought to mind their rescue from slavery in Egypt. God told the Israelites that in order to avoid being affected by the final plague, they were to take a lamb without defect and slaughter it. The blood of the lamb was to be painted on the doorframe, and the lamb was to be eaten. That night when the Lord passed through Egypt and struck down every firstborn, He passed over each door that had the blood on the top and sides of the doorframe. Jesus was about to fulfill the Passover, as the Lamb of God, without defect, without sin.

1. John 13:1 says that "having loved his own who were in the world, [Jesus] loved them to the end." That's how He loves you too.

   Describe God's love for you based on the following verses:

   Jeremiah 31:3

   Zephaniah 3:17

   Romans 5:8 and 1 John 4:9–10

   Romans 8:38–39

2. Who put it into the heart of Judas to betray Jesus? Why? What is he doing in our world today? See 1 Peter 5:8.

3. When Jesus rose from the table, He took off His outer garment and stood in a simple tunic, the clothing of a slave. What does this mean?

A. According to John 13:3, what did Jesus know as He prepared to wash the disciples' feet?

B. On what were Jesus' dignity and identity based? See also John 8:42 and CCC 423.

4. A. Think of someone you would find difficult to serve. Would you, in some sense, feel diminished or degraded if you served that person? Recall times when you may have thought, *I will look foolish if I serve my husband/mother-in-law/difficult work colleague in this way.* What is the basis for this kind of thinking?

B. What is the source of your dignity? Does it make it any easier to serve when you remember that you are God's precious daughter, full of grace and worth?

Quiet your heart and enjoy His presence...Take a moment to contemplate Philippians 2:3–4: "Do nothing from selfishness or conceit, but in humility count others better than yourselves. Let each of you look not only to his own interests, but also to the interests of others."

Ask God whom He wants you to serve today. Ask Him to help you see concrete ways that you can do so. Keep Jesus ever before you as the ultimate example. "For the Son of man also came not to be served but to serve, and to give his life as a ransom for many" (Mark 10:45).

Day Two: Washing the Disciples' Feet

Read John 13:5–17.

1. In John 13:8, How did Jesus react when Peter said that he didn't want Jesus to wash his feet?

2. To understand John 13:10, it's helpful to look at the original Greek words used for *"bathe"* and *"wash."* The Greek word for *"bathe"* is *loúō*, which means "to cleanse the entire person." Various forms of this word are used in the New Testament to describe Baptism (see 1 Corinthians 6:11, Ephesians 5:26, Titus 3:5, and Hebrews 10:22). The Greek word for *"wash"* is *nipto*, which means "to cleanse the hands, the feet, or the face." The study notes in the Ignatius Catholic Study Bible state, "Jesus' words hint at the distinction between Baptism, which washes away every stain of sin committed (actual) and contracted (Original), and the Sacrament of Reconciliation, which cleanses us of the accumulated dust of sins committed after our baptismal washing." [45]

   Read the following quote by Saint Gregory of Nazianzus, found in CCC 1216, underlining any phrases that are especially meaningful to you:

   > Baptism is God's most beautiful and magnificent gift…We call it gift, grace, anointing, enlightenment, garment of immortality, bath of rebirth, seal, and most precious gift. It is called gift because it is conferred on those who bring nothing of their own; grace since it is given even to the guilty; Baptism because sin is buried in the water; anointing for it is priestly and royal as are those who are anointed; enlightenment because it radiates light; clothing since it veils our shame; bath because it washes; and seal as it is our guard and the sign of God's Lordship.

3. A. In John 13:14, Jesus said, "You also ought to wash one another's feet." Share a real-life example of a time when someone has "washed your feet."

   B. "Love is not feelings; it is not noble desires; love is self-giving. Love is costly." [46] How can you follow Christ's example by displaying self-forgetful love today?

   LOVE NOT FEELING

---

45   Ignatius Catholic Study Bible, RSV, 187.

46   Bartunek, *The Better Part*, 929.

4. A. Luke's Gospel gives us added insight into this scene. According to Luke 22:24, what had the disciples been discussing just before Jesus washed their feet?

    B. How does Jesus define true greatness? See Matthew 23:11–12.

Quiet your heart and enjoy His presence…Take a moment to contemplate the following quote from Martin Luther King Jr. When you finish, ask God to help you to shed any selfishness that keeps you from true greatness as He defines it.

The setting is clear. James and John are making a specific request of Jesus—"when you establish your kingdom, let one of us sit on the right hand and the other on the left hand of your throne." What was the answer that Jesus gave these men? It's very interesting. One would have thought that Jesus would have condemned them. One would have thought that Jesus would have said, "You are out of your place. You are selfish. Why would you raise such a question?"

But that isn't what Jesus did; He did something altogether different. He said in substance, "Oh, I see, you want to be first. You want to be great. You want to be important. You want to be significant. Well, you ought to be. If you're going to be my disciple, you must be." But He reordered priorities. And He said, "Yes, don't give up this instinct. It's a good instinct if you use it right. It's a good instinct if you don't distort it and pervert it. Don't give it up. Keep feeling the need for being important. Keep feeling the need for being first. But I want you to be first in love. I want you to be first in moral excellence. I want you to be first in generosity. That is what I want you to do."

And He transformed the situation by giving a new definition of greatness. And you know how He said it? He said, "Now brethren, I can't give you greatness. And really, I can't make you first." This is what Jesus said to James and John. "You must earn it. True greatness comes not by favoritism, but by fitness. And the right hand and the left are not mine to give; they belong to those who are prepared."

And so Jesus gave us a new norm of greatness. If you want to be important—wonderful. If you want to be recognized—wonderful. If you want to be great—wonderful. But recognize that He who is greatest among you shall be your servant. That's a new definition of greatness.

And this morning, the thing that I like about it [is this]: By giving that definition of greatness, it means that everybody can be great, because everybody can serve. You don't have to have a college degree to serve. You don't have to make your subject and your verb agree to serve. You don't have family solidarity *to know about Plato and Aristotle to serve. You don't have to know Einstein's theory of relativity to serve. You don't have to know the second theory of thermodynamics in physics to serve. You only need a heart full of grace, a soul generated by love. And you can be that servant."* [47]

Day Three: Jesus Foretells His Betrayal

Read John 13:18–30.

1. Did the other disciples suspect Judas of duplicity and betrayal? See John 13:22 and 28.

2. What went wrong? How could Judas have been with Jesus for three years and not loved Him? At some point, something happened to Judas' heart. His actions must not have given away what was going on within, or the disciples would have recognized him as the betrayer. His was an *internal* battle. This interior battle is common to everyone. We all struggle to have the right intentions, desires, and thoughts. How does the progression of sin occur? Answer the following questions to see how we can stop the progression of sin in its tracks so that we aren't led down the same path of destruction that Judas followed.

   A. According to James 1:13–14, what does and does not lead a person into temptation?

   B. The Amplified Bible translates James 1:14 this way: "But each person is tempted when he is lured and enticed by his own desire." What might have been some of the passions or desires that caused Judas to betray Jesus? See also John 12:6.

   C. In your own life, what kinds of passions and desires most often tempt you to do things your way instead of God's way? Where do you notice chronic weakness within? Note that sometimes the desire is inherently good, but the way you are seeking to have that desire met is not.

---

47   Martin Luther King Jr., "Drum Major Instinct" (sermon), Ebenezer Baptist Church, Atlanta, February 4, 1968.

D. James 1:15 says, "Desire when it has conceived gives birth to sin." If we want to keep from sinning, we need to do something about our desires within. What do the following verses suggest as a safeguard against harmful desires?

Proverbs 4:23

2 Corinthians 10:5

3. What a contrast in relationships is painted in this passage of Scripture! Judas and John responded to Jesus in completely different ways. How did St. John describe himself in John 13:23? How did he describe his proximity to Jesus in this scene? Are these words reflective of your relationship with Jesus?

4. When Jesus handed the piece of bread to Judas, it wasn't just to show St. John who was to betray Him. In those times it was a special honor for the host to personally hand a piece of food to one of the guests; it was a gesture of deep friendship.[48] Looking at John 6:70–71, 12:4–8, and 13:10 and this week's lesson, what are some of the ways that Jesus encouraged Judas to reconsider his betrayal?

There were many opportunities for Judas' conscience to be pricked. In John 13:18, Jesus quoted Psalm 41 (a psalm David wrote after experiencing deep betrayal) and said, "He who ate my bread has lifted his heel against me." Jesus' words were meant to cause Judas to reconsider his course of action in a manner that was both subtle and pointed. When Jesus gave Judas the piece of bread, it was a last appeal of friendship. Culturally, sharing a meal was a sign of true friendship. The fact that Judas rose and betrayed Jesus after eating with Him was evidence of a heart hardened over time by choice after choice.

Quiet your heart and enjoy His presence…Take a moment to contemplate how the story of Judas ended.

He eventually felt remorse, but remorse is not the same as repentance. Judas wished he hadn't betrayed Jesus. He wished things hadn't turned out so horrifically. He never intended it to be so brutal. But Judas

---

48 Ray, *St. John's Gospel*, 259.

never repented. He never turned to Jesus to ask for forgiveness. In that same vein, we may regret certain actions and experience a great deal of guilt about them. But if our remorse doesn't lead to repentance, we'll never experience forgiveness and healing. True repentance involves saying we are sorry to God and then turning in a new direction. Talk to God about any area of your life in which you have expressed remorse but not repentance. Draw close to the mercy seat of Christ, where the answer to the sincere question "Do you forgive me?" is always yes.

Day Four: The New Commandment

Read John 13:31–38.

God was soon to be glorified in Jesus when Jesus willingly submitted to death on the cross in order to reconcile us to God. It was also to God's glory that He would have such love for mankind that He'd be willing to spare His own Son for our sake.

1. A. What was the new commandment that Jesus gave the disciples? See John 13:34.

    B. In what way was this commandment different from the Old Testament commandment found in Leviticus 19:18?

2. A. In what way are people to know that we are Christ's disciples? See John 13:35.

    B. According to Romans 5:5, how is it possible for us to love as Christ loved us?

3. What did Jesus prophesy about Peter in John 13:38? Did it occur? See John 18:17 and 25–27.

4. A. What are the two main lessons of John 13? See John 13:14–15 and 34–35.

ways to
impact

B. Do you think Christians stand out in our world today because of the radical way they love? Why or why not?

Quiet your heart and enjoy His presence…Take a moment to contemplate the way you love.

Read the words of 1 Corinthians 13:4–7, substituting your name in place of the word "love": "Love is patient and kind; love is not jealous or boastful; it is not arrogant or rude. Love does not insist on its own way; it is not irritable or resentful; it does not rejoice at wrong, but rejoices in the right. Love bears all things, believes all things, hopes all things, endures all things."

How do I love the lovable? How do I love the "unlovable"? How do I treat my enemies? How do I treat those who have hurt people I love? Ask God to reveal to you whom He wants you to love radically. Ask Him for the grace to obey Him and for the insight to see creative ways you can express love. Remember that love isn't a matter of feelings; it is a decision.

Remember a time when your life has exemplified the truth of the statement "It's by His grace that we love." Ask for His help in the areas of your life in which you struggle. He will be faithful to fill up your heart with love so that it overflows into the lives of those around you. But you have to ask Him to do it; He's a gentleman and won't force His way into your heart.

Day Five: Jesus, the Way, the Truth, and the Life

Read John 14:1–14.

Our passage for today begins with Jesus' words: "Let not your hearts be troubled." Troubles come our way; none of us are able to avoid them. So how can we have trouble-free hearts in the midst of unhappy circumstances? How can we have peaceful hearts if our marriages aren't what we hoped for? How can we have peaceful hearts when the medical report brings bad news? How can we have peaceful hearts when our children disappoint, finances are tight, or death robs us of a loved one?

Our emotions run wild when we face difficulties. Our imagination kicks into gear. We analyze every detail over and over again. Fear takes over and peace seems elusive.

Yet if Jesus told us not to have troubled hearts, then peace must be possible. Jesus never asks anything for which He doesn't give the means. He said, "Let not your hearts be troubled; believe in God, believe also in me." Therein lie the keys: trust and faith.

1. How is the Father's house described in John 14:2–3 and CCC 2795?

2. A. What will heaven be like? See CCC 1024 and 1025.

   B. How did Jesus say we are to reach the Father in heaven in John 14:6? What was He claiming by this statement? See also Acts 4:12.

   C. The single most important decision you will ever make is whether you will trust Jesus. This position of faith affects your experience of daily life as well as where you'll spend eternity. Have you placed your trust in Jesus or in something or someone else?

The following prayer is one way to express trust in Jesus:

> *Thank You, dear God, for Your limitless love for me. I need You. Without You I'll never experience the forgiveness and freedom that I desire. Thank You for Your sacrifice on the cross. Thank You for loving me and dying for me, even when I have been such a mess. Forgive me for all the times that I've chosen what I want instead of what You want for me. I don't deserve Your grace, yet You pour it out on me. Fill my emptiness with Your presence. Be my peace. May my will be changed so that what I want is what You want, when You want it, and how You want it. I've tried to run my life for so long. I want You to run it from this day forward. I want You to be in the driver's seat of my life. I trust You. Thank You for loving me. Thank You for forgiving me. Thank You for filling me. Amen.*

3. A. Describe Jesus' emotions in His response to Philip's statement "Lord, show us the Father, and we shall be satisfied."

   B. What was Jesus claiming when He said, "He who has seen me has seen the Father"? How does Colossians 1:15 affirm this truth?

4. A. What did Jesus promise in John 14:13? What was the stipulation in His promise? What was His purpose in fulfilling His promise?

   B. What does it mean to ask in Jesus' name? See CCC 2614.

Quiet your heart and enjoy His presence…Take a moment to contemplate the needs and desires that are on your heart today.

Write them down or mentally lay them before Christ. Ask Him to reveal to you if the things you are asking for correspond to His will. If they do not, ask Him for the strength to let them go. You might want to pray the words of the Surrender Novena, "Jesus, I surrender myself to you. Take care of everything." Then ask God to replace those desires with good ones from Him. Ask Him for the strength and wisdom to want His will above all things. Psalm 37:4 says, "Take delight in the Lord, and he will give you the desires of your heart." People sometimes misinterpret that verse to mean that God will give us whatever we want. We must make sure that we are first delighting ourselves in the Lord. When we do, and when pleasing God and loving Him are what bring us the most pleasure, the things that our hearts desire will be the things that God wants to do for us.

Conclusion

What does washing someone's feet and showing radical love look like in modern-day life? Years ago my husband went on a three-day men's retreat that ended with a Mass. Families were welcome to attend the Mass, so I got our children dressed up in their "Sunday best." I knew my husband was excited to fill the pew with our children, and we were looking forward to being there with him. After an hour-long ride, just as we were pulling into the parking lot, our six-year-old daughter threw up all over her lovely dress and the back of the car. It was disgusting. I truly think it was on a par with feet covered in animal dung and mud.

I sent the other children into the chapel, gathered some towels from the retreat center, and started cleaning up. A woman in the parking lot had a spare dress in her car (my daughter's size—quite remarkable), which she gave me. I cleaned up as best I could and brought all the soiled things into the retreat center to try to clean them. The priest who had been leading the retreat met me as I was headed to the bathroom and asked if I needed help. I laughed and said, "Definitely not with this. This is a mom's job."

He asked me if I'd been to Mass that day. I hadn't. He put out his hands and said, "Will you please let me clean these things for you so you can go to Mass?"

"Absolutely, positively *not*," I said. "This is revolting. This is disgusting for me, but I'm her mother. This goes with the job description. You've just taught a three-day retreat. I'm sure you're exhausted. This is a mom's job, it's nasty, and I'd never let you clean these things."

"I know this is hard for you," he said. "Pride makes it hard to accept this kind of help. But will you let me serve you in this way?"

How I related to Saint Peter in that moment! I didn't want to see anyone cleaning up my mess, least of all this priest who had already given so much. But I knew God was working in my life in the area of pride. Was refusing to receive help strengthening pride's hold on me?

As I handed over the towels and clothes and saw this man, who had never had biological children of his own, cleaning up after mine, I thought, *This is the love of Jesus in action. This is quiet service that will never gain the world's attention but reflects Jesus' sacrificial heart.*

My Resolution

In what specific way will I apply what I learned in this lesson?

Examples:

1. I now recognize that regret is not the same as repentance. I will truly repent. I'll go to Reconciliation and determine, by God's grace, to go in a new direction instead of back down the same path that leads me to sin.

2. I will perform a concrete act of service for the person I wrote about on day one, question 4A.

3. I want to experience the kind of intimacy that Saint John had with Jesus. I'm going to go to adoration this week for the sole purpose of letting His love wash over me.

My Resolution:

Catechism Clips

CCC 423 We believe and confess that Jesus of Nazareth, born a Jew of a daughter of Israel at Bethlehem at the time of King Herod the Great and the emperor Caesar Augustus, a carpenter by trade, who died crucified in Jerusalem under the procurator Pontius Pilate during the reign of the emperor Tiberius, is the eternal Son of God made man. He "came from God," "descended from heaven," and "came in the flesh." For "the Word became flesh and dwelt among us, full of grace and truth; we have beheld his glory, glory as of the only Son from the Father...And from his fullness have we all received, grace upon grace."

CCC 1024 This perfect life with the Most Holy Trinity—this communion of life and love with the Trinity, with the Virgin Mary, the angels and all the blessed—is called "heaven." Heaven is the ultimate end and fulfillment of the deepest human longings, the state of supreme, definitive happiness.

CCC 1025 To live in heaven is "to be with Christ." The elect live "in Christ," but they retain, or rather find, their true identity, their own name. For life is to be with Christ; where Christ is, there is life; there is the kingdom.

CCC 1216 Baptism is God's most beautiful and magnificent gift...We call it gift, grace, anointing, enlightenment, garment of immortality, bath of rebirth, seal, and most precious gift. It is called *gift* because it is conferred on those who bring nothing of their own; grace since it is given even to the guilty; Baptism because sin is buried in the water; anointing for it is priestly and royal as are those who are anointed; enlightenment because it radiates light; clothing since it veils our shame; bath because it washes; and seal as it is our guard and the sign of God's Lordship.

CCC 2795 The symbol of the heavens refers us back to the mystery of the covenant we are living when we pray to our Father. He is in heaven, his dwelling place; the Father's house is our homeland. Sin has exiled us from the land of the covenant, but conversion of heart enables us to return to the Father, to heaven. In Christ, then, heaven and earth are reconciled, for the Son alone "descended from heaven" and causes us to ascend there with him by his Cross, Resurrection, and Ascension.

Verse Study

See appendix 3 for instructions on how to complete a verse study.

John 14:6

1. Verse:

2. Paraphrase:

3. Questions:

4. Cross-references:

5. Personal Application:

Lesson 16

JESUS, THE TRUE VINE

Introduction

I remember well a lovely summer day in 1991 in Minneapolis. My boyfriend had flown in from England, and we went to Mass on our way home from the airport. The sermon was on marriage, which I found interesting, although it seemed to have an odd effect on my boyfriend, Leo. He was fidgeting and constantly looking at me. I later understood why, because after Mass ended, he asked if we could go up to the front and pray. As I was kneeling next to him, he took my hand and said, "If I promise to make you happy for the rest of your life, will you marry me?" How could I say no to an offer like that? If only I'd been able to record his words and play them back to him later. The deal was: if I said yes, he'd make me happy for always! So no one can fault me for entering marriage with that expectation.

We moved to Germany immediately following our honeymoon and it wasn't long at all before I found out I was pregnant with our first child, Amy. I was sick, and I was lonely. I couldn't speak German, I had no friends, and Leo traveled five days a week. I sat him down one day and informed him that there was a problem with our "deal." I wasn't happy! I then sat back to see how he would respond. To my great surprise and horror, he became very irritated and asked if I expected him to quit his job and sit home with me. Regardless of what he had said when he was proposing, he had no intention of taking on the responsibility of my personal happiness. I did not consider this good news.

I felt like Leo and I weren't connecting. He didn't want to talk to me about anything spiritual, so I set out to remedy that. I bought him some very helpful books, had some excellent advice about which friends he should hang out with (nice Christian ones), and *really* encouraged him to go to a men's retreat called Promise Keepers. Instead of thanking me, he very curtly informed me that he was *not* my father—to which I wanted to reply, "I *know* that. Look at all the broken things in the house! My dad would have fixed them!"

I had come into my marriage with expectations. I had left behind my family, my friends, my church, and my country when I got married. This left a huge void, and I expected Leo to fill it. I figured he should be grateful that I had been so generous.

While the fact that Leo didn't even try to fill that void in my life was very upsetting to me, it actually saved the two of us a great deal of heartache, because in attempting to fill it, he most certainly would have failed.

I would later learn that the void in my life was to be filled by a relationship with Jesus Christ. No other man or person would be able to satisfy me.

The late Ruth Bell Graham expressed this beautifully: "It is a foolish woman who expects her husband to be to her that which only Jesus Christ Himself can be: always ready to forgive, totally understanding, unendingly patient, invariably tender and loving, unfailing in every area, anticipating every need, and making more than adequate provision. Such expectations put a man under an impossible strain."[49]

This does not mean that our relationships with other people do not affect us deeply. They certainly do. But even the best relationship will never fill the void that is inside us. We were created with a God-shaped vacuum that only He can fill. Saint Augustine said it well: "Our hearts are restless until they rest in you."

The Bible is a love story. Starting at the very beginning, it tells the story of a prince who leaves His throne and comes to rescue the ones He loves. This lesson describes the intimate relationship that God wants to have with us. Story after story illustrates His love and sacrifice. The parable of the vine and the branches, which we'll study this week, is a word picture describing just how close He wants us to be to Him.

Day One: The Promise of the Holy Spirit

Read John 14:15–31.

1. How do we show God that we love Him? (See John 14:15, 21; 1 John 2:5–6.)

---

49 Debra Evans, *Blessing Your Husband: Understanding and Affirming Your Man* (Carol Stream, IL: Tyndale House, 2003), 30.

2. A. God knew that on our own, we would never be able to be truly holy. Whom did He send to help us? How does He help us? See John 14:16–17 and the following note:

    > Counselor (John 14:16) *Parakletos* (Gk.): an "advocate" or "helper." The word is used five times in John's writings, always with reference to Jesus or the Holy Spirit. It is a legal term for an attorney or spokesman who defends the cause of the accused in a courtroom. Jesus uses it for a heavenly intercessor who is called to the side of God's children to offer strength and support. Jesus is a "Paraclete" because in heaven he pleads to the Father for believers still struggling on earth (1 John 2:1). The Spirit, too, is a "Paraclete" because he is sent to strengthen the disciples in Jesus' absence (John 14:16), instruct them in the truth (John 14:26; 15:26), and defend them against the prosecutions of the devil (John 16:7–11), who is the "accuser" of the family of God (Rev. 12:10).[50]

    B. What else did Jesus teach about the Holy Spirit, in John 14:25–26?

3. A. In John 14:27, Jesus differentiated between the peace He gives and the peace the world gives. How would you describe the difference between the two?

    B. In what area of your life would you most like to experience greater peace?

4. Why did Jesus tell His disciples that He was going to be leaving them? See John 14:29.

5. What did Jesus tell His disciples about Satan in John 14:30? Why? How does this reinforce His previous words to them in John 10:17–18?

---

50   Ignatius Catholic Study Bible, RSV, 190.

Quiet your heart and enjoy His presence…Take a moment to contemplate these words from the Lord, spoken through Saint Catherine of Siena:

> *Why don't you have confidence in me, your creator? Why do you rely on yourself? Am I not faithful and loyal to you? Redeemed and restored to grace by virtue of the blood of my only son, man can then say that he has experienced my fidelity. And, nevertheless, he still doubts, it would appear, that I am sufficiently powerful to help him, sufficiently strong to help and defend him against his enemies, sufficiently wise to illuminate the eyes of his intelligence or that I have sufficient clemency to want to give him whatever is necessary for his salvation. It would appear that I am not sufficiently rich to make his fortune, not beautiful enough to make him beautiful; one might say that he is afraid not to find enough bread in my home to nourish himself, nor clothing with which to cover himself.*[51]

Original sin causes us all to struggle with mistrust of God. We question whether He really wants what is best for us and whether He is powerful enough to deliver it. Ask God to help you to grow in confidence in Him. Contemplate the ways in which He has more than adequately provided for you spiritually, physically, and emotionally.

Day Two: Jesus, the True Vine

Read John 15:1–5.

1. Who is the vine? Who is the vinedresser? Who are we in this analogy? See CCC 2074.

2. A. What does the Father do to the branches that bear no fruit?

   B. What does He do to the branches that do bear fruit?

---

51 Father Jacques Philippe, *Searching for and Maintaining Peace* (New York: The Society of Saint Paul, 2002), 26–27.

3. What insights do the following verses give regarding the pruning process in the life of a Christian?

Hebrews 12:5–11

James 1:2–4

4. To abide in Christ means to remain close to Him. It's meant to be an intimate, dependent relationship. What did Jesus mean when He said that abiding in Him was the key to bearing fruit? How can He say, "Apart from me you can do nothing," when many great things are accomplished in our world by people who aren't connected to Christ?

5. What is the fruit produced in us that is spoken of in John 15:5? See CCC 2074 and Galatians 5:22–23.

Quiet your heart and enjoy His presence…Take a moment to contemplate an area of your life where you are experiencing difficulty.

Is it possible that God is doing some pruning in your life? Is He cutting away things that have fed your desire for people's approval so that you might more deeply long for His *approval? Is He pruning you financially so that your sense of blessing comes more from spiritual graces than from material things? Is He purifying your motives? Ask God to show you where He is pruning you. Ask Him for the grace to accept His work in your life. Renew your faith in His love for you. Remember that the Lord disciplines those He loves in order to produce beautiful holiness in them.*

Day Three: Abiding in Christ

Read John 15:6–11.

1. What does the burning of branches symbolize? In order to not wither and burn, what is required? See also Ezekiel 15:1–8 and Matthew 3:10.

2. In John 15:7, did Jesus mean that He would do whatever we want as long as we pray each day? See John 14:13 (lesson 15, day five, questions 4A and B) and James 4:3.

3. Practically speaking, how do we abide in the love of Christ? See also 1 John 4:15–16 and 3:23–24; John 15:7 and 6:56.

4. Where does the joy mentioned in John 15:11 come from?

Quiet your heart and enjoy His presence…Take a moment to contemplate that Jesus loves us in the same way that the Father loves Him (John 15:9).

People in our lives may love us imperfectly, but the perfect love of the One who created us and knows us intimately should be a source of deep joy. Sometimes we get so busy pursuing other interests or desires that we forget we hold the greatest riches within our hearts. Spend some time thanking God for His unconditional love. Be specific about ways in which you have experienced His personal care and compassion.

Day Four: Sacrificial Love

Read John 15:12–17.

1. A. What is the "new commandment" of Jesus? See CCC 1970.

   B. Note the progression of God's commandments regarding love in the following verses. How are we told to love in each verse?

   Leviticus 19:18

   Luke 6:32–36

John 15:12–13

The following quote by Saint Josemaría Escrivá sheds additional light on this passage:

> Even though Christ is purity itself, and temperance and humility, He does not make any one of these virtues the distinguishing mark of His disciples; He makes charity that mark. The Master's message and example are clear and precise. He confirmed His teaching with deeds. Yet I have often thought that, after twenty centuries, it is still a new commandment, for very few people have taken the trouble to practice it. The others, the majority of men, both in the past and still today, have chosen to ignore it. Their selfishness has led them to the conclusion: "Why should I complicate my life? I have more than enough to do just looking after myself."
>
> Such an attitude is not good enough for us Christians. If we profess the same faith and are really eager to follow in the clear footprints left by Christ when He walked on this earth, we cannot be content merely with avoiding doing unto others the evil that we would not have them do unto us. That is a lot, but it is still very little when we consider that our love is to be measured in terms of Jesus' own conduct. Besides, He does not give us this standard as a distant target, as a crowning point of a whole lifetime of struggle. It is—it ought to be, I repeat, so that you may turn it into specific resolutions—our starting point, for our Lord presents it as a sign of Christianity; "By this shall all men know that you are my disciples."[52]

2. A. Where is God currently asking you to love sacrificially?

    B. Where can we find the strength to love as He has commanded us? See CCC 1972 and 1 John 4:19.

---

[52] Navarre Bible: Saint John's Gospel, RSV (Dublin: Four Courts Press, 2003), 148.

Quiet your heart and enjoy His presence…Take a moment to contemplate 1 John 4:18: "There is no fear in love, but perfect love casts out fear."

When God asks us to love sacrificially, our first reaction is often anxiety; we're afraid that we'll be hurt or taken advantage of. Focusing on God's love for us helps drive out that fear. We can dwell on God's love for us by consciously noting the many blessings He sends our way. Make a list of the little ways that God has shown you love in the past week. Has mercy been shown to you? Did you see something beautiful in His creation? Did God answer a prayer? How has He provided for you? How has He sustained you? Thank Him for His love and faithfulness. Ask Him to cast out any fear in your heart with His perfect love.

Day Five: The World's Hatred

Read John 15:18–27.

1. Using the definition of *"world"* found after Catechism clip 1972 at the end of this lesson, as well as Catechism clips 408 and 409, describe the way Christ used the word *"world"* in John 15:18–25.

2. When we experience persecution because of our faith in Christ, how do the following verses say we should respond?

   Romans 12:14 (Note how we can apply this verse in practical ways.)

   1 Peter 4:12–16

We are wise to recognize that not all suffering that a Christian experiences is because of his or her faith. Sometimes a Christian will say, "She's just treating me that way because I'm a Christian," when the suffering actually being experienced is the consequence of the Christian's poor choices or behavior.

3. According to John 15:22–24, why do Jesus' listeners have no excuse for their sin?

4. What help has God sent us to strengthen us as we face the world's hatred?

Quiet your heart and enjoy His presence...Take a moment to contemplate Jesus' command to love one another.

If we live out our faith authentically and don't compromise to fit in with the world, we will inevitably experience some persecution. But the greatest pain often comes from within the Body of Christ. When the attack comes from sisters or brothers in the Lord, the feeling of betrayal or hurt goes deep. Let's endeavor to be agents of love within the Church. Ask God to help you to identify any small problems that you are allowing to get in the way of loving within the Body of Christ. Ask God for the strength to forgive and let things go.

Conclusion

"Do not look ahead to what may happen tomorrow. The same everlasting Father who cares for you today will take care of you tomorrow and every day. Either He will shield you from suffering or He will give you His unwavering strength that you may bear it. Be at peace, then, and set aside all anxious thoughts and worries."
—*Francis de Sales*

Daughter of God, do not need to look ahead to the changes and challenges of this life in fear. Instead, as they arise, make the choice to look at them with the full assurance that God, to whom you belong, will deliver you out of them. Hasn't He kept you safe up till now? So let's hold His loving hand tightly, and He will lead us safely through all things. And when we cannot stand, He will carry us in His arms.

My dear sister in Christ, *you are deeply loved.* You are loved by Christ so much more perfectly than an earthly father or husband could ever love! Someone has chosen *you*; someone loves *you.* You don't have to be perfect or pretty or productive or popular. If you are none of these things, Jesus may even have a particular delight in you! Jesus cherishes you! No matter how far from Him you may run, He will always outrun you and woo you back to Him. His love is never ending; it never diminishes, and He never gives up on you. In order to experience this love, abide in Christ. Connect with Him each day as a branch is connected to the vine. When you do this, the Father's love will flow through you, filling your emptiness and satisfying your desires with Him.

"You did not choose me, but I chose you" (John 15:16).

"For your Maker is your husband" (Isaiah 54:5).

"I have loved you with an everlasting love; therefore, I have continued my faithfulness to you" (Jeremiah 31:3).

My Resolution

In what specific way will I apply what I learned in this lesson?

Examples:

1. When I feel I don't have peace, I will check myself to see if I am:

    A. overanalyzing every detail repeatedly

    B. letting my imagination run wild

    C. becoming consumed with what-ifs and if-onlys

    I will acknowledge that this shows my lack of trust in God and His provision for me. I'll say a prayer about whatever is causing me anxiety, and then, I will thank God for answering my prayer.

2. I will start my day by praying an Act of Faith prayer. Each time I begin to worry or be afraid, I will pray it again.

    Act of Faith: O my God, I firmly believe that You are one God in three Divine Persons: Father, Son, and Holy Spirit. I believe that Your Divine Son became man and died for our sins, and that He will come to judge the living and the dead. I believe these and all the truths the Holy Catholic Church teaches because You have revealed them, who can neither deceive nor be deceived.

My Resolution:

Catechism Clips

CCC 408 The consequences of original sin and of all men's personal sins put the world as a whole in the sinful condition aptly described in St. John's expression, "the sin of the world." This expression can also refer to the negative influence exerted on people by communal situations and social structures that are the fruit of men's sins.

CCC 409 This dramatic situation of "the whole world [which] is in the power of the evil one" makes man's life a battle: The whole of man's history has been the story of dour combat with the powers of evil, stretching, so our Lord tells us, from the very dawn of history until the last day. Finding himself in the midst of the battlefield man has to struggle to do what is right, and it is at great cost to himself, and aided by God's grace, that he succeeds in achieving his own inner integrity.

CCC 1970 The Law of the Gospel requires us to make the decisive choice between "the two ways" and to put into practice the words of the Lord. It is summed up in the Golden Rule, "Whatever you wish that men would do to you, do so to them; this is the law and the prophets." The entire Law of the Gospel is contained in the "new commandment" of Jesus, to love one another as he has loved us.

CCC 1972 The New Law is called a *law of love* because it makes us act out of the love infused by the Holy Spirit, rather than from fear; a *law of grace* because it confers the strength of grace to act, by means of faith and the sacraments; a *law of freedom* because it sets us free from the ritual and juridical observances of the Old Law, inclines us to act spontaneously by the prompting of charity and, finally, lets us pass from the condition of a servant who "does not know what his master is doing" to that of a friend of Christ—"For all that I have heard from my Father I have made known to you"—or even to the status of son and heir.

WORLD Creation, or the earth, or even the universe. "All that is"—often called the "world" in Scripture—owes its existence to God's act of creation; God's creation is called "good" in the Bible, and human beings are said to have been created "in his own image and likeness" (282, 295). In the New Testament the "world" is sometimes used to indicate the forces of opposition to the work of Jesus and his Holy Spirit. In this sense it signifies the world that Jesus came to redeem from sin. The world will reach its goal and perfection when it has been renewed and transformed into "the new heaven and the new earth" in the fullness of God's kingdom (1043). ("World," glossary entry, *Catechism of the Catholic Church*)

CCC 2074 Jesus says, "I am the vine, you are the branches. He who abides in me, and I in him, he it is that bears much fruit, for apart from me you can do nothing." The fruit referred to in this saying is the holiness of a life made fruitful by union with Christ. When we believe in Jesus Christ, partake of his mysteries, and keep his commandments, the Savior himself comes to love, in us, his Father and his brethren, our Father and our brethren. His person becomes, through the Spirit, the living and interior rule of our activity. "This is my commandment, that you love one another as I have loved you."

Verse Study

See appendix 3 for instructions on how to complete a verse study.

John 15:5

1. Verse:

2. Paraphrase:

3. Questions:

4. Cross-references:

5. Personal Application:

Lesson 17

JESUS, THE INTERCESSOR

Introduction

In John 15, Jesus warned the disciples of the persecution and hatred they would experience in the future. Persecution, especially from the religious leaders, could have caused them to question whether they were to continue as followers of Christ. Jesus didn't want them to fall away, confused and disheartened.

The disciples were warned that they would be put out of the synagogues. Being expelled from the local synagogue would have meant being shunned by the Jewish community. Jesus also foretold that people would feel they were serving God by killing His disciples. All of this was devastating news to the disciples:

> Christians in John's day were being expelled from many local synagogues, perhaps under the influence of Palestinian Pharisaic propaganda. Hostile Jewish non-Christians in Asia Minor do not appear to have killed Christians directly, but their participation in Christians' deaths was no less significant. By betraying Jewish Christians to the Roman authorities and claiming that Christians were non-Jewish, they left Christians with no legal exemption from worshipping the emperor. Worried that Christians were a messianic and apocalyptic movement that could get them in trouble with Rome, many synagogue leaders may have thought their betrayal of Christians would protect the rest of their community.[53]

When Christians refused to worship the emperor, many were fed to the lions; some were crucified; others were sewn into animal skins and thrown to the dogs; and some were covered in pitch, nailed to wooden posts, and burned as torches.[54]

---

53 Craig S. Keener, *The IVP Bible Background Commentary: New Testament* (Downers Grove, IL: InterVarsity Press, 1993), 302–303.

54 Philip Schaff, *History of the Christian Church*, vol. 1 (Grand Rapids, MI: Eerdmans, 1910), 381–382.

How could they bear such a future? Jesus assured them that the work of the Holy Spirit would enable them not only to endure but also to be filled with joy in the midst of difficulty. God was going to allow them to be a part of His mission to change the world. Would it be easy? No. But they were to participate in a great adventure, one worth every ounce of struggle.

We, too, are invited on this adventure. We have been entrusted with the privilege of living out and sharing Christ's teachings. Perhaps we will not experience martyrdom; however, we'll have difficulties and challenges as we follow Christ. We, too, will always need the comfort, strength, and wisdom of the Holy Spirit.

As we follow Christ, we are assured that He intercedes for us in heaven (Hebrews 7:25) just as He prayed for His disciples and future followers in John 17. This allows us to say with confidence, "If God is for us, who is against us?" (Romans 8:31)

"It is better to be alone with God. His friendship will not fail me, nor his counsel, nor his love. In his strength, I will dare and dare and dare until I die."
—Saint Joan of Arc

Day One: The Work of the Holy Spirit

Read John 16:1–11.

1. It was difficult enough for the disciples to imagine being persecuted and thrown out of the synagogue. Hearing Jesus say that He was going away and that they'd have to face these challenges without His physical presence filled them with sorrow. Facing difficulties alone is hard. Have you ever experienced the loneliness that comes from feeling unknown, misunderstood, ignored, or unsupported? Explain. How did your solitude make your suffering worse?

2. A. What was Jesus' response to the disciples' impending loneliness?

   B. In what sense can Jesus' words to the disciples offer us comfort today?

3. The Holy Spirit's work is described in John 16:8–11. Jesus said that the Holy Spirit would convince (Revised Standard Version) or convict (New American Bible) the world of three things. What are they?

By the time the Holy Spirit came to the disciples, Jesus had been wrongly condemned, convicted, and executed. His reputation had been dragged through the mud. The Holy Spirit set to work convicting people of the sin of disbelief in Jesus, convincing them of Jesus' innocence (His righteousness), and communicating that disbelief in Him would result in judgment. That is still His work today.

> "Since Easter, the Holy Spirit has proved 'the world wrong about sin,' i.e., proved that the world has not believed in him whom the Father has sent. But this same Spirit who brings sin to light is also the Consoler who gives the human heart grace for repentance and conversion." (CCC 1433)

Quiet your heart and enjoy His presence…Take a moment to contemplate the work of the Holy Spirit described in John 16:8–9.

It's the Holy Spirit's job to convict people of their sin and of Jesus' righteousness. Have you ever tried to help the Holy Spirit by attempting to convince a loved one of his or her sin? Have you ever wished you could make another person love Jesus? We can't do either thing. Both are jobs of the Holy Spirit.

> *I entrust to you, Holy Spirit, the work of convicting others of their sin. I entrust to you the work of igniting love for Jesus in the heart of [name]. You desire conversion more intensely for [name] than I do. Contrition comes from you. The birth of desire for God within a person's heart comes from You. Turn my desire to cause these changes into a prayer that You cause these changes. Help me to discern when I am to speak and when I am to keep silent. Amen.*

Day Two: Sorrow Turned to Joy

Read John 16:12–24.

1. How do the words "he will not speak on his own" in verse 13 describe the unity of the Trinity?

2. What did Jesus mean by "A little while, and you will see me no more; again a little while, and you will see me"? See also John 20:19–20.

3. John 16:20 refers to Jesus' Resurrection but also to the joy that we will experience when He returns in the future. What insight do we receive from Revelation 7:17 and 21:4 regarding this?

4. Jesus wanted His disciples to fix their eyes on the future—on the day they would see Him again and the time when they would be with Him permanently in heaven. Saint Paul is a wonderful example of living this way. Read his words and apply them to your own present difficulties.

   Romans 8:18 and 2 Corinthians 4:16–18

The blessings we will receive in heaven aren't visible to us today, but they are real. The magnitude of what we suffer on earth is less than the glory and joy we'll experience in heaven. One day it will all be worth it. Saint Ignatius wrote the following on his way to Rome, where he was martyred for his faith: "Let the fire, the gallows, the wild beasts, the breaking of bones, the pulling asunder of members, the bruising of my whole body, and the torments of the devil and hell itself come upon me, so that I may win Christ Jesus."[55] He considered Jesus such a prize, he was willing to suffer anything for His sake. Many saints have gone before us, showing us that it is possible to live a life rife with difficulties and still stay faithful.

Quiet your heart and enjoy His presence…Take a moment to contemplate the full joy spoken of in John 16:24.

We can experience this joy when our focus shifts from ourselves to Christ. The acronym JOY can help us to remember this:

Jesus
Others
You

Ask God to reveal to you some practical ways you can keep your focus on Jesus and others today.

---

55 John Foxe, *Foxe's Book of Martyrs*, trans. *Marie Gentert King* (Old Tappan, NJ: Spire Books, 1968), 17.

Day Three: Peace for the Disciples

Read John 16:25–33.

1. What do you think Jesus meant in John 16:25 when He said, "I shall no longer speak to you in figures"?

2. In John 16:26–27, Jesus began to describe a new relationship that the disciples were going to experience with the Father because of Jesus' death and Resurrection. We, too, can experience a new relationship with God the Father because of Jesus. What do you learn from the following verses about how we are able to address God the Father? See CCC 2777 and Romans 8:15–17.

3. How would you describe your feelings when you approach God? Are you filled with fear? Awe? Confidence? Boldness?

"Let us then with confidence draw near to the throne of grace, that we may receive mercy and find grace to help in time of need" (Hebrews 4:16).

4. What virtue do we need if we are going to experience peace in the midst of tribulation? See CCC 1808.

Quiet your heart and enjoy His presence…Take a moment to contemplate how we grow in the virtue of fortitude through a close, dependent relationship with God.

Trust me and don't be afraid, for I am your Strength and Song. Think about what it means to have Me as your Strength. I spoke the universe into existence; My Power is absolutely unlimited! Human weakness, consecrated to Me, is like a magnet, drawing My Power into your neediness. However, fear can block the flow of My strength into you. Instead of trying to fight your fears, concentrate on trusting Me. When you relate to Me in confident trust, there is no limit to how much I can strengthen you.

Remember that I am also your Song. I want you to share My Joy, living in conscious awareness of My Presence. Rejoice as we journey together toward heaven; join Me in singing My Song.[56]

"The Lord is my strength and my song; he has become my salvation" (Psalm 118:14).

Day Four: Jesus Prays for the Church

John chapter 17 is called the high priestly prayer of Jesus. He first prays about His approaching sacrifice to God (John 17:1–5). He then prays for His disciples (John 17:6–19). Lastly He prays for future believers (John 17:20–26).

Read John 17:1–19.

1. How did Jesus describe eternal life in John 17:3? What does that description mean to you personally?

2. Jesus described our relationship to the world in John 17:11 ("they are *in* the world") and John 17:14 ("they are not of the world"). What do you think He meant by these words?

We are in the world, but we are focused on Christ rather than on what the world offers. This is not a call for us to retreat from anyone who doesn't believe what we believe. What hope would there be for the many people who don't know Christ if everyone who followed Him stayed in a holy huddle? We are called to interact with people but to do so in a way that brings honor to God. "Let your light so shine before men, that they may see your good works and give glory to your Father who is in heaven" (Matthew 5:16).

At the same time, we must recognize that being involved in certain activities can draw us away from faithfully following God's will for our lives. We need to continually ask God to guide our decisions regarding the use of our money and time and which relationships He wants us to invest in. What He will call each one of us to do will be different. Certain activities that would be fine for one person might lead another into a morally tempting situation. We must be careful not to judge other people, and instead pour that energy into seeking God's will for our own decisions.

---

56 Young, *Jesus Calling*, 84.

3. A. John 17:18: "As you sent me into the world, so I have sent them into the world." In what sense are *all* followers of Christ sent into the world to continue His mission? See CCC 1268 and 1270.

B. While all followers of Christ are to carry out His mission in the world, in what sense were the apostles sent out in a special way?

C. Who are the ordained successors who continue this work today? See CCC 858–862.

Quiet your heart and enjoy His presence…Take a moment to contemplate the enormous responsibility placed on the bishops of the Catholic Church. Pray for protection over them.

Dear Lord,

In the words of Saint Paul, I ask that You fill our bishops "with the knowledge of [Your] will in all spiritual wisdom and understanding, to lead a life worthy of the Lord, fully pleasing to [You], bearing fruit in every good work and increasing in the knowledge of [You]. May [they] be strengthened with all power, according to [Your] glorious might, for all endurance and patience with joy" (Colossians 1:9–11).

Day Five: The Prayer for Unity

Read John 17:20–26.

1. Whom was Jesus praying for in John 17:20–26?

2. What did Jesus specifically pray for in verses 21–23?

3. What are some ways we can foster unity among followers of Christ who may differ in terms of doctrinal beliefs? Share your own thoughts and gain insights from CCC 821.

4. How does the Catholic Church view members of the Protestant Church? See CCC 818 and 819.

"The fact that the Good News of reconciliation is preached by Christians who are divided among themselves weakens their witness. It is thus urgent to work for the unity of Christians so that missionary activity can be more effective. At the same time we must not forget that efforts toward unity are themselves a sign of the work of reconciliation which God is bringing about in our midst."[57]

Quiet your heart and enjoy His presence…Take a moment to contemplate how the visible unity of the early Church changed the world.

The Body of Christ was characterized by love. Tertullian wrote that the Roman people would exclaim, "See how they love one another!" Justin Martyr said, "We who used to value the acquisition of wealth and possessions more than anything else now bring what we have into a common fund and share it with anyone who needs it. We used to hate and destroy one another and refused to associate with people of another race or country. Now, because of Christ, we live together with such people and pray for our enemies." People saw this radical love and unity, and it gave validity to the Gospel message. Take a few moments to pray for unity within the Body of Christ. Ask God to help you see ways that you can demonstrate love and unity.

Conclusion

If we are going to take seriously Jesus' call to reach out to our hurting world with the message of His never-ending, always forgiving, heart-healing love, we will experience persecution. The minute we step into the battle, Satan will determine to stop us in our tracks. He'll use one of his favorite weapons—discouragement. He'll work through people (although they are rarely aware of this). He'll make a study of each of us and hit us where we are weakest.

---

57 Saint John Paul II in Alan Schreck, *The Legacy of Pope John Paul II: The Central Teaching of His 14 Encyclical Letters* (Steubenville, OH: Emmaus Road, 2012), 71.

When you are discouraged in the spiritual life, negative messages will flood your mind: *You're never going to be able to keep this up. You don't have the strength to stay faithful. You'll never be good enough. You are defined by your past mistakes. Just take a break from it all. Do something else with your time. If no one appreciates you, then why bother?* The messages will vary from person to person. They are tailor-made for each one of us by one who is bent on our destruction. Why does Satan care about us individually? It certainly isn't because he loves us. It's because he is terrified by the immense amount of good we can do and the enormous difference we can make in the lives of individuals the world over—not in our own strength but because "He who is in you is greater than he who is in the world" (1 John 4:4).

Perhaps the greatest discouragement happens when the persecution comes from within the Church. If we're all batting for the same team, shouldn't we simply be cheering one another on? Unfortunately this isn't always the case. It requires a lot of self-discipline to look past the hurt we are feeling to the person behind it. Hurting people hurt people. We never have the whole story regarding another person's life.

We must always try to let the hurt go and look for ways to build bridges and love others proactively. Within the Body of Christ, we won't agree on every issue. We all are uniquely gifted and have different issues that fire our hearts with holy discontent. Because of this, and because sin is always at work in each of us, we lack understanding of one another. But let's never give up the fight for unity. Instead let's pray that we, as followers of Christ, would look to the physical, emotional, and spiritual needs of others. Let's pray that God would give us *His* perspective on people so that we can see the very people with whom we disagree through His merciful, loving eyes.

My Resolution

In what specific way will I apply what I learned in this lesson?

Examples:

1. I will look at my calendar each day this week and rank my activities according to whether they concern Jesus, others, or me (**J**esus, **O**thers, **Y**ou). I'll make a point to put Christ and others before my own desires.

2. After I have prayed, if I find that anxiety continues to creep into my heart, I will thank God for having heard my prayer. I will thank Him for the answer that has already been set in motion, even though I cannot see it. Doing this will increase and reaffirm my trust in God.

My Resolution:

Catechism Clips

CCC 818 However, one cannot charge with the sin of the separation those who at present are born into these communities [that resulted from such separation] and in them are brought up in the faith of Christ, and the Catholic Church accepts them with respect and affection as brothers...All who have been justified by faith in Baptism are incorporated into Christ; they therefore have a right to be called Christians, and with good reason are accepted as brothers in the Lord by the children of the Catholic Church.

CCC 819 "Furthermore, many elements of sanctification and of truth" are found outside the visible confines of the Catholic Church: "the written Word of God; the life of grace; faith, hope, and charity, with the other interior gifts of the Holy Spirit, as well as visible elements." Christ's Spirit uses these Churches and ecclesial communities as means of salvation, whose power derives from the fullness of grace and truth that Christ has entrusted to the Catholic Church. All these blessings come from Christ and lead to him, and are in themselves calls to "Catholic unity."

CCC 821 Certain things are required in order to respond adequately to this call [toward unity]:

- a permanent *renewal* of the Church in greater fidelity to her vocation; such renewal is the driving-force of the movement toward unity;

- *conversion of heart* as the faithful "try to live holier lives according to the Gospel"; for it is the unfaithfulness of the members to Christ's gift which causes divisions;

- *prayer in common,* because "change of heart and holiness of life, along with public and private prayer for the unity of Christians, should be regarded as the soul of the whole ecumenical movement, and merits the name 'spiritual ecumenism'";

- *fraternal knowledge of each other;*

- *ecumenical formation* of the faithful and especially of priests;

- *dialogue* among theologians and meetings among Christians of the different churches and communities;

- *collaboration* among Christians in various areas of service to mankind. "Human service" is the idiomatic phrase.

The Apostles' Mission

CCC 858 Jesus is the Father's Emissary. From the beginning of his ministry, he "called to him those whom he desired...And he appointed twelve, whom also he named apostles, to be with him, and to be sent out to preach." From then on, they would also be his "emissaries" (Greek *apostoloi*). In them, Christ continues his own mission: "As the Father has sent me, even so I send you." The apostles' ministry is the continuation of his mission; Jesus said to the Twelve: "he who receives you receives me."

CCC 859 Jesus unites them to the mission he received from the Father. As "the Son can do nothing of his own accord," but receives everything from the Father who sent him, so those whom Jesus sends can do nothing apart from him, from whom they received both the mandate for their mission and the power to carry it out. Christ's apostles knew that they were called by God as "ministers of a new covenant," "servants of God," "ambassadors for Christ," "servants of Christ and stewards of the mysteries of God."

CCC 860 In the office of the apostles there is one aspect that cannot be transmitted: to be the chosen witnesses of the Lord's Resurrection and so the foundation stones of the Church. But their office also has a permanent aspect. Christ promised to remain with them always. The divine mission entrusted by Jesus to them "will continue to the end of time, since the Gospel they handed on is the lasting source of all life for the Church. Therefore...the apostles took care to appoint successors."

The bishops—successors of the apostles

CCC 861 "In order that the mission entrusted to them might be continued after their death, [the apostles] consigned, by will and testament, as it were, to their immediate collaborators the duty of completing and consolidating the work they had begun, urging them to tend to the whole flock, in which the Holy Spirit had appointed them to shepherd the Church of God. They accordingly designated such men and then made the ruling that likewise on their death other proven men should take over their ministry."

CCC 862 "Just as the office which the Lord confided to Peter alone, as first of the apostles, destined to be transmitted to his successors, is a permanent one, so also endures the office, which the apostles received, of shepherding the Church, a charge destined to be exercised without interruption by the sacred order of bishops." Hence the Church teaches that "the bishops have by divine institution taken the place of the apostles as pastors of the Church, in such wise that whoever listens to them is listening to Christ and whoever despises them despises Christ and him who sent Christ."

CCC 1268 The baptized have become "living stones" to be "built into a spiritual house, to be a holy priesthood." By Baptism they share in the priesthood of Christ, in his prophetic and royal mission. They are "a chosen race, a royal priesthood, a holy nation, God's own people, that [they] may declare the wonderful deeds of him who called [them] out of darkness into his marvelous light." Baptism gives a share in the common priesthood of all believers.

CCC 1270 "Reborn as sons of God, [the baptized] must profess before men the faith they have received from God through the Church" and participate in the apostolic and missionary activity of the People of God.

CCC 1808 Fortitude is the moral virtue that ensures firmness in difficulties and constancy in the pursuit of the good. It strengthens the resolve to resist temptations and to overcome obstacles in the moral life. The virtue of fortitude enables one to conquer fear, even fear of death, and to face trials and persecutions. It disposes one even to renounce and sacrifice his life in defense of a just cause. "The Lord is my strength and my song." "In the world you have tribulation; but be of good cheer, I have overcome the world."

CCC 2777 In the Roman Liturgy, the Eucharistic assembly is invited to pray to our heavenly Father with filial boldness; the Eastern liturgies develop and use similar expressions: "dare in all confidence," "make us worthy of…" From the burning bush Moses heard a voice saying to him, "Do not come near; put off your shoes from your feet, for the place on which you are standing is holy ground." Only Jesus could cross that threshold of the divine holiness, for "when he had made purification for sins," he brought us into the Father's presence: "Here am I, and the children God has given me."

Verse Study

See appendix 3 for instructions on how to complete a verse study.

John 16:33

1. Verse:

2. Paraphrase:

3. Questions:

4. Cross-references:

5. Personal Application:

 NOTES

Lesson 18: Connect Coffee Talk 5

JESUS, THE INTERCESSOR

The accompanying talk can be viewed via DVD or digital download purchase or accessed online at walkingwithpurpose.com/videos.

Key Verses

"'For my thoughts are not your thoughts, neither are your ways my ways,' says the Lord. For as the heavens are higher than the earth, so are my ways higher than your ways and my thoughts than your thoughts" (Isaiah 55:8–9).

"Simon, behold, Satan demanded to have you, that he might sift you like wheat, but I have prayed for you that your faith may not fail" (Luke 22:31).

"[Jesus withdrew from His disciples,] he fell on the ground and prayed that, if it were possible, the hour might pass from him. And He said, 'Abba, Father, all things are possible to you; remove this chalice from me; yet not what I will, but what you will'" (Mark 14:35–36).

"Jesus offered up prayers and supplications, with loud cries and tears, to him who was able save him from death" (Hebrews 5:7).

"In this is love, not that we loved God but that he loved us and sent his Son to be the expiation for our sins" (1 John 4:10).

"See what love the Father has given us, that we should be called children of God; and so we are" (1 John 3:1).

Jesus invites us to spend time in His presence with daily prayer.

I. **From Jesus' Own Prayers We Learn:**

    A. He didn't always see immediate results.

    B. In answering prayer, God does not limit human freedom.

    C. Jesus asked for plan B while being willing to follow God's plan A.

II. **Prayer Is a Relationship, Not a Transaction**

    A. We come close to God just to be with Him—not to get what we want.

    B. Prayer is remaining in God's presence, loving Him, letting Him love us.

        Remembering how He loves us—*being* loved by Him—draws us close to God. The closer we are to Him, the more we trust Him and desire His will.

    C. We can be real before God.

        There is no need to give Him a candy-coated version of who we are and what we feel.

Make it a goal to begin each day with fifteen minutes of prayer. Let Him love you. Let Him transform you. Love Him back by simply sitting in His presence.

Questions for Discussion or Journaling

1. Have your circumstances ever caused you to question whether prayer makes a difference? What has helped you to continue drawing close to God with your heart in prayer?

2. In the talk we learned that Jesus didn't see immediate results for His prayers, yet He prayed anyway. What are you praying for that you are waiting for?

3. In *Time for God,* Father Jacques Philippe writes, "Our main task in praying is to love. But in our relationship with God, loving means first of all letting ourselves be loved."[58] What have you found to be a helpful way to let yourself be loved by God?

---

58 Jacques Philippe, *Time for God* (New York: Scepter, 1992), 53.

NOTES

Lesson 19

JESUS, OUR TRUTH

Introduction

We have all experienced the little voice inside us that says, "It's not fair!" The issue may be small—we are misunderstood, someone treats us unkindly, or recognition due us goes to someone else. Or it may be large—we are taken advantage of in business, a spouse is unfaithful, a child responds to love and care with rebellion.

Our reading this week chronicles Jesus' religious and civil trials. The religious trials were, in a word, unfair. Keep your eye out as you read for instances in which Jesus was not given a fair trial. Some background about Jewish law will help:

Rules:[59]
1. No trials were to occur during the night hours.
   Mishnah: Sanhedrin 4:1

2. Trials were not to occur on the eve of a Sabbath or during festivals.
   Mishnah: Sanhedrin 4:1

3. All trials were to be public; secret trials were forbidden.
   Mishnah: Sanhedrin 1:6

4. All trials were to be held in the Hall of Judgment in the Temple area.
   Mishnah: Sanhedrin 11:2

5. Capital cases required a minimum of twenty-three judges.
   Mishnah: Sanhedrin 4:1

6. An accused person could not testify against himself.
   Mishnah: Sanhedrin 3:3–4

---

[59] Charles R. Swindoll, *Insights on John* (Grand Rapids, MI: Zondervan, 2010), 312–3.

7. Conviction required the testimony of two or three witnesses to be in perfect alignment.
    Deuteronomy 17:6–7, 19:15–20

8. Witnesses for the prosecution were to be examined and cross-examined extensively.
    Mishnah: Sanhedrin 4:1

9. Capital cases were to follow a strict order, beginning with arguments by the defense, then arguments for conviction.
    Mishnah: Sanhedrin 4:1

10. All Sanhedrin judges could argue for acquittal, but not all could argue for conviction.
    Mishnah: Sanhedrin 4:1

11. Voting for conviction and sentencing in a capital case was to be conducted individually, beginning with the youngest, so younger members would not be influenced by the voting of the elder members.
    Mishnah: Sanhedrin 4:2

12. Verdicts in capital cases were to be handed down only during daylight hours.
    Mishnah: Sanhedrin 4:1

As you note the instances of injustice and unfairness, pay attention to Jesus' reaction. How was He able to respond as He did? He knew His purpose and kept His eyes on the goal. He remained composed in spite of the abominable treatment He received.

Whenever we are mistreated—in small or large instances—we must honor God in our behavior. It's OK to be angry. It's OK to seek justice. But our feelings and actions must be checked by the Holy Spirit. We are called to be self-possessed even in the midst of rotten circumstances:

> Therefore, since we are surrounded by so great a cloud of witnesses, let us also lay aside every weight, and sin which clings so closely, and let us run with perseverance the race that is set before us, looking to Jesus the pioneer and perfecter of our faith, who for the joy that was set before him endured the cross, despising the shame, and is seated at the right hand of the throne of God. Consider him who endured from sinners such hostility against himself, so that you may not grow weary or fainthearted. (Hebrews 12:1–3)

Day One: The Arrest of Jesus

Read John 18:1–11.

1. What was Jesus doing and what might He have been feeling while in the garden across the Kidron Valley? See Mark 14:32–41 and Luke 22:44.

2. Judas was accompanied by a band of soldiers and some officers from the chief priests and Pharisees. A band of soldiers was a detachment of several hundred Roman troops accompanied by Temple policemen.[60] What emotions and thoughts might Jesus and the disciples have experienced as they saw Judas approach?

3. How did the soldiers react when Jesus said, "I am he"?

4. Peter so loved his master that he leapt to Jesus' defense, cutting off the high priest's slave's ear, because he didn't understand the necessity of Jesus' suffering and death. What did Jesus do to rectify the situation? See Luke 22:51.

Quiet your heart and enjoy His presence…Take a moment to contemplate the swirl of emotions—fear, anger, betrayal—that consumed the disciples.

Everything must have seemed so out of control! But precisely when it seemed things couldn't get worse, Jesus was taking steps toward the fulfillment of the boldest, bravest rescue plan ever undertaken. What aspect of your life is out of control? Remember that God is at work, even if you don't see evidence of it. Ask Him to help you to grow in faith. In prayer affirm your trust in Him even when you can't see proof of His care and providence. He is there. He is at work. He is in control. He loves you and His will is to prosper and not to harm you, to give you hope and a future (Jeremiah 29:11).

---

60 Ignatius Catholic Study Bible, RSV, 194.

Day Two: The Religious Trials and Peter's Denial

Read John 18:12–27.

Today's passage chronicles Jesus' religious trials. Keep in mind that these took place throughout the night. Civil trials with Pilate and Herod followed the religious trials.

1. Was Jesus forcefully bound by the soldiers, or did He allow them to bind Him? See John 8:59 and 10:17–18; Matthew 26:53.

2. Jesus' first religious trial was conducted before which man?

Annas had been the high priest of Israel from AD 6 to 15. The Romans deposed and replaced him with his five sons, one grandson, and now, his son-in-law, Caiaphas.[61] This was against the rules of the Torah, so many of the Jews continued to consider Annas their head.[62] The Jewish leaders had been plotting Jesus' death for quite some time. They knew that they needed to prepare trials both for the Jewish religious authorities and for the Romans (civil trials). They wanted to be sure that they had a strong enough case to ensure that Jesus would be executed. His religious trials were before Annas, Caiaphas, and the Sanhedrin. The civil trials were before Pilate and Herod.

3. John 18:24 says that Jesus was sent from the house of Annas to the house of Caiaphas. This was His second religious trial. What happened during the trial in Caiaphas' home? See Matthew 26:57–68.

4. A. In John 13:37, Peter promised that he would lay down his life for Jesus. Jesus responded by predicting Peter's denial. List the verses from John 18 that describe Peter's denial. What emotion superseded Peter's desire to stay faithful to Jesus?

---

61 F. F. Bruce, *The Gospel of John* (Grand Rapids, MI: Eerdmans, 1983), 343.

62 Ignatius Catholic Study Bible, RSV, 195.

B. How can you apply this to your own life?

Fear is a powerful emotion. When we fear, we can sometimes magnify potentially negative outcomes and ignore God's love for us, His protection, and His promise to make good come from all suffering. When we focus on our fears, we are less apt to seek God's will and follow it and more likely to do whatever it takes to escape.

C. Luke 22:59–62 tells what happened immediately following Peter's denial. Jesus was probably being led from the home of Annas to the home of Caiaphas, His hands bound behind His back. What happened, and what was Peter's reaction?

Quiet your heart and enjoy His presence…Take a moment to contemplate what Jesus' gaze must have been like when He looked at Peter in the courtyard.

Beth Moore reflects on this in her book Jesus, the One and Only:

> *I do not doubt that Christ's face was painted with pain when their eyes met in the courtyard, but I think the conspicuous absence of condemnation tore through Peter's heart. I wonder if Christ's fixed gaze might have said something like this: "Remember, Peter, I am the Christ. You know that and I know that. I called you. I gave you a new name. I invited you to follow Me. Don't forget who I am. Don't forget what you are capable of doing. And, whatever you do, don't let this destroy you. When you have turned back, strengthen your brothers." Surely nothing leads to repentance in those who are tender like the kindness of God.*[63]

Reread those words, inserting your name in place of Peter's. This is God's message to you, too, when you fall. We'll all fall at one time or another. The important thing isn't that we never fall but that we get back up and allow God's mercy to fuel us toward accomplishing greater things in and through Him.

---

[63] Beth Moore, *Jesus, the One and Only* (Nashville, TN: Broadman & Holman, 2002), 299.

Day Three: Jesus Before Pilate

Read John 18:28–32.

According to Mark 15:1, there was a final consultation held in the morning by the chief priests, elders, scribes, and entire counsel (the Sanhedrin). They concluded that Jesus was to be put to death (Matthew 27:1).

1. A. The praetorium was the home of Pilate, the Roman governor in Jerusalem. It was his headquarters during Israel's annual feasts and other times when it was necessary to ensure that peace was kept in the city. Why didn't the Jewish leaders enter the praetorium? See also Acts 10:28.

   B. Their actions were further proof that they hadn't learned the lesson that Jesus tried to teach them in Matthew 23:23–28. What was this lesson? Give a modern-day example of a way that we can fall into this same behavior.

Anytime we focus on outward behavior and ignore the state of our hearts, we are guilty of cleansing the outside of the cup but not the inside. An example of this is being fastidious about exercise and dieting while starving your spirit day after day.

2. Why were the Jewish religious leaders determined to have Jesus tried and convicted in a civil court? See John 18:31.

3. What type of charge had to be levied against Jesus in order for Him to be crucified? See CCC 596.

Only the Romans could condemn a person to death. A Roman citizen was beheaded, and noncitizens and insurrectionists were crucified.[64] Because Jesus was not a Roman

---

64 Ignatius Catholic Study Bible, RSV, 196.

citizen, crucifixion was the only option. Jesus had indicated which type of death He would die in John 3:14: "As Moses lifted up the serpent in the wilderness, so must the Son of man be lifted up."

Quiet your heart and enjoy His presence…Jesus chose to enter the world without fanfare or status, out of love for you.

Take a moment to contemplate the fact that God could have chosen for Jesus to be born a Roman citizen. (It was possible for a Jew to be a Roman citizen. Saint Paul was a Roman citizen, as mentioned in Acts 22:27–29.) It was possible to purchase Roman citizenship or have it conferred as a gift for exemplary service to the empire. Roman citizens weren't crucified and couldn't be scourged as a means of torturous examination.[65]

But God chose for Jesus to be born to simple Jewish people, which meant His death would involve much more suffering. It has been said that when Jesus died for us, He showed us His love. But when He suffered for us, He showed us His trustworthiness. There is nothing *that He will not do for you, His beloved.*

Day Four: Jesus Sentenced to Death

Read John 18:33–38.

1. A. What did Pilate ask Jesus in verse 33?

    B. Why had King Herod been interested in this same question years before? See Matthew 2:1–4.

2. A. In John 18:36–37, Pilate was trying to understand Jesus' kingship. Pilate, and rulers like him, couldn't imagine a kingship that didn't depend on force, violence or oppression. What kind of authority and power characterizes Jesus' kingship? See Matthew 20:25–28.

---

[65] Ignatius Catholic Study Bible, RSV, 245.

B. How does Jesus respond to Pilate's question in John 18:37, "So you are a king?" Why do you think he responds in this way?

3. A. Do you think our society resembles Pilate when he asked, "What is truth?" Share an example or two.

Many people consider truth to be relative, believing that there is no absolute truth. Pope Emeritus Benedict XVI had this to say about relativism: "We are moving toward a dictatorship of relativism which does not recognize anything as definitive and has as its highest value one's own ego and one's own desires…The church needs to withstand the tides of trends and the latest novelties…We must become mature in this adult faith, we must guide the flock of Christ to this faith."[66]

B. In John 14:6, how did Jesus answer Pilate's question?

4. Truth was staring Pilate in the face, and he chose to walk away. How interested are you in truth? How often do you ask Jesus to show you the truth about your heart or your decisions? What does Proverbs 2:3–4 have to say about this?

Quiet your heart and enjoy His presence…Take a moment to contemplate the fact that Jesus is the Truth.

When life seems confusing and we need to discern the right path to take, we must draw close to Christ. As we quiet our hearts and minds and spend time in silence in His presence, the Holy Spirit will help us to discover what decisions we should make. He'll guide us toward the truth. When we rely on ourselves, we often end up bound by worry and fear of the future. When we rely on Christ and ask Him to reveal the truth to us, we are set free.

---

66 "Homily of His Eminence Card. Joseph Ratzinger, Dean of the College of Cardinals," Vatican City, Italy (April 18, 2005): https://www.vatican.va/gpII/documents/homily-pro-eligendo-pontifice_20050418_en.html.

Day Five: Jesus and Herod

Read Luke 23:6–12 and John 18:38b–40.

1. What insight do you gain from Matthew 27:17–19 that explains why Pilate wanted to avoid making a judgment about Jesus?

2. A. When did Pilate send Jesus to Herod? See Luke 23:6–12.

    B. Why was Herod glad to see Jesus? Did Jesus give him what he wanted?

3. Herod's stepdaughter had provocatively danced one evening before his court. He was so pleased that he made a careless oath in front of his guests, offering her any reward, up to half his kingdom. She asked for the head of John the Baptist on a platter, and he delivered. Mark 6:20 reveals that Herod considered John the Baptist a righteous and holy man and liked listening to him speak. Herod had been given a great deal of spiritual light. But when he was confronted with his sin, he didn't respond with repentance. Passively listening to the truth means nothing if it doesn't result in action. How easy it is for us to fall into this same habit. When have you passively listened, failing to respond to truths as they were revealed to you?

Quiet your heart and enjoy His presence...Take a moment to contemplate Jesus' silence toward Herod.

Throughout Jesus' ministry, He recognized hearts that were genuinely seeking truth, and He took the time to reach out to those people. But He also recognized a hardened heart that asked questions for the sake of debate or a show. Ask God to soften your heart so that you seek to hear His voice at all times. Ask Him for the strength to respond with obedience to whatever He asks of you. If God seems far away and His words no longer touch your heart, go back to the moment when this began, and ask Him if there is an area of unconfessed sin in your life. Remember that He will always respond to a repentant heart with mercy.

Conclusion

John 18 ends with Pilate's offer to release Jesus, saying that he finds no reason to convict our Lord. Each Passover Pilate released a man. This year would it be Jesus or Barabbas, the equivalent of a modern-day terrorist? The people were allowed to decide. Why would anyone have chosen Barabbas over a gentle, peaceful teacher? Perhaps Barabbas wasn't requiring the people to lay aside their preconceived notions about religion. He didn't talk about cleaning the inside of their lives. Barabbas didn't require anyone to relinquish control.

Jesus, on the other hand, challenged the status quo. He was casting aside a religion that consisted of checking off boxes to indicate outward piety. He wanted *more*. He wanted people's hearts. He wanted them to surrender their will to God. This loss of power was terrifying to the religious leaders. It can feel a little scary to us too. We all must wrestle with Pilate's question, "What is truth?" When the truth is revealed to us, it requires a response. Will we embrace the truth revealed through Christ, or will we run from it?

Pilate asked Jesus, "Are you the King of the Jews?" When the people wanted to crown Jesus a king after He multiplied the loaves and fishes, He fled. Yet when He stood bound in ropes, questioned by Pilate, He accepted that title.

"For this I was born, and for this I have come into the world, to bear witness to the truth" (John 18:37). Jesus came to reveal Himself as the King of love. As King, He asks for our allegiance. He asks for our trust. He knows how difficult it is for us to relinquish control when we fear what might happen. He knows how difficult it is for us to open our hearts to His love if we've been hurt before. But Jesus, the tender King who knows our weaknesses, will only bring what is for our benefit. He is not only the King; He is also the Great Physician. He heals our hurts and restores us. We only need to give Him full access to our hearts. This is Truth. How will you respond?

My Resolution

In what specific way will I apply what I learned in this lesson?

Examples:

1. If I find myself in a situation this week that feels unfair, I will think about how Jesus reacted in the midst of His trial. I'll practice self-control in my response, paying attention to my words and tone. I'll ask God to give me the strength to respond with grace.

2. I will take some time this week (in addition to weekly Mass) to go into a chapel and meditate on Jesus' choice to be mistreated for my sake. I'll look at the cross, recognizing that every second He endured pain and suffering, He had the power to quit. He stayed there out of love for me. I will respond in prayer by thanking Him.

3. This week I will go to confession and acknowledge my weakness and dependence on the Truth, with the intention of receiving the strengthening grace that comes from the sacrament.

My Resolution:

Catechism Clips

CCC 596 The religious authorities in Jerusalem were not unanimous about what stance to take towards Jesus. The Pharisees threatened to excommunicate his followers. To those who feared that "everyone will believe in him, and the Romans will come and destroy both our holy place and our nation," the high priest Caiaphas replied by prophesying: "It is expedient for you that one man should die for the people, and that the whole nation should not perish." The Sanhedrin, having declared Jesus deserving of death as a blasphemer but having lost the right to put anyone to death, hands him over to the Romans, accusing him of political revolt, a charge that puts him in the same category as Barabbas who had been accused of sedition. The chief priests also threatened Pilate politically so that he would condemn Jesus to death.

Verse Study

See appendix 3 for instructions on how to complete a verse study.

John 18:37

1. Verse:

2. Paraphrase:

3. Questions:

4. Cross-references:

5. Personal Application:

Lesson 20

JESUS, OUR REDEEMER

Introduction

How easy it is to hear the story of Christ's crucifixion and gloss over the details. We already know what's going to happen. We know how it ends. It's possible to read John 19 with our hearts unmoved.

It's harder to do this with the images of Mel Gibson's movie *The Passion of the Christ* in mind. I remember the first time I saw this film. Our fifth child, Jane, was just a couple of months old. I went to the movie with her in my arms. I desperately wanted to look away or to close my eyes. The reality of what Jesus suffered was just too terrible. Tears ran down my cheeks as I forced myself to watch, knowing that He endured this for me. He endured this for little Jane. He endured it for all of us to show how much He loves us. He kept His focus on His goal—reconnecting people with their heavenly Father through His sacrifice.

Humanity had been suffering for thousands of years. People needed healing. They were desperate for hope. They needed a bridge to lead them back to an intimate relationship with their Creator. A price needed to be paid.

Jesus was to suffer the consequences of man's rebellion against God. Now was the time. Now was His hour, when Jesus would offer Himself as the ransom. His love was so great that the very One who had been wronged offered to take the punishment for the people who had hurt Him.

Reading over John 19, you'd probably find the details very familiar. So this week, we're going to make a special effort to place ourselves in the scene and see things as they really were, to the best of our ability. Let's pray that this time we will see the events of Christ's last hours with fresh eyes and with hearts overwhelmed with gratitude.

Day One: The Scourging

Read John 19:1–3.

1. How was Jesus treated in John 19:1–3?

A Roman scourging (or flogging) was such a horrific event that many victims did not survive it. "Tied to the ends of the whip were fragments of bone or metal designed to tear up the skin, causing injuries that were sometimes fatal."[67] The heavy whip was lashed with full force again and again—across Jesus' legs, His back, His shoulders. Initially it would have broken the skin. As the flogging went on and on, it cut deeper into Jesus' tissue, into the muscle, until the skin was an unrecognizable wound.

Imagine His mother's reaction to this treatment of her Son. The Bible doesn't tell us, but we can feel fairly certain that by this time, someone had run to tell the Blessed Mother that her Son had been arrested. She would have been as close as she possibly could have been. How she must have been desperate to protect Him or to at least strengthen Him with a look that said, "I love you, Son." Even as she trusted God and His wisdom, she felt complete anguish of soul watching the extent of human cruelty. This was her little boy. She had nurtured Him as an infant, tucked Him in at night, washed away His tears when He stumbled, made His meals, encouraged Him during His ministry. What could she do now in the midst of this torture? She could pray. She could be there. She could refuse to leave His side, no matter how much it agonized her to watch Him suffer. She could enter into His suffering in a mystical way and share it.

2. Read Matthew 27:27–31. Describe what followed the scourging in your own words.

3. "He himself bore our sins in his body on the tree, that we might die to sin and live to righteousness. By his wounds you have been healed" (1 Peter 2:24). What does this verse mean to you personally?

---

67 Ignatius Catholic Study Bible, RSV, 196.

Quiet your heart and enjoy His presence…Take a moment to contemplate Jesus' scourging.

My dear kind, gentle, loving Jesus,

What strength it took to submit to the hands of sinful men—men who delighted in seeing You suffer. You created them. Let me never forget that You are God. What restraint You showed when You endured this pain. How can I respond in any other way than to fall to my knees in awareness of how little I deserve Your mercy? My sins are too many to count. But You stood up and said, "Punish me instead of her." Why do You love me like this? As crazy as it seems, there are times my heart doubts Your love. People haven't loved me unconditionally, and I have a hard time remembering that You don't love like other people do. Help me to understand the meaning of the cross, because that's where You proved that Your love goes far beyond the best human love.

Day Two: Pilate Finds No Crime

Read John 19:4–11.

1. Including John 18, how many times did Pilate say he found no crime in Jesus?

2. In a word, what was the charge the Jewish leaders brought against Jesus? See also Leviticus 24:16. What is the irony in that charge?

3. As Pilate debated what to do with Jesus, what thoughts might have been running through his mind? See Matthew 27:17–19.

4. Pilate said, "Do you not know that I have power to release you and power to crucify you?" What does John 19:11 indicate about who was really in control of the situation? See also CCC 600. Does this offer you encouragement when situations in your life seem out of control?

Quiet your heart and enjoy His presence...Take a moment to contemplate Jesus' incredible self-control.

The physical pain He was experiencing from the flogging as well as the contemplation of the suffering He was about to endure on the cross would have tempted Jesus to escape. Yet He refrained from exercising control over the situation, and instead He controlled His reactions and emotions. Do you know that the same power that gave Jesus remarkable strength and endurance is available to you? God has placed within His children the fruits of the Spirit. One of these fruits is self-control (Galatians 5:23). When we are facing situations that are affecting our emotions and we want to react in a way that is not consistent with godliness, we can call on the Holy Spirit to fill us with self-control.

Never forget "what is the immeasurable greatness of his power in us who believe, according to the working of his great might which he accomplished in Christ when he raised him from the dead" (Ephesians 1:19–20).

Thank God for giving you the power, through the indwelling Holy Spirit, to overcome your emotions and to react to the small and big difficulties in life with grace.

Day Three: Pilate's Final Decision

Read John 19:12–16.

1. A. How did the Jewish people respond when Pilate said to them, "Here is your King"?

    B. Does the Church blame the Jews for Jesus' death? See CCC 597.

2. Who are the true authors of Christ's Passion? See CCC 598.

3. "We, however, profess to know him. And when we deny him by our deeds, we in some way seem to lay violent hands on him" (CCC 598). How do those words change the way you think about sin and the sacrament of Reconciliation?

4. "So when Pilate saw that he was gaining nothing, but rather that a riot was beginning, he took water and washed his hands before the crowd, saying, 'I am innocent of this righteous man's blood; see to it yourselves'" (Matthew 27:24). The personal sin of Pilate is known to God alone, but it is clear that his desire for position and power was stronger than his desire to protect someone falsely accused. Can you think of an example in your own life when you were tempted, as was Pilate, to look out for yourself instead of for another?

Quiet your heart and enjoy His presence…Take a moment to contemplate the fact that every time we sin, it causes Jesus pain.

How He wants us to experience the abundant life He promises in John 10:10! Recall the words of Jesus in Luke 19:42: "Would that even today you knew the things that make for peace! But now they are hidden from your eyes." So often the obedience that God asks of us seems like the harder route to take. We think that our own plans will lead to greater peace and ease. But the big picture is hidden from our eyes. His way is always the best. His plan always leads us to abundance. Our shortcuts and best-laid plans often lead us away from God's best plan for us. Pray that God will give you the strength to trust Him with the things you cannot see and to obey even when the road ahead is unclear.

Day Four: The Crucifixion

Read John 19:17–27.

1. Describe in your own words what it would have felt like for Jesus to carry a heavy wooden cross on His back after experiencing a severe scourging.

2. The purple robe had been torn from Jesus' back, and His garments were divided among the soldiers. Spiritually speaking, what was He wearing when He hung on the cross? See 2 Corinthians 5:21.

3. A. In the midst of unimaginable agony, what did Jesus say regarding those who were hurting Him? See Luke 23:34.

    B. Do you believe it was easier for Jesus to forgive His enemies than it is for us to forgive those who wrong us? Whom do you need to forgive?

4. Who stayed by Jesus' side until the end?

5. What does the Catholic Church teach is the significance of Jesus' words to Mary, "Woman, behold your son," and to John, "Behold, your mother"? See also CCC 501 and 964.

Venerable Fulton Sheen writes of this in his book *Life of Christ*:

> [Jesus] looked longingly at Her, who had sent Him willingly to the Cross and who is now standing beneath it as a cooperator in His Redemption; and He said, "Woman, this is thy son." He did not call him John; to do that would have been to address him as the son of Zebedee and no one else. But in his anonymity, John stood for all mankind. To His beloved disciple He said: "This is thy mother."

> Here is the answer, after all these years, to the mysterious words in the Gospel of the Incarnation which stated that Our Blessed Mother laid her "firstborn" in the manger. Did that mean that Our Blessed Mother was to have other children? It certainly did, but not according to the flesh. Our Divine Lord and Savior Jesus Christ was the unique Son of Our Blessed Mother by the flesh. But Our Lady was to have other children, not according to the flesh, but according to the spirit![68]

Quiet your heart and enjoy His presence...Take a moment to contemplate what Jesus has done for you.

---

68 Sheen, *Life of Christ*, 547.

So many religions are characterized by man lifting himself up to God, hoping that He will think man is good enough. Only in Christianity do we see God reaching down to man. God knew that even our best efforts would fall short of the holiness that He wants for us. So He came down to fill in the gap between our best efforts and His ideal for man. Jesus took our sins upon Himself on the cross and experienced the punishment that was ours. Contemplate this divine exchange: He takes our sins, our failings, our inadequacies and, by the power of the cross, applies His forgiveness and mercy, transforming us into His image and likeness. He does this because He loves us. He does this to create a way for us to spend eternity with Him. How are we to respond? With hearts of gratitude. Our motivation for doing the right thing should be a heart overflowing with appreciation for all our Savior sacrificed for us. Each act of kindness should be a thank-you to Him. If a person saved your life on earth, would it not be true that you would do anything that he or she asked of you? In that same way, we show our gratitude to Jesus by the way we live. We show our gratitude by the way we love.

Day Five: Jesus' Side Is Pierced

Read John 19:28–42.

1. When Jesus' side was pierced, water and blood came out. The water and blood symbolize which sacraments? See CCC 1225 and 694.

2. Galatians 2:20 says, "I have been crucified with Christ; it is no longer I who live, but Christ who lives in me; and the life I now live in the flesh I live by faith in the Son of God, who loved me and gave himself for me."

    A. How are we crucified with Christ? See Romans 6:3–4.

    B. How does Christ live in us? See 1 Corinthians 6:19.

    C. How did Jesus show His love for the world collectively and for you individually? See CCC 616.

3. Joseph of Arimathea and Nicodemus (note the change in him!) bound Jesus' body in linen clothes with spices. What other burial preparation had previously taken place for Jesus? See Matthew 26:6–12.

Quiet your heart and enjoy His presence…Take a moment to contemplate what we can offer Christ to show Him our gratitude.

Think of Mary of Bethany. People judged her, saying that her costly perfume was wasted when she washed Jesus' feet with it. Sometimes people look at the sacrifices we make for Jesus and think they are a waste. Have you ever been judged for something that you offered Him? Be assured He sees your sacrifice and considers it a beautiful thing. It offers consolation to His heart. How it must gladden His heart when you receive and relish His love.

Conclusion

The crucifix we see in church is a sanitized version of Jesus on His cross. In reality He was covered in blood and wounds. Had we stood at the foot of the cross, that image of Jesus would have been emblazoned on our memory for the rest of our lives. We could never have thought of His death with a callous heart.

Dr. C. Truman Davis, a physician, has studied the practice of crucifixion in order to more fully appreciate all that Christ suffered for his sake. He writes the following description:

> Jesus is offered wine mixed with myrrh, a mild analgesic mixture. He refuses to drink. Simon [of Cyrene] is ordered to place the patibulum on the ground and Jesus is quickly thrown backward with His shoulders against the wood. The legionnaire feels for the depression at the front of the wrist. He drives a heavy, square, wrought-iron nail through the wrist and deep into the wood. Quickly, he moves to the other side and repeats the action, being careful not to pull the arms too tightly, but to allow some flexion and movement…
>
> The left foot is now pressed backward against the right foot, and with both feet extended, toes down, a nail is driven through the arch of each, leaving the knees moderately flexed. The Victim is now crucified. As He slowly sags down with more weight on the nails in the wrists, excruciating pain shoots along the fingers and up the arms to explode in the brain—the nails in the wrists are

putting pressure on the median nerves. As He pushes Himself upward to avoid this stretching torment, He places His full weight on the nail through His feet. Again there is the searing agony of the nail tearing through the nerves between the metatarsal bones of the feet.

At this point, as the arms fatigue, great waves of cramps sweep over the muscles, knotting them in deep, relentless, throbbing pain. With these cramps comes the inability to push Himself upward. Hanging by His arms, the pectoral muscles are paralyzed and the intercostal muscles are unable to act. Air can be drawn into the lungs, but cannot be exhaled. Jesus fights to raise Himself in order to get even one short breath. Finally, carbon dioxide builds up in the lungs and in the blood stream and the cramps partially subside. Spasmodically, he is able to push Himself upward to exhale and bring in the life-giving oxygen. It was undoubtedly during these periods that He uttered the seven short sentences recorded.[69]

And what were His words? Did He cry out for relief? No. His words spoke forgiveness to those who hurt Him, offered mercy to a thief by His side, took care of His mother, and offered Mary to the Church. Even in such agony, His thoughts were of love for those He had come to save.

We are reminded of these lines from the hymn "When I Survey the Wondrous Cross": "Love so amazing, so divine, demands my soul, my life, my all."

My Resolution

In what specific way will I apply what I learned in this lesson?

Examples:

1. When I begin to feel my emotions getting the better of me, I will stop and remember that the same power that raised Jesus from the dead is within me through the indwelling Holy Spirit. I'll ask the Holy Spirit to calm me and help me to react as I should. I'll read Ephesians 1:19–20 and remember that "the immeasurable greatness of his power [is] in us who believe."

---

[69] C. Truman Davis, "The Crucifixion," Gospel Outreach Ministries Online: gospeloutreach.net/crucifixion.html.

2. Has Christ asked me to sacrifice something for Him? Has He asked me to obey Him in an area that I find difficult? I will take time to pray about what is holding me back. Am I worried about what other people will think? Do I not want to leave a place of comfort? I'll ask God for help to let go and to obey. I will take a concrete step of obedience in this area within the week. I'll share my desire to obey with a friend and ask her to hold me accountable.

My Resolution:

Catechism Clips

CCC 501 Jesus is Mary's only son, but her spiritual motherhood extends to all men whom indeed he came to save: "The Son whom she brought forth is he whom God placed as the first-born among many brethren, that is, the faithful in whose generation and formulation she co-operates with a mother's love."

CCC 597 The historical complexity of Jesus' trial is apparent in the Gospel accounts. The personal sin of the participants (Judas, the Sanhedrin, Pilate) is known to God alone. Hence we cannot lay responsibility for the trial on the Jews in Jerusalem as a whole, despite the outcry of a manipulated crowd and the global reproaches contained in the apostles' calls to conversion after Pentecost. Jesus himself, in forgiving them on the cross, and Peter in following suit, both accept "the ignorance" of the Jews of Jerusalem and even of their leaders. Still less can we extend responsibility to other Jews of different times and places, based merely on the crowd's cry: "His blood be on us and on our children!" a formula for ratifying a judicial sentence. As the Church declared at the Second Vatican Council:

> [N]either all Jews indiscriminately at that time, nor Jews today, can be charged with the crimes committed during his Passion...[T]he Jews should not be spoken of as rejected or accursed as if this followed from Holy Scripture.

CCC 598 In her Magisterial teaching of the faith and in the witness of her saints, the Church has never forgotten that "sinners were the authors and the ministers of all the sufferings that the divine Redeemer endured." Taking into account the fact that our sins affect Christ himself, the Church does not hesitate to impute to Christians the gravest responsibility for the torments inflicted upon Jesus, a responsibility with which they have all too often burdened the Jews alone:

> We must regard as guilty all those who continue to relapse into their sins. Since our sins made the Lord Christ suffer the torment of the cross, those who plunge themselves into disorders and crimes crucify the Son of God anew in their hearts (for he is in them) and hold him up to contempt. And it can be seen that our crime in this case is greater in us than in the Jews. As for them, according to the witness of the Apostle, "None of the rulers of this age understood this; for if they had, they would not have crucified the Lord of glory." We, however, profess to know him. And when we deny him by our deeds, we in some way seem to lay violent hands on him.

Nor did demons crucify him; it is you who have crucified him and crucify him still, when you delight in your vices and sins.

CCC 600 To God, all moments of time are present in their immediacy. When therefore he establishes his eternal plan of "predestination," he includes in it each person's free response to his grace: "In this city, in fact, both Herod and Pontius Pilate, with the Gentiles and the peoples of Israel, gathered together against your holy servant Jesus, whom you anointed, to do whatever your hand and your plan had predestined to take place." For the sake of accomplishing his plan of salvation, God permitted the acts that flowed from their blindness.

CCC 616 It is love "to the end" that confers on Christ's sacrifice its value as redemption and reparation, as atonement and satisfaction. He knew and loved us all when he offered his life. Now "the love of Christ controls us, because we are convinced that one has died for all; therefore all have died." No man, not even the holiest, was ever able to take on himself the sins of all men and offer himself as a sacrifice for all. The existence in Christ of the divine person of the Son, who at once surpasses and embraces all human persons, and constitutes himself as the Head of all mankind, makes possible his redemptive sacrifice for all.

CCC 694 The symbolism of water signifies the Holy Spirit's action in Baptism, since after the invocation of the Holy Spirit it becomes the efficacious sacramental sign of new birth: just as the gestation of our first birth took place in water, so the water of Baptism truly signifies that our birth into the divine life is given to us in the Holy Spirit.

CCC 964 Mary's role in the Church is inseparable from her union with Christ and flows directly from it. "This union of the mother with the Son in the work of salvation is made manifest from the time of Christ's virginal conception up to his death"; it is made manifest above all at the hour of his Passion:

> Thus the Blessed Virgin advanced in her pilgrimage of faith, and faithfully persevered in her union with her Son unto the cross. There she stood, in keeping with the divine plan, enduring with her only begotten Son the intensity of his suffering, joining herself with his sacrifice in her mother's heart, and lovingly consenting to the immolation of this victim, born of her: to be given, by the same Christ Jesus dying on the cross, as a mother to his disciple, with these words: "Woman, behold your son."

CCC 1225 In his Passover Christ opened to all men the fountain of Baptism. He had already spoken of his Passion, which he was about to suffer in Jerusalem, as a "Baptism" with which he had to be baptized. The blood and water that flowed from the pierced side of the crucified Jesus are types of Baptism and the Eucharist, the sacraments of new life. From then on, it is possible "to be born of water and the Spirit" in order to enter the Kingdom of God.

> See where you are baptized, see where Baptism comes from, if not from the cross of Christ, from his death. There is the whole mystery: he died for you. In him you are redeemed, in him you are saved.

Verse Study

See appendix 3 for instructions on how to complete a verse study.

John 19:30

1. Verse:

2. Paraphrase:

3. Questions:

4. Cross-references:

5. Personal Application:

NOTES

Lesson 21

JESUS, OUR RESTORER

Introduction

I recently traveled to speak to a Walking with Purpose group and sat in the chapel, preparing to give a talk. To my left I saw a woman, clearly distressed. She was hunched over, rocking back and forth, muttering something. It didn't feel right to ignore her in order to better prepare my talk, so I asked the Lord if He wanted me to speak with her. I sensed that He wanted me to go to her, so I walked over and sat behind her, intending to offer her comfort. I wasn't really sure what I was supposed to say to her; I just knew it would be wrong to ignore her distress. As I got closer, I could hear she was praying the Our Father, but her tone and body language lacked any peace.

I gently tapped her on the shoulder. Quick as lightning she spun around, eyes crazy with fear or anger; I wasn't sure which one it was. "What are you doing?" she screamed. "Who do you think you are? How dare you touch me! Don't touch me! Don't come near me! What's wrong with you, touching a stranger?" I was afraid. She was clearly very upset by me. I had made things worse, not better. She moved away but continued to scream.

As quickly as possible, I headed toward the room where the ladies were gathered for my talk. The woman came out of the chapel. She had seen where I was. I became all the more nervous that she might interrupt the talk. What would she say?

She passed in the hallway but didn't come in. My shoulders lost their tension. Then just before I was to start, she came through the door and came straight to me. Her look of terror was gone. She was calm and put out her hand. "Please forgive me," she said. "Will you please pray for me?" I said I would, and she left.

As I reflected on our interaction, my first thought was to say to God, "That is the last time I'm following through on what I think is a little nudge from you!" But as her face has stayed in my memory and I'm often prompted to pray for her, I feel more certain that God connected us. I've often asked Him, "Please break my heart with the things that break yours." I believe He was simply answering that prayer. God sees this woman day after day, and He loves her. He has seen the terrible things that have happened to her—wrongs that have left her a hurt, broken woman. He cares about her deeply, and He wants others to as well.

Our reading today begins with Mary Magdalene at Jesus' tomb. According to Luke 8:1–2, Jesus had cast seven demons out of her. What did she look like when He first met her? What did people think of her? What did they say about her? Did her demon possession terrify those in her path?

God had seen Mary Magdalene in her distress. In His compassion He sent His Son to restore her dignity. She had been chained to demons bent on destroying her. Jesus gave her freedom. Her sins were burned up in the furnace of God's mercy. Sheer love invaded her soul. For the first time, she felt beautiful. As long as she kept her eyes on Jesus, she was assured of her dignity and goodness. So she stayed close. When He was nailed to the cross, she bravely remained at His feet. The minute the Sabbath was over—early, while it was still dark—she ran to the tomb. She desperately wanted to see if what He had said would happen had come true—that He would rise again in three days. How could she live without Him? He had looked past her ugliness and seen a beloved daughter of God. She had seen herself reflected in His eyes.

Day One: The Resurrection of Jesus

Read John 20:1–18.

1. A. How did the apostle John refer to himself in verse 2?

   B. Does this strike you as egotistical? Would you describe yourself with similar words? Why or why not?

2. John was the faster runner, but he didn't go in the tomb. Instead he waited for Peter. Why might he have waited? See Matthew 16:16–19.

3. What did Mary Magdalene think had happened to Jesus' body? How did the state of affairs within the tomb cause the disciples to look for another explanation?

The state of the linen cloths and napkin in the tomb made a significant impression on the apostle John. "The linen clothes lying there": the Greek participle translated as "lying there" seems to indicate that the clothes were flattened, deflated, as if they were emptied when the body of Jesus rose and disappeared—as if He had come out of the clothes and bandages without their being unrolled, passing right through them. This would explain the clothes being fallen, flat, lying, which is how the Greek literally translates, after Jesus' body—which had filled them—left them.[70]

4. A. At what point did Mary Magdalene recognize Jesus?

B. What did Jesus ask Mary Magdalene to say to the disciples?

C. Why was it significant that Jesus said, "I am ascending to my Father and *your Father*" (emphasis added)? See Galatians 4:4–7. What does this teach you in terms of how God wants you to view yourself?

The way in which people were able to approach God the Father dramatically changed after Jesus' death and Resurrection. In the Old Testament, the Israelites were told to build a tabernacle (later the Temple) for God. God dwelled within the tabernacle in a place called the holy of holies. Outside the holy of holies was the holy place. A "veil of blue and purple and scarlet stuff and fine twined linen; in skilled work it shall be made, with cherubim" was hung on four gold-plated columns of acacia wood (Exodus 26:31–32). This was to separate the holy place from the holy of holies. It served as a lovely Do Not Enter sign. There was another veil, equally ornate, separating the holy place from the outer courts. When the Israelites wanted to get close to God, they couldn't just stroll into the holy place and then the Holy of Holies. Only priests were allowed in the holy place, and only once a year was the high priest allowed to go into the holy of

---

70 Navarre Bible: Saint John's Gospel, RSV, 293–294.

holies. He entered there to present a blood sacrifice as a way of asking for forgiveness for the nation of Israel.

When Jesus died on the cross, the curtain of the Temple was torn in two from top to bottom (Mark 15:38). "As the curtain ripped from top to bottom, the barrier between the face of God and his people was removed."[71]

Quiet your heart and enjoy His presence…as the Lord delights in your presence.

Take a moment to contemplate what it would have been like to feel the earth shake, see the sky darken, and witness the veil of the Temple ripping even though nothing had touched it. Can you imagine peeking into the holy places that you'd never been allowed to enter? What a privilege it is that we can approach God whenever we'd like to with the confidence of a beloved child visiting her father. Thank Him for what it cost Him to offer you this priceless intimacy.

Day Two: The Power to Forgive Sins

Read John 20:19–31.

1. How would you describe Jesus' resurrected body? See John 20:20, Luke 24:36–42, and CCC 645.

2. In what way did Jesus ensure that His disciples would never be left alone? See John 20:22 and CCC 788.

3. What power did Jesus give to the disciples in John 20:23?

The Church has always understood—and has in fact defined—that Jesus Christ here conferred on the apostles authority to forgive sins, a power that is exercised in the sacrament of penance: "The Lord then especially instituted the Sacrament of Penance when, after being risen from the dead, He breathed upon His disciples and said: 'Receive the Holy Spirit…' The consensus of all the Fathers has always acknowledged that by

---

71 Ignatius Catholic Study Bible, RSV, 96.

this action so sublime and words so clear the power of forgiving and retaining sins was given to the Apostles and their lawful successors for reconciling the faithful who have fallen after Baptism."[72]

4. The reason the Gospel of John was written is listed in John 20:31. What was the apostle John's purpose when he wrote?

Quiet your heart and enjoy His presence…as the Lord delights in your presence.

"And this is the testimony, that God gave us eternal life, and this life is in his Son. He who has the Son has life; he who has not the Son of God has not life" (1 John 5:11–12).

God gave us the way to eternal life by giving us His Son. Life in Jesus' name is eternal life. We must embrace God's gift, uniting ourselves with Christ, to find our way to the Father and eternal life. What difference has Christ made in your life? Has He freed you from bad habits? Has He softened your heart with His unconditional love? Has He given you peace in the midst of difficult circumstances? How different would your life be if He were not a part of it?

Father John Bartunek states it beautifully in The Better Part*: "Our hearts seem unsatisfied even by all that life offers us: We always want more. God made us like that. He made us thirsty for a happiness that only he can give, in order to make sure that we would seek him. Our life is a quest for Jesus Christ."[73]*

Day Three: Jesus Appears to the Disciples

Read John 21:1–14.

1. Why did the disciples leave Jerusalem and go to the Sea of Tiberias? See John 6:1 and Matthew 28:10.

---

72 Navarre Bible: Saint John's Gospel, RSV, 196.

73 Bartunek, *The Better Part*, 999.

2. A. Sitting in a boat all night long gave the disciples plenty of time to reflect. How do you think Peter felt when he thought back on his words, recorded in Mark 14:27–29? How would those thoughts have influenced his desire to get back up and follow Christ's command to lead the Church?

    B. Peter had experienced a life-changing lesson in humility. Never again would he count on his own strength to remain faithful. It's so easy to succumb to the temptation of relying on ourselves. Whose strength are we to rely on? See 2 Corinthians 12:9–10.

3. There have been many discussions regarding the significance of the catch of 153 fish. Saint Jerome said that Greek zoologists at that time had discovered 153 different species of fish.[74] In what way might that interpretation relate to the Church? See also Matthew 28:19–20 and Revelation 7:9 and 14:6.

4. Jesus prepared breakfast over a charcoal fire. According to Scripture, what had happened the last time Peter was in front of a charcoal fire? See John 18:15–18, 25–27.

Quiet your heart and enjoy His presence…as He delights in your presence.

Take a moment to contemplate Peter's response when he heard it was Jesus on the shore. "He sprang into the sea" to get to Him as quickly as possible. Peter recognized Jesus in the miraculous catch of fish. He threw aside his pride. Oh, that we would respond the same way when we feel we've let Jesus down! So often we retreat, hide, or distract ourselves with other things instead of rushing to Him for restoration. Is there something in your heart that needs to be forgiven? He's waiting for you with open, loving arms.

---

74   Ignatius Catholic Study Bible, RSV, 200.

Day Four: The Restoration of Peter

Read John 21:15–19.

1. The full meaning of this passage is lost in the translation from Greek to English. Greeks used four distinct words to distinguish the different types of love: *storge*, *philia*, *eros*, and *agape*. As described in *Our Sunday Visitor's Catholic Encyclopedia*, *storge* is a familial love, describing the bond between one who loves and those who surround him or her. *Philia* describes the love between friends. *Eros* is a passionate love, often used to describe sexual love. *Agape* is a divine love—a generous, self-giving love with no concern for reward.[75]

    Note the verb choices John used in John 21:15–17. "Jesus said to Simon Peter, 'Simon, son of John, do you love [agape] me?' He said to him, 'Yes, Lord; you know that I love [philia] you.'…A second time he said to him, 'Simon, son of John, do you love [agape] me?' He said to him, 'Yes, Lord; you know that I love [philia] you.'… He said to him the third time, 'Simon, son of John, do you love [philia] me?'…And he said to him, 'Lord, you know everything; you know that I love [philia] you.'"

    What do you think is the significance of the verb changes in this passage?

2. *Philia* love, the love of friendship, would help Peter follow Christ's call to feed and tend His sheep. But Peter would need a deeper love to live out the sacrifice that Jesus spoke of in John 21:18, predicting Peter's martyrdom. If Peter were to follow Jesus to the death, his heart would need to be filled with a love that goes deeper than friendship. He would need *agape* love to remain faithful.

    Where does one find agape love? See Romans 5:5 and CCC 1813.

3. How many times did Peter publicly deny Jesus? How many times did Jesus give him the chance to publicly reaffirm his love for Him?

---

75 Reverend Peter M. J. Stravinskas, ed., *Our Sunday Visitor's Catholic Encyclopedia* (Huntington, IN: Our Sunday Visitor, 1998), 633.

4. What is the significance of Jesus asking Peter to feed His lambs, tend His sheep, and feed His sheep? See also CCC 881.

Jesus had already forgiven Peter. This conversation by the charcoal fire was all about restoration. In forgiveness the debt is paid. In restoration trust is given again. Jesus not only forgave Peter; He trusted him with what was most precious to Him—His sheep.

Quiet your heart and enjoy His presence…as He delights in your presence.

Take a moment to contemplate Peter's words in 1 Peter 1:8. The indwelling Holy Spirit changed him so much that he was able to say, "Without having seen him you love [agape] him; though you do not now see him you believe in him and rejoice with unutterable and exalted joy." Although we can't see Jesus, we can still love Him with agape love because the Holy Spirit pours that love into our hearts. We need that kind of love to follow Christ. Life is not easy. Much personal sacrifice is required. In order to respond to tough circumstances and difficult people with grace, we need divine love. Ask God to fill you with His love so that it overflows into all areas of your life.

Day Five: Peter Is Given a Command

Reread John 21:15–25.

1. A. While this passage is about the mission given to St. Peter to shepherd those entrusted to His care, we can apply some of these lessons to our own lives. Who are the sheep that God has entrusted to your care? Who are the souls that He has asked you to encourage spiritually?

    B. Often those entrusted to our care are children. They, like us, are wired to worship. Either they will worship God, or they will worship something else. Remaining neutral is not an option. *We are made to worship.* What are some practical ways that we can encourage children to worship God instead of their peers, popularity, pleasure and instant gratification, or sports?

2. We relate to the words of the beloved hymn "Come, Thy Fount of Every Blessing": "Prone to wander…Lord I feel it! Prone to leave the God I love!" Sheep are prone to wander.

   A. What are some specific ways that you can resist the temptation to wander spiritually?

   B. Do you know anyone who has wandered away from God? What can you do to encourage her to come back to the Good Shepherd? How can you be the voice of the Good Shepherd, calling her name?

   C. Take a moment to contemplate John 10:11: "I am the good shepherd. The good shepherd lays down his life for the sheep." Caring for sheep requires sacrificial love. It's so easy to lose sight of this high calling when we are weary, feel constantly interrupted, and aren't feeling appreciated. If our hearts are ruled by the desire for comfort, control, appreciation, or success, we can easily look to those entrusted to our care to satisfy those needs. In the words of author Paul Tripp, "Instead of seeing moments of struggle as God-given doors of opportunity, we will view them as frustrating, disappointing irritants, and we will experience growing anger against the very [ones] to whom we have been called to minister."[76] Ask God to reveal to you what is ruling your heart. Is your desire for appreciation, respect, success, comfort, or control getting in the way of tending to the sheep in your care?

3. How did Jesus respond in John 21:22 when Peter wanted to know God's plan for John?

---

76 Paul David Tripp, *Age of Opportunity: A Biblical Guide to Parenting Teens* (Phillipsburg, NJ: P&R), 38.

Quiet your heart and enjoy His presence…as He delights in your presence.

"But there are also many other things which Jesus did; were every one of them to be written, I suppose that the world itself could not contain the books that would be written" (John 21:25).

St. Jerome said the Scriptures are like "a pool that is deep enough for scholars to swim in without ever touching bottom and yet shallow enough for children to wade in without ever drowning."[77] We'll never plumb its depths, but it's accessible to all. May we come not just to the Bible but to the whole life of faith with a hungry heart. God is continually communicating with us; He wants to be known. May we have eyes to see and a thirst for His Revelation. May we not just hear His words but do what He says, and may we take all that He has so generously passed on to us and share it with others. This is our commission, not just Saint Peter's. May we "see to it that no one misses the grace of God" (Hebrews 12:15).

Conclusion

Dear Friends,

I pray this journey through John's Gospel has been as encouraging to you as it has been to me. We've learned about so many aspects of Jesus' personality. We've seen Him as the Lamb of God, who loved us enough to suffer in our place. We've seen that just as He filled the jars at the wedding at Cana with the best wine, He can fill us when we're empty and transform us. We've learned that He is the greatest gift-giver, offering us eternal life, just as He offered it to Nicodemus. When we are thirsting for real love, just like the Samaritan woman at the well, Jesus will fill us with living water that refreshes and restores. We've met Jesus in the Eucharist and watched many leave because that teaching was too different from what they expected of the Messiah. We saw Jesus persecuted and were inspired by His fidelity, His commitment to stay strong and faithful to the Father's will. We've met Jesus as the Light of the World and learned that He can dispel the darkness in our lives. We watched Him reach out and touch the marginalized, and we saw that He desires to console each one of us in our places of hurt and need. And what would He not do for His sheep as the Good Shepherd? He laid down His life for His sheep and tenderly calls each one by name. As the Resurrection and the Life, He can enter our most desolate places and bring new life and hope. He's the King who rules by serving. He washes feet and cleanses souls. He's the Vine who promises growth if we'll stay connected to Him. He calls out to God on our behalf, praying for us because He loves us. Jesus is the Truth, and He brings clarity to our confused lives. He is our Redeemer, who came to set us free. He is our freedom, breaking our bonds to sin and

---

77   Frederick Dale Bruner, *The Gospel of John: A Commentary* (Grand Rapids, MI: Eerdmans, 2012), 1206.

offering us a fresh start. He is our Restorer, the One who brings back our dignity and trusts us to carry forth His message of grace and healing.

Never forget, Jesus loves you with an unending, passionate, unconditional love. I pray that by knowing Him more, you love Him more. May the journey of your heart, growing closer and closer to your Savior, continue always.

My Resolution

In what specific way will I apply what I learned in this lesson?

Examples:

1. When I am in a situation that feels hopeless, I will remember what God has told me. I'll remind myself of His promises: "I will never fail you nor forsake you" (Hebrews 13:5). "For this slight momentary affliction is preparing for us an eternal weight of glory beyond all comparison" (2 Corinthians 4:17). "Neither death, nor life, nor angels, nor principalities, nor things present, nor things to come, nor powers, nor height, nor depth, nor anything else in all creation, will be able to separate us from the love of God in Christ Jesus our Lord" (Romans 8:38–39).

2. I'll stop making excuses and will take the time to receive the sacrament of Reconciliation this week. I'll take time beforehand to think through the areas where I most need to grow, asking the Holy Spirit to reveal to me what I should confess. I'll remember that I'm going to the mercy seat of Christ, where nothing is beyond the reach of His forgiveness.

My Resolution:

Catechism Clips

CCC 645 By means of touch and the sharing of a meal, the risen Jesus establishes direct contact with his disciples. He invites them in this way to recognize that he is not a ghost and above all to verify that the risen body in which he appears to them is the same body that had been tortured and crucified, for it still bears the traces of his Passion. Yet at the same time this authentic, real body possesses the new properties of a glorious body: not limited by space and time but able to be present how and when he wills; for Christ's humanity can no longer be confined to earth, and belongs henceforth only to the Father's divine realm. For this reason too the risen Jesus enjoys the sovereign freedom of appearing as he wishes: in the guise of a gardener or in other forms familiar to his disciples, precisely to awaken their faith.

CCC 788 When his visible presence was taken from them, Jesus did not leave his disciples orphans. He promised to remain with them until the end of time; he sent them his Spirit. As a result communion with Jesus had become, in a way, more intense: "By communicating his Spirit, Christ mystically constitutes as his body those brothers of his who are called together from every nation."

CCC 881 The Lord made Simon alone, whom he named Peter, the "rock" of his Church. He gave him the keys of his Church and instituted him as shepherd of the whole flock. "The office of binding and loosing which was given to Peter was also assigned to the college of apostles united to its head." This pastoral office of Peter and the other apostles belongs to the Church's very foundation and is continued by the bishops under the primacy of the Pope.

CCC 1813 The theological virtues are the foundation of Christian moral activity; they animate it and give it its special character. They inform and give life to all the moral virtues. They are infused by God into the souls of the faithful to make them capable of acting as his children and of meriting eternal life. They are the pledge of the presence and action of the Holy Spirit in the faculties of the human being. There are three theological virtues: faith, hope, and charity.

Verse Study

See appendix 3 for instructions on how to complete a verse study.

John 21:22

1. Verse:

2. Paraphrase:

3. Questions:

4. Cross-references:

5. Personal Application:

NOTES

Lesson 22: Connect Coffee Talk 6

JESUS, OUR RESTORER

The accompanying talk can be viewed via DVD or digital download purchase or accessed online at walkingwithpurpose.com/videos.

Key Verses

"Abide in me, and I in you. As the branch cannot bear fruit by itself, unless it abides in the vine, neither can you, unless you abide in me. I am the vine, you are the branches. He who abides in me, and I in him, he it is that bears much fruit, for apart from me you can do nothing" (John 15:4–5).

"For my thoughts are not your thoughts, neither are your ways my ways, says the Lord. For as the heavens are higher than the earth, so are my ways higher than your ways and my thoughts than your thoughts" (Isaiah 55:8–9).

"He himself gives to all men life and breath and everything" (Acts 17:25).

"To all who received him, who believed in his name, he gave power to become children of God; who were born, not of blood nor of the will of flesh nor of the will of man, but of God" (John 1:12–13).

"Before I formed you in the womb I knew you, and before you were born I consecrated you; I appointed you as a prophet to the nations" (Jeremiah 1:5).

"To each is given the manifestation of the Spirit for the common good" (1 Corinthians 12:7).

Jesus draws close. He calls us. He invites us. But we decide.

I. **Jesus Restores Us Through His Unconditional Love**

    A. Jesus' love for us is not based on our accomplishments—and it is not withdrawn based on our failures. He will never leave us.

    B. Just as Peter ran to Jesus while carrying the weight of his denials, we must own our failures, bring them to the foot of the Cross, and ask God to restore us.

II. **Jesus Directs Us to Our Personal Calling**

    A. Each of us has a purpose for which God uniquely designed and gifted us.

    B. If we cooperate with Him, God can redeem our mistakes and turn them into wonderful opportunities for us to minister to others.

III. **Jesus Gives Us the Opportunity to Publicly Accept His Offer of Unconditional Love**

    A. Baptism

    "Through Baptism we are freed from sin and reborn as sons of God" (CCC 1213). Our journey of faith begins among a community of believers with this incredible outpouring of grace.

    B. Confirmation

    God publicly marks us with "an indelible spiritual mark" (CCC 1304), which imprints on our soul that *we are His.*

Open your heart and let His love rush in. It's a decision you'll never regret.

Questions for Discussion or Journaling

1. Can you share a time in your life when you've faced failure but later experienced restoration? What did you learn from it?

2. What blocks your ability to abide in Christ, to depend on Him, to cast aside self-reliance? What action step might you take to grow in this critical area of your spiritual life?

3. We were not meant to journey alone. Community is key to our restoration. Who is one person in your life you can trust with your honest self? Whom can you invite into your spiritual journey to walk and grow alongside you?

 NOTES

Appendices

 NOTES

Appendix 1
Saint Thérèse of Lisieux

Patron Saint of Walking with Purpose

Saint Thérèse of Lisieux was gifted with the ability to take the riches of our Catholic faith and explain them in a way that a child could imitate. The wisdom she gleaned from Scripture ignited a love in her heart for her Lord that was personal and transforming. The simplicity of the faith that she laid out in her writings is so completely Catholic that Pope Pius XII said, "She rediscovered the Gospel itself, the very heart of the Gospel."

Walking with Purpose is intended to be a means by which women can honestly share their spiritual struggles and embark on a journey that is refreshing to the soul. It was never intended to facilitate the deepest of intellectual study of Scripture. Instead the focus has been to help women know Christ: to know His heart, to know His tenderness, to know His mercy, and to know His love. Our logo is a little flower, and that has meaning. When a woman begins to open her heart to God, it's like the opening of a little flower. It can easily be bruised or crushed, and it must be treated with the greatest of care. Our desire is to speak to women's hearts no matter where they are in life, baggage and all, and gently introduce truths that can change their lives.

Saint Thérèse of Lisieux, the little flower, called her doctrine "the little way of spiritual childhood," and it is based on complete and unshakable confidence in God's love for us. She was not introducing new truths. She spent countless hours reading Scripture and she shared what she found, emphasizing the importance of truths that had already been divinely revealed. We can learn so much from her:

> The good God would not inspire unattainable desires; I can, then, in spite of my littleness, aspire to sanctity. For me to become greater is impossible; I must put up with myself just as I am with all my imperfections. But I wish to find the way to go to Heaven by a very straight, short, completely new little way. We are in a century of inventions: now one does not even have to take the trouble to

climb the steps of a stairway; in the homes of the rich, an elevator replaces them nicely. I, too, would like to find an elevator to lift me up to Jesus, for I am too little to climb the rough stairway of perfection. So I have looked in the books of the saints for a sign of the elevator I long for, and I have read these words proceeding from the mouth of eternal Wisdom: "He that is a little one, let him turn to me" (Proverbs 9:16). So I came, knowing that I had found what I was seeking, and wanting to know, O my God, what You would do with the little one who would answer Your call, and this is what I found:

"As one whom the mother caresses, so will I comfort you. You shall be carried at the breasts and upon the knees they shall caress you" (Isaiah 66:12–13). Never have more tender words come to make my soul rejoice. The elevator which must raise me to the heavens is Your arms, O Jesus! For that I do not need to grow; on the contrary, I must necessarily remain small, become smaller and smaller. O my God, You have surpassed what I expected, and I want to sing Your mercies.[78]

---

[78] Saint Thérèse of the Infant Jesus, *Histoire d'une Ame: Manuscrits Autobiographiques* (Paris: Éditions du Seuil, 1998), 244.

Appendix 2
Scripture Memory

"The tempter came and said to him, 'If you are the Son of God, command these stones to become loaves of bread.' But He answered, 'It is written: Man shall not live by bread alone, but by every word that proceeds from the mouth of God'" (Matthew 4:3–4).

Jesus was able to respond to Satan's temptations because He knew God's Truth. When He was under fire, He didn't have time to go find wisdom for the moment. It had to be in His head already. He had memorized Scripture and found those words to be His most effective weapon in warding off temptation.

Do you ever feel tempted to just give in? To take the easy way when you know the hard way is right? Does discouragement ever nip at your heels and take you to a place of darkness? If you memorize Scripture, the Holy Spirit will be able to bring God's Truth to your mind just when you need to fight back.

Ephesians 6:17 describes Scripture as an offensive weapon ("the sword of the Spirit"). How does this work? When negative thoughts and lies run through our minds, we can take a Bible verse and use it as a weapon to kick out the lie and embrace the truth. Verses that speak of God's unconditional love and forgiveness and our new identity in Christ are especially powerful for this kind of battle. When we feel defeated and like we'll never change, when we falsely assume that God must be ready to give up on us, the Holy Spirit can remind us of 2 Corinthians 5:17: "If anyone is in Christ, [she] is a new creation; the old has passed away, behold, the new has come."

That's not the only way memorized Scripture helps us. The Holy Spirit can bring one of the truths of the Bible to our mind just before we might make a wrong choice. It's like a little whisper reminding us of what we know is true, but there's power in it, because we know they are God's words. For example, in the midst of a conversation in which we aren't listening well, the Holy Spirit can bring to mind Proverbs 18:2: "Fools take no delight in understanding, but only in displaying what they think." This enables us to make a course correction immediately instead of looking back later with regret. As it says in Psalm 119:11, "I have laid up your word in my heart *that I might not sin against you*" (emphasis added).

You may think of memorizing Scripture as an activity for the über-religious, not for the average Christian. A blogger at She Reads Truth (shereadstruth.com) described it this way: "Recalling Scripture isn't for the overachievers; it's for the homesick." It's for those of us who know that earth isn't our home—heaven is. It's for those of us who don't want to be tossed all over the place by our emotions and instead long to be grounded in truth.

But how do we do it? Kids memorize things so easily, but our brains are full of so many other bits of information that we wonder if we're capable of doing it. Never fear. There are easy techniques that can help us to store away God's words in our minds and hearts. Pick a few that work for you. YOU CAN DO IT!

Touching the Divine **Memory Verses:**

"For God so loved the world that he gave his only Son, so that everyone who believes in him might not perish but might have eternal life" (John 3:16).

"I am the vine, you are the branches. Whoever remains in me and I in him will bear much fruit, because apart from me you can do nothing" (John 15:5).

1. **Learning Through Repetition**

   Every time you sit down to do the first eleven lessons, begin by reading one of the memory verses for *Touching the Divine*. Then begin the remaining eleven lessons by reading the other memory verse. The more you read it, the sooner it will be lodged in your memory. Be sure to read the reference as well. Don't skip that part—it comes in handy when you want to know where to find the verse in the Bible.

2. **Learning Visually**

   Write the memory verse lightly *in pencil* on a piece of paper. Read the entire verse, including the reference. Choose one word, and erase it well. Reread the entire verse, including the reference. Choose another word, and erase it well. Reread the entire verse, including the reference. Repeat this process until the whole verse has been erased and you are reciting it from memory.

   Go to our website under Bible Studies and save the *Touching the Divine* Memory Verse image to your phone's lock screen. Practice the verse every time you grab your phone.

3. **Learning by Writing It Down**

   Grab a piece of paper and write your verse down twenty times.

4. **Learning by Seeing It Everywhere**

   Display the gorgeous WWP Memory Verse cards somewhere in your house. Recite each verse whenever you pass by it. But don't stop there. Write the verses down on index cards and leave them in places you often linger: the bathroom mirror, the car dashboard, the coffeepot, whatever works for you.

5. **Learning Together**

If you are doing this Walking with Purpose™ study in a small group, hold one another accountable and recite the Memory Verse together at the start and end of each lesson. If you are doing this study on your own, consider asking someone to hold you accountable by listening to you say your verse from memory each week.

For God so Loved the World that He gave His only Son so that everyone who believes in Him might not perish but might have ETERNAL Life

JOHN 3/16

I AM THE VINE YOU ARE THE BRANCHES WHOEVER REMAINS IN ME and I IN HIM will BEAR MUCH FRUIT BECAUSE APART from ME YOU CAN DO NOTHING

JOHN 15:5

Appendix 3
How To Do A Verse Study

A verse study is an exciting Bible study tool that can help to bring the Scriptures to life! By reading, reflecting on, and committing a verse to memory, we open ourselves to the Holy Spirit, who reveals very personal applications of our Lord's words and actions to our daily lives.

Learning to do a verse study is not difficult, but it can be demanding. In this Walking with Purpose™ study, a Bible verse has been selected to reinforce a theme of each lesson. To do the verse study, read the verse and then follow these simple instructions. You'll be on your way to a deeper and more personal understanding of Scripture.

- **Read the verse and the paragraph before and after the verse.**

- **Write out the selected verse.**

- **Paraphrase.**
  Write the verse using your own words. What does the verse say?

- **Ask questions.**
  Write down any questions you have about the verse. What does it say that you don't understand?

- **Use cross-references.**
  Look up other Bible verses that help to shed light on what the selected verse means. A Bible will often list cross-references in the margin or in the study notes. Another excellent resource is Biblehub.com. This website allows you to enter a specific Bible verse, and it will provide many cross-references and additional insights into the passage of Scripture you selected. Record any insights you gain from the additional verses you are able to find.

- **Make a personal application.**
  What does the verse say to you personally? Is there a promise to make? A warning to heed? An example to follow? Ask God to help you find something from the verse that you can apply to your life.

The recommended Bible translations for use in Walking with Purpose™ studies are: The New American Bible, which is the translation used in the United States for the readings at Mass; The Revised Standard Version, Catholic Edition; and The Jerusalem Bible.

A Sample Verse Study

1. **Verse:**

   "I am the vine, you are the branches. Those who abide in me and I in them bear much fruit, because apart from me you can do nothing" (John 15:5).

2. **Paraphrase:**

   Jesus is the vine; I am the branch. If I abide in Him, then I'll be fruitful, but if I try to do everything on my own, I'll fail at what matters most. I need Him.

3. **Questions:**

   What does it mean to abide? How does Jesus abide in me? What kind of fruit is Jesus talking about?

4. **Cross-references:**

   "He who eats my flesh and drinks my blood abides in me, and I in him" (John 6:56). This verse brings to mind the Eucharist and the importance of receiving Christ in the Eucharist as often as possible. This is a very important way to abide in Jesus.

   "If you abide in me, and my words abide in you, ask whatever you will, and it shall be done for you" (John 15:7). How can Jesus' words abide in me if I never read them? I need to read the Bible if I want to abide in Christ.

   "You did not choose me, but I chose you and appointed you that you should go and bear fruit and that your fruit should abide; so that whatever you ask the Father in my name, he may give it to you" (John 15:16). Not all fruit remains. Some is good only temporarily—on earth. I want my fruit to remain in eternity—to count in the long run.

   "The fruit of the Spirit is love, joy, peace, patience, kindness, goodness, faithfulness, gentleness, self-control" (Galatians 5:22–23). These are some of the fruits that will be seen if I abide in Christ.

5. **Personal Application:**

   I will study my calendar this week, making note of where I spend my time. Is most of my time spent on things that will last for eternity (fruit that remains)? I'll reassess my priorities in light of what I find.

Appendix 4
Conversion Of Heart

The Catholic faith is full of beautiful traditions, rituals, and sacraments. As powerful as they are, it is possible for them to become mere habits in our lives instead of experiences that draw us close to the heart of Christ. In the words of Saint John Paul II, they can become acts of "hollow ritualism." We might receive our first Communion and the sacraments of Confession and Confirmation yet never experience the interior conversion that opens the heart to a personal relationship with God.

Pope Benedict XVI has explained that the "door of faith" is opened at one's baptism, but we are called to open it again, walk through it, and rediscover and renew our relationship with Christ and His Church.[79]

So how do we do this? How do we walk through that door of faith so we can begin to experience the abundant life that God has planned for us?

Getting Personal

The word *"conversion"* means "the act of turning." This means that conversion involves a turning away from one thing and a turning toward another. When you haven't experienced conversion of heart, you are turned *toward* your own desires. You are the one in charge, and you do what you feel is right and best at any given moment. You may choose to do things that are very good for other people, but the distinction is that *you are choosing.* You are deciding. You are the one in control.

Imagine driving a car. You are sitting in the driver's seat, and your hands are on the steering wheel. You've welcomed Jesus into the passenger's seat and have listened to His comments. But whether or not you follow His directions is really up to you. You may follow them, or you may not, depending on what seems right to you.

When you experience interior conversion, you decide to turn, to get out of the driver's seat, move into the passenger's seat, and invite God to be the driver. Instead of seeing Him as an advice giver or someone nice to have around for the holidays, you give Him control of every aspect of your life.

More than likely, you don't find this easy to do. This is because of the universal struggle with pride. We want to be the ones in charge. We don't like to be in desperate need. We

---

79 Pope Benedict XVI, Apostolic Letter: Porta Fidei, for the Induction of the Year of Faith, October 11, 2011.

like to be the captains of our ships, charting our own courses. As William Ernest Henley wrote, "I am the master of my fate: I am the captain of my soul."

Conversion of heart isn't possible without humility. The first step is to recognize your desperate need for a savior. Romans 6:23 states that the "wages of sin is death." When you hear this, you might be tempted to justify your behavior or compare yourself with others. You might think to yourself, *I'm not a murderer. I'm not as bad as this or that person. If someone were to put my good deeds and bad deeds on a scale, my good ones would outweigh the bad. So surely, I am good enough? Surely I don't deserve death!* When this is your line of thought, you are missing a very important truth: Just one mortal sin is enough to separate you from a holy God. Just one mortal sin is enough for you to deserve death.

The Catholic Church teaches that "mortal sin requires *full knowledge and complete consent.* It presupposes knowledge of the sinful character of the act, of its opposition to God's law" (CCC 1859). By contrast, "*unintentional ignorance* can diminish or even remove the imputability of a grave offense" (CCC 1860). But before we let ourselves off the hook too quickly, claiming that "unintentional ignorance" is what is at play when we sin, we would be wise to keep reading CCC 1860, which reminds us, "No one is deemed to be ignorant of the principles of the moral law, which are written in the conscience of every man." The truth is, we all have sinned willfully at certain times in our lives. That means that the starting point for each one of us must be an acknowledgement that we have messed up and we need a savior.

Even your best efforts to do good fall short of what God has required in order for you to spend eternity with Him. Isaiah 64:6 says, "All our righteous deeds are like a polluted garment." If you come to God thinking that you are going to be accepted by Him based on your "good conduct," He will point out that your righteousness is nothing compared to His infinite holiness.

Saint Thérèse of Lisieux understood this well and wrote, "In the evening of my life I shall appear before You with empty hands, for I do not ask You to count my works. All our justices are stained in Your eyes. I want therefore to clothe myself in Your own justice and receive from Your love the eternal possession of Yourself."[80]

She recognized that her works, her best efforts, wouldn't be enough to earn salvation. Salvation cannot be earned. It's a free gift. Saint Thérèse accepted this gift and said that if her justices or righteous deeds were stained, then she wanted to clothe herself in Christ's

---

80 Saint Thérèse of Lisieux, "Act of Oblation to Merciful Love," June 9, 1895.

own justice. We see this described in 2 Corinthians 5:21: "For our sake he made him to be sin who knew no sin, so that in him we might become the righteousness of God."

How did God make Him who had no sin to be sin for you? This was foretold by the prophet Isaiah: "But he was wounded for our transgressions, he was bruised for our iniquities; upon him was the chastisement that made us whole, and with his stripes we are healed" (Isaiah 53:5).

Jesus accomplished this on the cross. Every sin committed, past, present, and future, was placed on Him. Now *all the merits of Jesus can be yours.* He wants to fill your empty hands with His own virtues.

But first you need to recognize, just as Saint Thérèse did, that you are little. You are weak. You fail. You need forgiveness. You need a savior.

When you come before God in prayer and acknowledge these truths, He looks at your heart. He sees your desire to trust Him, to please Him, to obey Him. He says to you, "My precious child, you don't have to pay for your sins. My Son, Jesus, has already done that for you. He suffered, so that you wouldn't have to. I want to experience a relationship of intimacy with you. I forgive you.[81] Jesus came to set you free.[82] When you open your heart to me, you become a new creation![83] The old you has gone. The new you is here. If you will stay close to me and journey by my side, you will begin to experience a transformation that brings joy and freedom.[84] I've been waiting to pour my gifts into your soul. Beloved daughter of Mine, remain confident in Me. I am your loving Father. Crawl into my lap. Trust me. Love me. I will take care of everything."

This is conversion of heart. This act of faith lifts the veil from your eyes and launches you into the richest and most satisfying life. You don't have to be sitting in church to do this. Don't let a minute pass before opening your heart to God and inviting Him to come dwell within you. Let Him sit in the driver's seat. Give Him the keys to your heart. Your life will never be the same again.

---

81 "If we confess our sins, he is faithful and just, and will forgive our sins and cleanse us from all unrighteousness" (1 John 1:9).

82 "So if the Son makes you free, you will be free indeed" (John 8:36).

83 "Therefore, if anyone is in Christ, he is a new creature; the old has passed away, behold, the new has come" (2 Corinthians 5:17).

84 "I will sprinkle clean water upon you, and you shall be clean from all your uncleanness, and from all your idols I will cleanse you. A new heart I will give you, and a new spirit I will put within you; and I will take out of your flesh the heart of stone and give you a heart of flesh" (Ezekiel 36:25, 26).

Appendix 5
Litany of Humility

Composed by Cardinal Rafael Merry del Val (1865–1930)

Jesus! Meek and humble of heart, *Hear me.*

From the desire of being esteemed, *Deliver me, Jesus.*

From the desire of being loved, *Deliver me, Jesus.*

From the desire of being extolled, *Deliver me, Jesus.*

From the desire of being honored, *Deliver me, Jesus.*

From the desire of being praised, *Deliver me, Jesus.*

From the desire of being preferred to others, *Deliver me, Jesus.*

From the desire of being consulted, *Deliver me, Jesus.*

From the desire of being approved, *Deliver me, Jesus.*

From the fear of being humiliated, *Deliver me, Jesus.*

From the fear of being despised, *Deliver me, Jesus.*

From the fear of suffering rebukes, *Deliver me, Jesus.*

From the fear of being calumniated, *Deliver me, Jesus.*

From the fear of being forgotten, *Deliver me, Jesus.*

From the fear of being ridiculed, *Deliver me, Jesus.*

From the fear of being wronged, *Deliver me, Jesus.*

From the fear of being suspected, *Deliver me, Jesus.*

That others may be loved more than I, *Jesus, grant me the grace to desire it.*

That others may be esteemed more than I, *Jesus, grant me the grace to desire it.*

That others may be chosen and I set aside, *Jesus, grant me the grace to desire it.*

That others may be praised and I unnoticed, *Jesus, grant me the grace to desire it.*

That others may be preferred to me in everything, *Jesus, grant me the grace to desire it.*

That others may become holier than I, provided that I may become as holy as I should, *Jesus, grant me the grace to desire it.*

Appendix 6
"You, Take Russia!"[85] By Father John Riccardo

A priest friend of mine recently passed away who used to work intimately with the Missionaries of Charity. He knew Mother Teresa well and was able to offer retreats for her and the sisters all over the globe.

He once told me a story of accompanying Mother as she was visiting a hospital. They walked into one room where, if I remember correctly, there were two brothers, both of whom were suffering mightily. She stood at the foot of their beds and, smiling as only she could, looked at the first one and said, "You, take Russia!" Turning to his brother, she said, "And you, take China!"

That story has been on my mind because of the seemingly countless number of people I know who are suffering in body, mind, and spirit, feeling and fearing that their pain is in vain. What Mother knew well was those who are suffering, in whatever way, are spiritual heavy artillery.

Perhaps no verse in the Bible is as difficult to understand as Colossians 1:24. St. Paul says, "I fill up in my flesh what is lacking in the sufferings of Christ for the sake of His Body, which is the Church." Excuse me? What in the world is "lacking" in the sufferings of Christ? Does Paul mean to convey that what Jesus did in going to war to rescue us was close but not quite enough to accomplish all that He came to do? Hardly. The only thing "lacking" in Jesus' suffering is our participation in it. This is immensely important, since it's not a question of if we're going to suffer in this life, only how and when.

The culture around us considers suffering of absolutely no value, almost a fate worse than death. Hence the movement over the past decades to enthusiastically promote euthanasia. It is an all-too-common part of parish life, whether as a priest, deacon, or volunteer, to spend much of our time visiting the sick and the dying, be they in hospitals, nursing homes, hospice, prison, or their own homes. Men and women in those places are more often than not inclined to think that what they are going through has no point and is in vain. The disciple of Jesus knows a different story.

If you and I had been there on that Friday we call "Good" and had seen Jesus nailed to that cross, we would certainly have said to each other, "What a waste." We would have thought that nothing good could or would come from that.

---

85 Father John Riccardo, *Thoughts from the Trailer: Where God Makes His Plans Known,* email newsletter March 2, 2022.

And we would have been wrong.

Frank Sheed, the great English author of the twentieth century, once wrote that the most active moment in Jesus' life was when He was hanging on the cross. As a disciple of Jesus, he understood that the Lord rescued us precisely by His loving suffering on the cross, whereby He revealed to us the Father's love, made atonement for our sins, and went to war to defeat the powers of Sin, Death, and Satan. As it was with Jesus on the cross, so it is with us when we suffer. It is not a waste, or in vain, or at least it need not be. I don't at all mean to imply that suffering is romantic. It's not. That's why we call it suffering. Still, when we suffer, we can use it. And God can do great things through it.

It was once common to hear someone encourage another who was suffering to "offer it up." I always recoiled at that expression, perhaps because I found it so passive (though Pope Benedict XVI favorably used it in his Encyclical Spe Salvi). Calling to mind Paul's words to the Christians in Colossae, I have found it helpful to remind myself and others to unite what we're going through, whether it's a migraine, chronic back pain, chemotherapy, depression, or any other way that suffering comes to us, to the cross of Jesus, trusting that one day we will understand how God used it. Nothing you and I are enduring right now, no matter how painful it may be, need be in vain!

Whenever I visit someone who is suffering, after praying and talking with them, I remind them what Jesus was doing on the cross. I then ask them if they will unite what they're going through to that same cross for the sake of someone specific: a marriage in trouble, a young person away from the Church, a world leader, or maybe someone struggling with an addiction. Sometimes I'll write the name of the person to suffer for on the board in the hospital room. I suggest to them that though I know they're tempted to think their pain is meaningless, they are, in fact, "the Armed Forces" in the Church, and no one's prayers are more powerful than theirs, for the simple reason that when we suffer we are most inclined to be selfish. After all, I hurt! But when we actively unite our pain to the cross for another, it's the most powerful display of love possible. And over and over again, the transformation that takes place in the suffering person's demeanor is amazing. Though the pain doesn't leave, suddenly, they have a purpose, and what they're going through isn't useless anymore. And they trust that one day, even if it's not until the Lord returns, they will see how He used their suffering and prayer and the great good that came from it.

Answer Key

Lesson 2, Day One

1. **A.** In the beginning was the Word. The Word was with God. The Word was God. The Word was in the beginning with God. All things were made through the Word.

   B. The Word is God's beloved Son, Jesus. In Jesus, "all things were created, in heaven and on earth…all things were created through him and for him. He is before all things, and in him all things hold together" (Colossians 1:16–17).

   C. Answers will vary.

2. **A.** Life is found in Jesus, and that life is the light of men.

   B. Jesus is the light, and the darkness is evil. No matter how bleak and hopeless things may seem, evil will never overpower or extinguish God's light.

   C. Answers will vary.

3. **A.** John the Baptist was sent to "bear witness to the light" (John 1:7) so that all people could believe. John the Baptist wasn't the light; his purpose was to bear witness and point others to the Light—Jesus.

   B. He came into the world to enlighten every man.

   C. "I will lead the blind by ways they have not known. Along unfamiliar paths I will guide them; I will turn the darkness into light before them and make the rough places smooth" (Isaiah 42:16). When we are confused and we don't know what to do, Jesus promises to provide light to guide us.

Lesson 2, Day Two

1. He wasn't recognized for who He really was; "the world knew him not" (John 1:10). Even His own people didn't receive Him. His attempts to minister to them were often rejected or resisted.

2. **A.** Jesus gave power to become children of God to all who received Him, who believed in His name.

   B. This help is the grace of God. According to CCC 1996, "Our justification comes from the grace of God. Grace is favor, the free and undeserved help that God gives us to respond to his call to become children of God, adoptive sons, partakers of the divine nature and of eternal life."

   C. Answers will vary.

3. **A.** In John 1:14, John describes Jesus in this way: "And the Word became flesh and dwelt among us, full of grace and truth; we have beheld his glory, glory as of the only-begotten Son from the Father."

   B. "Have this mind among yourselves, which was in Christ Jesus, who, though he was in the form of God, did not count equality with God a thing to be grasped, but emptied himself, taking the form of a servant, being born in the likeness of men. And being found in human form he humbled himself and became obedient unto death, even death on a cross" (Philippians 2:5–8).

4. **A.** We have received grace upon grace.
    B. We receive it from Christ's fullness.
    C. Answers will vary.

Lesson 2, Day Three

1. **A.** He called Jesus the Lamb of God.
    B. On the night of the final plague in Egypt, the Israelites were to take a lamb without defect and slaughter it. The blood of the lamb was to be painted on the doorframe, and the lamb was to be eaten. That night when the Lord passed through Egypt and struck down every firstborn, He passed over every door that had the blood on the top and sides of the doorframe.

2. Calling Jesus "the Lamb of God" would have caused the Israelites to think of both the Passover and their ritual sacrifices. During the Passover it was the blood of the lamb that saved them. In that same way, it is the blood of Christ that saves us from our sins ("The blood of Jesus…cleanses us from all sin," 1 John 1:7). And isn't it interesting that the Israelites had to eat the lamb? Doesn't that make you think of the Eucharist? It's amazing when the Old and New Testaments collide like this! When the Israelites sacrificed lambs in the Temple, their sins were transferred to the animal, and the lamb paid the price for those sins. Jesus did the same for us; the punishment we deserved was paid by Him. "The Lord has laid on Him the iniquity of us all" (Isaiah 53:6). "For our sake he made him to be sin who knew no sin, so that in him we might become the righteousness of God" (2 Corinthians 5:21).

3. We pray the Lamb of God, or Agnus Dei, before receiving the Eucharist. In this prayer we are meditating on Jesus, the Lamb of God, who suffered and died so we could live. This should humble us and fill us with gratitude—that we are so loved that we are worth suffering for. This should fill us with love for Jesus, and a desire to give Him our whole hearts—all we desire, all we are. This should make us run up the aisle to receive our Savior as intimately as we do in the Eucharist!

Lesson 2, Day Four

1. Answers will vary.
2. After Peter declared that Jesus was the Christ, the Son of the living God (Matthew 16:16), Jesus said, "You are Peter, and on this rock I will build my Church, and the gates of Hades shall not prevail against it." The Church fathers taught that in saying this, Jesus was promising to build the Church on the foundation of Peter's

leadership. As through Abraham and Israel before him, the Lord intended to reveal Himself to the world through this man and his anointed descendants.

For example, Cyprian of Carthage wrote:

> The Lord says to Peter: "I say to you," he says, "that you are Peter, and upon this rock I will build my Church, and the gates of hell will not overcome it. And to you I will give the keys of the kingdom of heaven..." [Matthew 16:18–19]. On him [Peter] he builds the Church, and to him he gives the command to feed the sheep [John 21:17], and although he assigns a like power to all the apostles, yet he founded a single chair [cathedra], and he established by his own authority a source and an intrinsic reason for that unity. Indeed, the others were that also which Peter was [i.e., apostles], but a primacy is given to Peter, whereby it is made clear that there is but one Church and one chair...If someone does not hold fast to this unity of Peter, can he imagine that he still holds the faith? If he [should] desert the chair of Peter upon whom the Church was built, can he still be confident that he is in the Church?[86]

3. Answers will vary.

Lesson 2, Day Five

1. As Jesus was looking for followers who were to carry His Gospel to the world, He knew He needed people who were genuine and honest. They would need to know their own weaknesses and be transparent about them. They would need to be willing to speak the truth, even if it was unpopular. Those qualities are just as essential today. Most people long to see Christians who are real and transparent. We need to be honest about our weaknesses instead of trying to act like we have it all together. We also need to be honest about spiritual truth, not saying one thing while believing another.

2. **A.** Jacob renamed the place where he slept the house of God and the gate to heaven.
    B. Jesus said the angels of God would ascend and descend upon the Son of man.
    C. Jesus is claiming that He is the true house of God and the gateway to heaven. He's saying, "Do you want to be where God dwells? Do you want to go to heaven? Then come to me!"

Lesson 3, Day One

1. **A.** Jesus confirmed the goodness of marriage and, through His presence at the wedding, proclaimed that from that time forward, marriage would be a sign of His presence.

---

86 Cyprian of Carthage, *The Unity of the Catholic Church* 4th ed. (AD 251).

B. Answers will vary.

C. The display of Jesus' love in this miracle was free. The Blessed Mother invited Jesus to intervene, but He was not coerced or guilted into doing this miracle. It was the result of His free will– a free choice. He showed a total, selfless love for the couple. In saving them from the embarrassment of running out of wine, He also sped up the timeline of His public ministry. Things would change and start moving toward the cross once this miracle took place. Jesus was willing to make a personal sacrifice to "enrich the other with the gift of self."[87] Jesus' love then, and always, was faithful, until death. This fidelity to His bride, the Church, cost Him everything. Lastly, Jesus' love was fruitful. Water turned into a superabundance of wine. Something new was created.

2. She immediately turned to Jesus. She didn't know how to fix the problem, so she went to the One who could. Her confidence in Him is something we should emulate. We, too, should turn first to Him, instead of trying out every other option and then considering prayer only as a last resort. Mary's intercession continues today. She will go to Jesus on our behalf when we ask her to pray for our needs.

3. The final result would be His crucifixion. His miracles drew a great deal of attention—some good and some bad. It was the miracle of the raising of Lazarus that sent the Pharisees over the edge, and from that day on, they began to plot how they could put Jesus to death.

4. She tells the servants to do whatever Jesus asked of them. In other words, "Thy will be done." She has complete faith in the goodness of Jesus. There is evidence here of the intimate relationship that the Blessed Mother shares with Jesus. We see her entrustment. We see her awaiting. We see her confidence in Him. She knows she's thinking about doing something about the wine. She doesn't need to control things—she trusts Jesus and His plan.

5. "The Church rightly honors 'the Blessed Virgin with special devotion. From the most ancient times the Blessed Virgin has been honored with the title of "Mother of God," to whose protection the faithful fly in all their dangers and needs…This very special devotion…differs essentially from the adoration which is given to the incarnate Word and equally to the Father and the Holy Spirit, and greatly fosters this adoration'" (CCC 971).

6. It's beautiful that our Savior inaugurated His plan of redemption where spousal love and a new family was formed and celebrated. The wedding setting makes his love more intimate and obvious.

---

87 Pope Paul VI; Humane Vitae; https://www.vatican.va/content/paul-vi/en/encyclicals/documents/hf_p-vi_enc_25071968_humanae-vitae.html; accessed April 25, 2022.

Lesson 3, Day Two

1. **A.** The Jewish people were to make sacrifices of animals and grain at the Temple.

   B. It would be difficult to travel a long distance with animals.

   C. The merchants were selling animals for travelers to use for their sacrifices. The money changers were exchanging foreign currency so the purchases could be made.

   D. Many varieties of coin and currency would be brought to Jerusalem for purchasing animals for sacrifice and to pay the Temple tax (Matthew 17:24). But only the Temple currency (ancient half-shekel) was allowed. Any currency with the image of a foreign sovereign would defile the Temple. Money changers were there to provide the necessary service of exchanging currency.[88]

2. The merchants were charging exorbitant prices to the pilgrims, taking advantage of them. They were selling the animals and changing money for the Temple tax in the Court of the Gentiles. There were several courts in the Temple. Non-Jewish people weren't allowed past this court. This was the only place where a Gentile was allowed to worship. The cacophony made it almost impossible for a person to pray there.

3. **A.** Jesus' anger reacted against the sins of injustice and dishonoring God. Jesus was focused on "His Father's house." It was about His Father—not Himself. Jesus confronted the money changers and merchants but did so without screaming, cursing, or losing control.

   B. When Jesus was personally attacked, He did not respond in anger. He didn't seek revenge.

   C. We should first check the reason for our anger. Is it wounded pride or a feeling of being personally wronged? Is it reacting against actual sin? What is the focus—personal concerns or God's concerns? How is the anger expressing itself?

Lesson 3, Day Three

1. **A.** He thought Jesus was a great teacher, and he was impressed with the signs that He had displayed. As a Pharisee Nicodemus was focused on keeping the law; this was the key to salvation. More than likely he felt proud and self-satisfied regarding his efforts in rule keeping. Comparing himself to the average Jew, he would have thought that God must be quite pleased with him and his religious

---

88 Stephen K. Ray, St. John's Gospel: A Bible Study Guide and Commentary (San Francisco: Ignatius Press, 2002), 87.

leadership and fervor. The Holy Spirit, he knew, had inspired certain of his ancestors, but it certainly wasn't available to everyone.

B. Perhaps Nicodemus was trying to avoid the crowds. Some believe that he was afraid of what people would think, so he came at a time when no one would see him. The night can represent the spiritual darkness that surrounded Nicodemus, since he had not yet experienced a spiritual rebirth. But even if it was night, Nicodemus was still taking his own small, hesitant steps, testing the waters before risking his reputation among the Pharisees.

2. A. The Catechism tells us that this is referring to the sacrament of Baptism. "Baptism is necessary for salvation for those to whom the Gospel has been proclaimed and who have had the possibility of asking for this sacrament" (CCC 1257). Catholics believe that being "born again," or "reborn of water and the Spirit," describes the process experienced when God's transforming love, called grace, purifies us in Baptism. Saint Peter spoke of this in Acts 2:38: "Be baptized every one of you in the name of Jesus Christ for the forgiveness of your sins; and you shall receive the gift of the Holy Spirit."

"But he himself is not bound by his sacraments" (CCC 1257). We are bound to come to God by the means He has laid out for us (when we are aware of it). This does not put a limit on God's ability to save souls outside of those parameters. CCC 1260 says, "Every man who is ignorant of the Gospel of Christ and of his Church, but seeks the truth and does the will of God in accordance with his understanding of it, can be saved." Ignorance is not sin. Inability is not sin.

B. We are saved not by our righteous deeds but by the washing of regeneration and renewal in the Holy Spirit.

C. Although the effects of Baptism are unseen, grace is at work, transforming the heart. This verse states clearly that Baptism brings salvation. "Baptism... now saves you, not as a removal of dirt from the body but an appeal to God for a clear conscience, through the resurrection of Jesus Christ" (1 Peter 3:21).

3. Answers will vary.

4. A. Ezekiel wrote that during the Messianic age (when the Messiah would arrive), God's Spirit would be poured out like water. The Holy Spirit would be put within God's children. His Spirit would cleanse the people from their impurities and idols. God would give the people new hearts in place of stone hearts. Hearts are hardened by sin. It takes the redemptive, transforming, purifying work of God to cleanse us, soften our hearts, and make us new.

B. This verse depicts the Holy Spirit being poured out like water, bringing blessing and nourishment to dry and hungry souls.

5. Jesus was referring to the time that God punished the Israelites by sending serpents, which bit the people and killed many. Moses prayed for the people, and God told him to mount a bronze serpent on a pole. He told Moses that if the people who were bitten would look to the bronze serpent, they would be healed. This came to pass—if they looked, they recovered.

This Old Testament story reminds us of Christ's crucifixion, of His death on the cross. Without Him, we are without hope. The bite of the serpent in our lives is sin and its lethal effects. Without Christ's death on the cross, we would need to pay the price for our sins, and that price would be death ("For the wages of sin is death" [Romans 6:23]). Christ's death on the cross paid the price for our sins, but we need to turn to Him to receive this gift.

Lesson 3, Day Four

1. **A.** God loved and so He gave. Whom did He love? He loved the world. He loved all the people He created, even though so many of them would reject Him. He loved broken people, sinful people, and hurting people. What did He give? He gave what was most precious to Him: His Son.
    B. God asks that we would believe in Jesus.
    C. We are promised eternal life. This is describing both eternal life in heaven and the abundant life on earth that we'll experience as Christ rules in our hearts.
2. No. God didn't send Jesus into the world to condemn it. He sent Him to save people. He doesn't want anyone to perish; He wants everyone to repent and turn to Him. God will not reject a single person who turns his or her heart to Him in humility and repentance. But He is a just God, and wickedness will be punished. There's much in the world that we want to see punished. We just don't want God to take our failings so seriously. We have a choice. Either we can accept Jesus as our substitute and live a life filled with gratitude toward Him for taking our sins on Himself and paying the penalty for them, or we can pay the penalty ourselves. God wants us to accept His gracious gift of redemption, freedom, and forgiveness.
3. Jesus says, "Light has come into the world, and men loved darkness rather than light, because their deeds were evil. For every one who does evil hates the light, and does not come to the light, lest his deeds should be exposed" (John 3:19–20).
4. Answers will vary.

Lesson 3, Day Five

1. God has specific ways that He has gifted each of us (1 Corinthians 12:4–11). He has a specific plan for each one of us (Jeremiah 29:11). If we spend our time wanting what He has chosen for another person, we not only spiral into discontent; we also

miss out on the abundant life God has crafted for us personally. John focused on God's will for his life, not on being successful in his own ministry. We, too, are called to be faithful where God has put us, using the gifts that He has given us. Doing this leads to the most fulfilling and joyful life.

2. "He must increase, but I must decrease" (John 3:30).

3. **A.** Jesus comes from above and is above all. He bears witness to what He has seen and heard. He utters the words of God. God has given the Son the Holy Spirit, without measure. God loves His Son and has given all things into Jesus' hand.

   B. It's described as the Spirit of the Lord resting upon Jesus—the spirit of wisdom and understanding, the spirit of counsel and might, the spirit of knowledge and the fear of the Lord.

4. **A.** We are to believe in the Son and obey the Son in order to have eternal life.

   B. Answers will vary.

Lesson 4, Day One

1. **A.** The Samaritans blended and mixed the worship of the God of Abraham with the worship of the pagan gods, called Baals. "So they feared the Lord but also served their own gods, after the manner of the nations from whom they had been carried away" (2 Kings 17:33).

   B. The Jews considered the Samaritans pagans or heretics. The Samaritans had disregarded the covenant made between God and the twelve tribes of Israel, in which they had promised not to venerate other gods.

2. **A.** The Samaritan woman was likely an outcast in her community due to her lifestyle. She wanted to avoid contact with the other women of her community so much that she chose to walk for her water at the hottest time of the day.

   B. She probably felt like used goods. All the accumulated hurts, disappointments, and loss of reputation had more than likely taken away her hope. She might have been a little jaded, perhaps cynical, after so much relational brokenness.

   C. Answers will vary.

Lesson 4, Day Two

1. The "living water" is the Holy Spirit.

2. **A.** Word, God

   B. Liturgy, Church

   C. Theological virtues, faith, hope, love

   D. Today

   E. Answers will vary.

3. **A.** In the Old Testament, God spoke to the Israelites through the prophet Jeremiah at a time when they were not remaining faithful to God. First of all, they had forsaken God and worshipped idols. Then they searched for satisfaction from man-made sources instead of from God.
    B. Answers will vary.

Lesson 4, Day Three

1. **A.** Jesus' tone must have been gentle, or the Samaritan woman wouldn't have continued to converse with Him. He knew her whole story and knew what had caused her to look for love in the wrong places. He would have been compassionate, aware that He was discussing a very tender part of her heart.
    B. Jesus loved the Samaritan woman too much to leave her in a place of bondage to sin. Walking in freedom requires knowing the truth and confessing it.
    C. **Ephesians 3:17–19:** We need to approach the throne of mercy remembering that God's love for us is wide and long and high and deep. He loves us so much that we can't begin to comprehend it. He longs to fill us, to satisfy us, to complete us. When we go to confession, we are approaching the source of love, forgiveness, and mercy. Reconciliation is a clearing out and a healing to make room for a greater outpouring of grace and every good thing.
    2 Corinthians 5:17–19: We go to confession for a fresh start! When we leave the confessional, we are given a new beginning. We are new creations in Christ. The old has gone; the new has come!
2. Jesus said that God was looking for people who worship in spirit and truth.
3. Answers will vary.

Lesson 4, Day Four

1. **A.** She left her water jar, went into the city, and told the people she saw about Jesus.
    B. Answers will vary.
    C. Answers will vary.
2. Jesus said that He had food to eat that the disciples didn't know about, and this food was doing God's will. There is nothing more satisfying than playing a part in God's overarching plan for the world.
3. The harvest refers to people whose hearts are ripe for conversion. Many are suffering and recognize their need for something more—for a Savior. These hearts are ready to abandon their broken lives and broken ways to put their faith, hope, and trust in God alone—if only someone would offer them the living water. Certainly He was speaking of the Samaritans, but this was also true then (and today) of the whole world.

4. Jesus said that their work in the harvest would be rewarded (He who reaps receives wages), that the good of their work would last forever (gathers fruit for eternal life), and that every worker in the harvest would rejoice together in their work.

Lesson 4, Day Five

1. It required humility for the royal official to track down Jesus and beg Him to come heal his son. Many people around him would have looked down on the Jewish religion and upstart preachers. He was admitting that he was out of resources and without hope and that he believed Jesus could make a difference. He was motivated by love for his son. No loss of reputation mattered in the face of his son's suffering.
2. Jesus healed the official's son with His Word. He wasn't physically present, but when He said, "Go; your son will live," the boy recovered. The official took Jesus at His word without seeing the result, obeyed Him, and went home.
3. Answers will vary.

Lesson 6, Day One

1. Answers will vary.
2. **A.** We can be blind to beauty, hope, God's love for us, and our need for Him. We can be blind to our own faults and to others' perspectives. We can be spiritually lame, limping along in the Christian life, never experiencing the spiritual fullness that God intends for us. We can be paralyzed by fear, guilt, grief, and shame.
   B. Answers will vary.
3. **A.** They were blind to their own need and inadequacy.
   B. They were encouraged to go to Jesus for the supernatural things that they really needed.
   C. "So, because you are lukewarm, and neither cold nor hot, I will spew you out of my mouth" (Revelation 3:16).

Lesson 6, Day Two

1. **A.** Jesus asked, "Do you want to be healed?"
   B. Answers will vary.
   C. Sir, there's no one here to help me. I don't have any friends who can lift me up and carry me down when the water starts to bubble. The other people here—they always get there ahead of me! Essentially I'm doing everything I can do… but it doesn't seem like enough!

2. **A.** Jesus told the man to get up, pick up his mat, and walk. With these words He communicated that the man didn't need someone to take him to the water. There was no magic in the bubbling water. All that was needed was Jesus' healing touch.

   B. Answers will vary.

   C. **Mark 1:35:** Get up! We are to follow Christ's example, to get up and pray—even if we're tired.

   Philippians 4:4–7: Don't be anxious about anything. God is our authority. He's almighty, and He brings us peace.

   Philippians 4:8–9: Think of positive things. Rather than dwell on anything negative, dwell on God's Word, put it into practice, and be filled with peace.

Lesson 6, Day Three

1. **A.** He was breaking the Sabbath.

   B. The purpose of the Sabbath law was not doing work and keeping the Sabbath day holy.

   C. Jesus considered the purpose of the Sabbath to honor God. This is accomplished by "doing good rather than harm, for saving life rather than killing. The Sabbath is the day of the Lord of mercies" (CCC 2173).

2. **Matthew 7:1–5:** We are not supposed to judge. We tend to notice the things that are wrong with other people, while we are blind to our own faults. This verse tells us to deal with our own issues instead of focusing on others' shortcomings.

   1 Samuel 16:7: We tend to judge by appearances—what we observe on the outside. God is able to look into a person's heart—to see the past hurts that contribute to the current behavior, to see the motives, and to see the desire to change or be different. We can't see that, and so our judgment is impaired.

   Ephesians 4:32: Instead of judging we are to be kind to one another, tenderhearted, offering forgiveness.

3. Answers will vary.

4. **A.** "This was why the Jews sought all the more to kill him, because he not only broke the Sabbath but also called God his Father, making himself equal with God" (John 5:18).

   B. In judging Jesus the Jews were considering themselves on par with God's authority. We are not to judge—that is God's job.

Lesson 6, Day Four

1. The Jews wanted to kill Jesus because He had healed on the Sabbath, and He called God His Father, making Himself equal to God.

2. **A.** Jesus has been given the right to judge the living and the dead. This authority was given to Him by God, His Father.

    B. Jesus earned the right to judge when He redeemed the world through His death on the cross.

3. **A.** Those who have done good will experience the resurrection of life, which leads to eternal life. Those who have done evil will experience the resurrection of judgment, which leads to eternal punishment.

    B. "Death puts an end to human life as the time open to either accepting or rejecting the divine grace manifested in Christ" (CCC 1021). "It is appointed for men to die once, and after that comes judgment" (Hebrews 9:27).

4. **John 3:17:** His is not a heart of condemnation. He didn't come to condemn us. He came to offer us all salvation.

    2 Peter 3:9: Jesus doesn't want anyone to perish. He wants everyone to turn to Him, repent, and receive eternal life. Sometimes we want His judgment to fall quickly on someone who we feel has done something heinous. When we don't see that judgment come according to our timetable, could it be that God is being patient, giving that person one more chance to turn to Him and repent? We're grateful for His patience with us; we need to trust His timing with other people and not judge.

5. It is our choice whether we make it through the gate. "By rejecting grace in this life, one already judges oneself, receives according to one's works, and can even condemn oneself for all eternity by rejecting the Spirit of love" (CCC 679).

Lesson 6, Day Five

1. John the Baptist's testimony (v. 33)

    The works (or miracles) that He's been doing (v. 36)

    The Father's witness to Jesus' authority and trustworthiness when He spoke at Jesus' baptism (v. 37)

    Moses spoke of Jesus coming. If they had open hearts, they'd recognize this (v. 46).

2. Jesus wasn't trying to win the Jews' approval. He loved them and spoke directly in hopes that their hearts would be softened. He said these things so that the Jews could be saved.

3. **A.** The Jews accepted praise from one another but made no effort to obtain God's praise.

    B. Answers will vary.

Lesson 7, Day One

1. Answers will vary.
2. **A.** The boy risked getting nothing back. He was hungry, too, and could easily have thought, *It's too bad no one else came prepared…I'm glad I'm covered!*
    B. His act was unselfish, trusting, obedient, and generous.
    C. Answers will vary.
    D. Philippians 4:19: God will supply all my needs, according to His riches in Christ Jesus.
    2 Corinthians 9:8: God is able to provide us with every blessing in abundance. He can make sure that we have enough of everything. We need to check, however, that we are asking for the right blessings. The blessings that He loves to give are the ones that last throughout eternity.
    Matthew 19:26: Even when things seem impossible, God is able to enter a situation and completely change things for the better.
3. This miracle prefigures "the superabundance of this unique bread of his Eucharist" (CCC 1335).

Lesson 7, Day Two

1. **A.** Jesus told them to do so. They were obeying Him.
    B. God sometimes allows us to be in difficult situations so that we learn essential lessons, but He is always there for us. We have only to turn to Him.
2. Jesus was up in the hills, praying. He knew exactly where they were the whole time. He was in control and waiting for the perfect time to rescue them.
3. **A.** Answers will vary.
    B. Jesus sits at the right hand of God (Romans 8:34) and intercedes for us (Hebrews 7:25). He is praying for you right now.
    C. Trials and difficulties are experienced by everyone. We may feel alone in our struggle, but we are not. God is working for our good. He knows our strength and never sends us more than we can bear. He takes our efforts to persevere and provides what we are lacking. We grow and mature as a result.
4. **A.** Jesus said, "It is I; do not be afraid."
    B. Deuteronomy 3:22: We do not need to be afraid of people or hide emotionally. God promises that He will fight for us.
    Isaiah 41:10: God promises that we don't need to fear, because He will always be with us. He promises to strengthen us, help us, and uphold us with His victorious right hand.

Psalm 23:4: Even when we walk through the valley of the shadow of death, we don't need to be afraid, because God will be with us. He will comfort us.

Matthew 10:19–20: We are not to be anxious about what we are to say, because God promises to give us the words that we need in the hour that we need them. If we invite Him to, the Holy Spirit will speak through us.

Lesson 7, Day Three

1. In both cases Jesus was telling them to satisfy their spiritual hunger and thirst with Him. Don't settle for what the world offers. It might bring temporary relief and pleasure, but it won't satisfy in the long run.

2. **A.** The two invitations are an invitation to faith (come to Jesus and believe in Him for salvation) and an invitation to the Eucharist (come to Jesus and eat His flesh and drink His blood).

   B. Without faith we can't be united with Christ or recognize His presence in the Eucharist. "Without faith it is impossible to please him" (Hebrews 11:6).

   If we don't respond to Christ's invitation to receive Him in the Eucharist, we are missing the greatest opportunity for intimacy with Him. We're turning away from a gift of grace that He longs to give to us. Jesus said, "I am the living bread which came down from heaven; if any one eats of this bread, he will live for ever; and the bread which I shall give for the life of the world is my flesh" (John 6:51).

   C. "This is the work of God, that you believe in him whom he has sent" (John 6:29).

   D. We must express our belief in deeds. God has prepared specific works for us to do (Ephesians 2:10). We work out our salvation in obedience to God as we endeavor to live out the Gospel (Philippians 2:12). Our belief and our faith in God are genuine only if they affect the way we live. True belief isn't just head knowledge; it is a belief that transforms us. Faith is a gift given to us by God. We need to receive that gift of faith and keep it until the end. True faith will be manifested in the way we live. Without works our faith is dead.

3. "Him who comes to me I will not cast out" (John 6:36). "And this is the will of him who sent me, that I should lose nothing of all that he has given me, but raise it at the last day. For this is the will of my Father, that every one who sees the Son and believes in him should have eternal life; and I will raise him up at the last day" (John 6:39–40).

Lesson 7, Day Four

1. **A.** Four times
    B. We won't have life in us.
    C. We'll have eternal life. We'll be raised on the last day. We'll abide in Him.
2. Jesus was speaking literally and sacramentally. In John 6:55, He said, "For my flesh is food indeed, and my blood is drink indeed." Catholics take a literal interpretation of this passage. Jesus' words point to the sacrament of the Eucharist, where Christ is present: body, blood, soul, and divinity (CCC 1374).
3. God had told Christ's followers not to drink any blood. To drink blood was to consume "life," as "life" was in the blood. The blood was to be put on the altar for atonement.
4. The principal fruit of receiving the Eucharist is an intimate union with Jesus Christ.

Lesson 7, Day Five

1. Many of His followers were shocked and abandoned Him. "After this many of his disciples drew back and no longer walked with him" (John 6:66). Jesus did not respond by calling them back and clarifying or moderating His earlier statements. He had been very clear. They hadn't misunderstood. He hadn't been speaking metaphorically. He meant what He said literally. They took it literally. They responded by leaving. He respected their free choice and let them go.
2. **A.** He said, "Lord, to whom shall we go? You have the words of eternal life; and we have believed, and have come to know, that you are the Holy One of God" (John 6:68–69). He reaffirmed his faith and belief in Jesus.
    B. Peter didn't yet understand the mystery of the Eucharist. The Last Supper and Jesus' sacrificial death on the cross hadn't yet occurred. Even though Jesus' words were hard to understand, Peter chose to believe Him. He displayed the virtue of faith—believing even when he couldn't see.
    C. Answers will vary.
3. Answers will vary.

Lesson 8, Day One

1. The Jews sought to kill Jesus because He healed on the Sabbath day, forgave sins, spent time with public sinners, and expelled demons. Some thought He was demon possessed. He was accused of blasphemy and false prophecy, which were religious crimes.
2. **Water Pouring Ceremony**: When the people were thirsty in the wilderness, Moses struck a rock, and water flowed out.

Festival of Lights: When the Israelites were in the wilderness, God's presence manifested itself through a pillar of fire by night and a cloud by day. It was called Shekinah and reminded the Israelites that they were not alone; God was with them.

3. **A.** Jesus' brethren didn't believe in Him (John 7:5) and weren't focused on God's timetable. They saw life from their own perspective. They were dictating to Jesus what seemed right to them with their limited understanding.

    B. Answers will vary.

Lesson 8, Day Two

1. Jesus was speaking of the miracle of the healing of the paralytic by the pool of Bethesda. The Jews were angry because He healed the man on the Sabbath.
2. Jesus pointed out that the Jews had no problem with circumcising on the Sabbath. If they were willing to tend to a part of the body on the Sabbath day, why would they have a problem with Him healing the whole body?
3. Jesus said, "If any man's will is to do [his Father's] will, he shall know whether the teaching is from God or whether I am speaking on my own authority" (John 7:17). Jesus was making the point that a heart fully surrendered to doing God's will has the discernment needed to recognize spiritual truth. The fact that they didn't recognize that Jesus was speaking the truth indicates that they had hearts that weren't fully surrendered to God's will.
4. Answers will vary.
5. Answers will vary.

Lesson 8, Day Three

1. The people believed that no one would know the origin of the Messiah, and they knew where Jesus came from (Nazareth).
2. Two traditions regarding the birth and origin of the Messiah circulated in ancient Judaism. (1) Some expected the Messiah to grow up in obscurity and be manifested to the world only as an adult. (2) Others expected the Messiah to come from Bethlehem in accordance with the prophecy of Micah 5:2. The irony here is that both are true of Jesus: his heavenly origin in the Trinity is unknown to his audience (8:14) as is his birth in Bethlehem (Luke 2:4–7).[89]
3. We live in a culture that takes less and less time to learn all the facts before making a decision. The fast pace of life gets in the way of studying, asking questions, and exploring truth. As a result many people have never taken the time to read the Bible before determining whether to reject the message contained in it. It has been said

---

89 Ignatius Catholic Study Bible, RSV, 176.

that Satan knows better than to try to convince us that Jesus doesn't exist. Instead he lulls us into believing that there is always tomorrow. There is no need to make a decision right now. We fill our lives with activities so that there's little time left for truly exploring the claims of Christ. To avoid this mistake, we need to take time for the things that matter most. Exploring what God says about Himself in Scripture is essential. Participating in Bible study with a prayerful and eager heart helps us learn more about Christ through Scripture. We should be lifelong learners of Scripture. We'll only do this if we make study and reflection a daily priority.

4. The "hour" refers to the hour of Jesus' Passion. "In this hour, the Son of man was glorified, meaning it was the time when Jesus was handed over to sinners and darkness: it was the hour of the Passion. The use of the term underscores the Passion as the fulfillment of Christ's life and ministry, and the completion of the divine plan of salvation at one particular point in time."[90]

5. Jesus would live only thirty-three years and was soon to die. He'd then return to His Father in heaven. The unbelieving Jews would look for Him after hearing rumors of His Resurrection, but they'd never find Him. They wouldn't see Him on earth, nor in heaven, as their disbelief would prevent them from seeing Him there.

Lesson 8, Day Four

1. Jesus was speaking of the Holy Spirit.
2. **A.** The rock was Jesus.
   B. Just as the water that poured from the rock sustained and refreshed the Israelites, Jesus sustains and refreshes us. Our thirst is quenched through union with Him.
3. Answers will vary.

Lesson 8, Day Five

1. Answers will vary.
2. Jesus had told Nicodemus that he needed to be born anew, born of water and the Spirit. He was speaking of a spiritual rebirth—Baptism. At the Feast of Tabernacles, Jesus pointed to Himself as the source of the Holy Spirit, who was described as streams of living water. Nicodemus was beginning to learn these lessons. He was letting go of a lot of preconceived notions about the Messiah and religion, and each teaching revealed a bit more of the truth. We know from later readings that Nicodemus did become a follower of Christ. This shows that he not only heard the teachings of Christ, but he received them and accepted them. He had an open

---

90 *Scott Hahn, Catholic Bible Dictionary (New York: Doubleday, 2009), 371–2.*

heart. By contrast the other Pharisees heard Jesus' teachings, but refused to open their hearts, humble themselves, and recognize God's movement in the world.

3. Jesus continued to give to others because He knew that God had a plan. He was filled with the Holy Spirit, so when He was pressed, blessings flowed out.

4. Answers will vary.

Lesson 9, Day One

1. **A.** If Jesus had said to let the woman go, He would have been opposing the Law of Moses, which stated that the penalty for adultery was stoning. Had He done this, He would have been guilty of injustice.

   If He had said she should be stoned, the Pharisees could use this to turn the Roman government against Jesus, because only the Roman government had the right to issue the death penalty. In addition to breaking the Roman law, Jesus would have been guilty of lacking mercy.

   B. Jesus avoided the trap by saying that the penalty should be carried out by the person who had no sin.

   This verse is not excusing sin. Jesus wasn't saying that it didn't matter that the woman had committed adultery. He was pointing out to the Pharisees and scribes that the sin in their own hearts should be their greater concern.

2. Answers will vary.

3. Jesus was full of grace and truth. He showed grace to the woman when He didn't condemn her. He spoke truth when He told her, "Go, and do not sin again." That was (and is) God's standard. Jesus didn't lie to her and say that how she lived didn't matter. That wouldn't have been truthful. He struck the perfect balance between lack of condemnation and encouragement to change her life for the better.

Lesson 9, Day Two

1. **A.** **1 John 1:9:** Acknowledge your sins.

   1 John 2:3: Keep God's commandments.

   1 John 2:6: Live just as Jesus lived.

   1 John 2:10: Love your brother.

   1 John 2:15: Do not love the world or the things of the world. Keep an eternal perspective.

   1 John 2:24: Let what you heard remain in you. Don't just listen to good teaching and then quickly forget it. Take notes, review them, and apply what you learn.

   1 John 2:28: Remain close to Christ.

   B. Answers will vary.

2. Answers will vary.

Lesson 9, Day Three

1. **Exodus 3:13–15:** God chose to identify Himself with the name I AM. This is how He wanted Moses to describe Him. This is the title God gave Himself.

   John 8:58: In this verse, Jesus was identifying Himself as God by referring to Himself with the Old Testament name for God.

   CCC 211: This Catechism quote teaches that the divine name I AM is not only God's title; it expresses something of His character, His faithfulness. God's faithfulness and mercy are seen throughout the Old Testament. Jesus revealed His faithfulness, mercy, and divine character when He gave His life for us on the cross.

   Isaiah 43:10–11 and Acts 4:12: We are to know and believe that no god was formed before our God, and no god will be formed afterward. No one is greater than our God. There is no Savior besides God. Acts 4:12 tells us that salvation is only through Jesus.

2. Jesus' crucifixion and the events surrounding His death confirmed His divinity. Darkness from 12:00 to 3:00 p.m., the veil in the sanctuary being torn in two from top to bottom, an earthquake, rocks splitting, tombs opening, and bodies being raised from the dead confirmed Jesus was no ordinary man. He also knew that the way in which He would suffer would deliver a powerful message. A hardened heart is unlikely to be swayed by artfully crafted words—it may lead to interesting debate but not a change in heart. However observing a person willing to suffer, proving love in the most difficult way imaginable, penetrates the heart and leaves an indelible mark.

3. Jesus claimed that He always did what was pleasing to the Father. We are to endeavor to live in this way, conforming our will to God's. We need to learn obedience. We read in CCC 2825 that we are incapable of doing this in our own strength. John 15:5 says, "Apart from [Jesus] you can do nothing." When we unite ourselves in a personal relationship with Jesus and are filled with the Holy Spirit, we are able to surrender our will to God's. But it is God's Holy Spirit in us that causes us to want to obey and gives us the ability to let go of our selfish desires. "For God is at work in you, both to will and to work for his good pleasure" (Philippians 2:13).

Lesson 9, Day Four

1. God's Word is truth (John 17:17). God's Truth is found in Jesus (Ephesians 4:21). The Holy Spirit is truth (1 John 5:8). CCC 2466 tells us that "In Jesus Christ, the whole of God's Truth has been made manifest. 'Full of grace and truth,' he came as the 'light of the world,' he is the Truth. 'Whoever believes in me may not remain in darkness.' The disciple of Jesus continues in his Word so as to know 'the truth

[that] will make you free' and that sanctifies. To follow Jesus is to live in 'the Spirit of truth,' whom the Father sends in his name and who leads 'into all the truth.'"
We can pursue truth through knowing Jesus Christ, studying Scripture and Church teachings, and nurturing a relationship with the indwelling Holy Spirit.

2. Many people exchange God's Truth for a lie, worshipping what God has created instead of God. We see this in the pursuit of money, pleasure, and fame instead of God's Truth (Romans 1:25).
Sometimes the truth makes us uncomfortable. It's more pleasant to listen to someone who tells you what you want to hear. Instead of welcoming challenge and good teaching, many people flock to "teachers to suit their own likings" (2 Timothy 4:3–4).

3. It's a spiritual battle against powers, rulers, and spiritual hosts that want to keep us in darkness. We need to put on God's armor in order to fight this battle—we need to keep truth around our waists and righteousness on our chests, stand firmly on the Gospel, and hold the shield of faith up, because Satan will fire arrows of doubt at us continually. The helmet of salvation will protect our minds.
Our offensive weapon, we are told, is the Spirit, who speaks to us the very words of God within our own hearts, through the Scriptures and through the teachings of the Magisterium of the Church. We need to pray to hear the Spirit in our hearts. We need to study the Scriptures to know God's Word. And we need to learn and adhere to the Church's teachings in order to fight in spiritual warfare.

4. **A.** Answers will vary.
   B. Answers will vary.
   C. Answers will vary.

Lesson 9, Day Five

1. **John 8:42:** We must love Jesus.
   John 8:47: We must hear the Word of God.
   John 1:12: We must receive Christ and believe in His name.
   1 John 3:10: Whoever does not do what is right is not of God. We need to love our brother.

2. Jesus said their father was the devil and described him as a murderer, a liar, and the father of lies.

3. Answers will vary.

Lesson 11, Day One

1. **A.** The disciples asked who had sinned (the man or his parents) that he was born blind. The Jews believed that sickness was punishment for sin. Tobit 3:3 reveals the Old Testament belief that children could be punished for the sins of their parents.

   B. We are each held responsible for our own actions. God does not hold a child responsible or consider a child guilty for the actions of his or her parent. Nor is a parent guilty for a child's sin.

2. **A.** The man was born blind so that the works of God might be made manifest in him. It was a part of God's plan, so that He could be glorified.

   B. When we are weak, we can't rely on our own abilities and power. We are desperate and need God. It's in our need that God can do the most amazing things. When we come with arms outstretched, aware that we can do nothing without Him, He comes in with His strength. Anything that is accomplished then brings glory to Him, not to us. It's when we're in that weak state that He can teach us wonderful lessons about His sufficiency and faithfulness. His power is made perfect in weakness. Colossians 1:24 describes the suffering that remains for followers of Christ as they experience trials in their lives. Suffering is one way in which we become more like Christ. (Note that this verse referenced in CCC 1508 does not mean that the suffering of Christ wasn't sufficient for our redemption.)

3. **A.** **John 2:7–11:** He used water when He turned the water to wine. He could have just created wine out of nothing.
   John 6:8–13: He used a young boy's fish and loaves of bread to create a feast for the multitudes.
   Mark 14:22–25: He used wine and bread to institute the first Eucharist—the giving of His body and blood to fill us and transform us by His grace.

   B. It brings to mind Baptism, in which a person is washed in the baptismal waters.

4. Answers will vary.

Lesson 11, Day Two

1. **A.** The Pharisees wanted to know how the miracle happened and concluded that "This man is not from God, for he does not keep the sabbath" (John 9:16). Members of the crowd of people figured that a man who was a sinner wouldn't be able to do a miracle like this. The parents didn't want to get involved at all, and instead of rejoicing in their son's healing, they told the Pharisees to talk directly to their son. They were afraid of the consequences of being connected to this controversial healing.

B. The man's parents didn't want to get in trouble by being associated with Jesus, so they told the Pharisees to ask their son for the details. They acknowledged that he had been blind from birth and had been healed, but they weren't willing to stick their necks out for Jesus or their son. His boldness was probably mortifying to them, and they would have felt embarrassed and ashamed when their son was thrown out of the synagogue.

C. Answers will vary.

D. Our loyalty needs to lie with God. We need to be prepared to give an answer to anyone who asks for the reason for the hope within us or the difference they see in us. We are wise to recognize when a person is spiritually hungry and wants to know more and when he or she is simply not asking. We make a mistake when we come on too strong, thinking that our words are going to cause another person to change. Far more powerful is the silent witness of a changed life. If we live out our faith, love sacrificially, respond with grace when treated unfairly, and suffer without bitterness, then our actions will speak louder than our words.

2. **John 9:11–12:** He acknowledged that Jesus was his healer and had changed him.
   John 9:17: He acknowledged Jesus as a prophet.
   John 9:31–33: He concluded that because Jesus was able to perform this miracle, and only God could create sight, God must have listened to Jesus. He acknowledged that Jesus was from God and that God was the ultimate source of the healing.

3. **Psalm 34:19:** God is close to the broken-hearted. He saves those who are crushed in spirit.
   Psalm 18:17: God reaches down from on high and takes hold of us. He draws us out of deep waters of self-pity, fear, sadness, and grief.
   Psalm 23:4: Even when we walk through dark valleys of suffering, we are never alone. God is always by our side. His rod and staff should give us courage. They are a picture of God offering us guidance and discipline (the rod) and pulling us out of danger (the staff).

4. The Pharisees consistently failed to see their need for Jesus. Their self-righteousness blinded them. They also failed to see that Jesus was the Son of God. They ignored the evidence of His miracles, His extraordinary wisdom, the witness of John the Baptist, and His fulfilment of Old Testament prophecies. Finally they failed to see the consequences of their actions in the lives of the people they were supposed to spiritually lead. As leaders they bore even greater responsibility, as many people blindly followed them. We see the consequence of their lack of belief in the lives of the blind man's parents.

Lesson 11, Day Three

1. Jesus described the religious leaders as thieves and robbers—strangers the people wouldn't follow. He described Himself as one whom the sheep recognized and trusted.

2. **Isaiah 43:1:** Jesus has called you by name, saying, "You are mine." When you pass through trials, He will be with you. As horrible as the circumstances may be, His presence will get you through.

    Isaiah 49:1: Jesus knew you even when you were in your mother's womb. He gave you a name, which signifies a designation for a special purpose.

    Isaiah 49:16: God engraves our name on the palm of His hand. In the ancient world, a slave would have had the name of his master engraved on his hand to keep him from wandering away. Here God makes Himself our slave, fulfilled in Christ. As our slave God has marked Himself as permanently belonging to us. In this image of God, He shows us His profound humility.

3. **A.** Jesus is the gate or, in some translations, the door.

    B. If we go through Jesus, the gate, we will be saved. The gate is narrow, but doesn't God, the Creator of all, have the right to say how He'll be approached? Yet it's so wide. John 10:9 says that whoever enters through Jesus will be saved.

4. **A.** I am the Good Shepherd.

    B. **John 10:11:** A Good Shepherd dies for His sheep.

    John 10:14: He knows His sheep.

    John 10:16: He brings other sheep (meaning Gentiles, non-Jews) into the flock.

    John 10:17–21: He takes up His life again. This refers to the Resurrection. Only God could make this claim, because only He has power over life and death.

Lesson 11, Day Four

1. Jesus said that they didn't believe because they didn't belong to His sheep.

2. A person must hear God's voice and follow Him.

3. **Psalm 25:8–9, 12:** God calls us to be humble if we're going to hear His voice. We need fear of the Lord if we want His guidance. Fearing the Lord means respecting Him and being in awe of Him. When we seek God's guidance, we aren't coming to Him as a peer to get a little extra perspective. We're going to our Creator to hear from the One who knows all things and is uniquely qualified to guide us. We approach Him with an attitude of humility.

    Proverbs 2:6–9: This passage talks about the importance of being upright—of piety and holiness. Sin builds up a wall between God and us. It affects our friendship with Him and must be confessed in order for us to clearly hear His voice.

Proverbs 11:14: God can lead us and speak to us through the wise counsel of other people.

Exodus 14:14: How will we hear Him if we are constantly making noise? We must quiet our hearts and close our mouths.

John 16:13: The Holy Spirit, who dwells within us, is our guide. He guides us into all truth.

4. Nothing except our own will. We are free to reject or accept God's love. If we accept it, then no hardship, or death, or anything that we worry about can separate us from God's love. We are in His hands, lovingly held and protected. No trial is deeper than His love.

Lesson 11, Day Five

1. In their minds this was blasphemy. He was making Himself equal with God. It was the clearest statement Jesus had made regarding His divinity, and they recognized this.

2. Jesus was making the point that if God, in Scripture, called human judges "gods," how could the Jews stone Jesus for using that title for Himself? The human judges were given that title because of their authority and because of their duties. Certainly Jesus was entitled to that same description because of His lack of sin and the fact that He spoke the words of God to the people.

3. Jesus was visibly consecrated by the Father at His baptism and transfiguration.

4. **John 1:19–34:** Jesus was revealed through John the Baptist's testimony.
   John 2:13–22: He was revealed through the fulfillment of all Old Testament prophecies concerning the Messiah.
   John 10:37–38: He was revealed through His works (His miracles).
   CCC 548: He was revealed through His works (His miracles).

Lesson 12, Day One

1. Mary and Martha referred to Lazarus as the one whom Jesus loved (John 11:3). In John 11:4, Jesus sent Mary and Martha a message of hope to encourage them. He knew He'd be keeping them waiting and that these would be words to which they would cling. John 11:5 says, "Now Jesus loved Martha and her sister and Lazarus." Jesus referred to Lazarus as "our friend" in John 11:11.

2. Jesus' waiting was not a miscalculation or a mistake. It was purposeful and an indication that He was following His Father's timetable. Something great happened because of the wait.

3. Answers will vary. But in every case, when Jesus doesn't answer our prayer as we desire, we can be sure that He has something better in mind.

4. Answers will vary.

5. The twelve hours of daylight represent the life span. Jesus wasn't worried about going to Judea, even though the Jews were plotting His death. He knew that His life was following God's timetable. Nothing was going to happen to Him that was unexpected for His Father. God knew the hour of Jesus' death. He would be safe to take this trip to Bethany.

6. Our circumstances are not the way that we should measure how much God loves us. We should measure His love for us by the cross. That's where He proved just how much He loves us.

Lesson 12, Day Two

1. **A.** Mary sat at Jesus' feet and soaked up His wisdom. She clearly loved and adored Him. She cared more about being close to Jesus than gaining the approval of her sister, Martha. Our relationship with Christ comes before our duty to serve. She knew that it is only through knowing Christ that we can serve in His name. In our fast-paced lives, we can easily lose sight of our first priority. By taking time to pray every day, we imitate Mary. Our service will then be blessed and will draw us even closer to Christ.

   B. Martha went out to meet Jesus; Mary stayed in the house. Mary may have been overcome with grief and may have been feeling hurt by Jesus, wondering why He hadn't come right away. Maybe her heart was raw because she didn't understand why He hadn't answered her request the way she'd hoped. She might have been angry with Jesus.

2. Answers will vary.

3. Answers will vary.

4. **A.** God, the Father.

   B. It's Jesus Himself. Jesus is the source of resurrected life. He is the One who will raise all to new life after death. He's not just a good teacher, an amazing healer, and a great example of selfless love. He is the Resurrection and the Life. Our hope of life after death rests solely in Him.

   C. Answers will vary.

Lesson 12, Day Three

1. Mary didn't need a theology lesson. She didn't need someone explaining doctrine to her. She needed Jesus. She needed His comfort and presence. She needed hope. This is what He gave her. So often when we see someone grieving, we feel the need to give advice. But this is not what a hurting person needs at this time. What he or she needs is our presence, our comfort.

2. No. In Isaiah 53:3, Jesus is described by the prophet Isaiah as a man of sorrows, acquainted with deepest grief. In Isaiah 63:8–9, Jesus was distressed over His people's distress. Scripture tells us in Romans 12:15 that we are to enter into other people's grief, weeping with those who weep.

3. When we are in heaven, there will be no more suffering, sorrow, or death. God will wipe every tear from our eyes.

4. **A.** He was deeply moved and troubled in spirit. Jesus wept. In John 11:35, "the Greek word means that Jesus broke into silent tears."[91]

   B. Answers will vary.

Lesson 12, Day Four

1. The Jewish people believed that bodily decay begins on the fourth day after death. Lazarus' body would have begun decomposing. There would have been a stench. Martha must have been horrified at the thought of seeing her beloved brother in that state.

2. **A.** The situation seemed pretty hopeless. People would have envisioned Lazarus' body as decaying and his soul gone.

   B. Answers will vary.

   C. **1 Timothy 1:1:** Jesus is our hope. Our hope doesn't lie in our circumstances or in our ability to overcome difficulty. It lies in Him.

   Ephesians 1:18: God has called us to hope because of the spiritual riches we have inherited. We may not have all that we want in this life circumstantially or materially, but we do have great spiritual wealth—redemption, freedom, power through the indwelling Holy Spirit, purpose, and strength.

   1 Peter 1:3–4: We have the hope of heaven. We have an inheritance in heaven that is imperishable, undefiled, and unfading. If we keep our eyes on the here and now, as if this life is all that there is, we will lose hope. If we keep our focus on heaven, we will find the strength to endure hardship in this life.

3. He was teaching us how to pray when we are facing hopeless situations. He began with thanks, and before God gave the gift, Jesus committed Himself to Him, recognizing that the real gift was God Himself. "The Giver is more precious than the gift; he is the 'treasure'; in him abides his Son's heart" (CCC 2604).

4. Psalm 86:12–13 says, "I give thanks to you, O Lord my God, with my whole heart, and I will glorify your name forever. For great is your merciful love toward me; you have delivered my soul from the depths of Sheol." We are thrilled any time we

---

91 Stephen K. Ray, *St. John's Gospel* (San Francisco: Ignatius Press, 2002), 231.

get a second chance or a fresh start. But neither of those experiences can begin to compare to the miracle of being raised from the dead.

5. Answers will vary.

Lesson 12, Day Five

1. The chief priests and the Pharisees were concerned that as more and more people believed in and followed Jesus, political unrest would follow. They feared that the Romans, who ruled Palestine, would take away their lucrative jobs for failing to keep order. Instead of causing them to be amazed at God's work in their midst, this miracle led to them plotting Jesus' death.

2. The end doesn't justify the means. A good intention doesn't make immoral behavior acceptable. "There are concrete acts that it is always wrong to choose, because their choice entails a disorder of the will, i.e., a moral evil. One may not do evil so that good may result from it" (CCC 1761).

3. The high priest, Caiaphas, prophesied that Jesus would die, not just for the nation of Israel but for the scattered children of God as well. Caiaphas was looking for a way to keep peace in the nation, removing political trouble. This isn't the kind of peace Jesus brings. Caiaphas' words came true, just not with his intended meaning.

4. **Psalm 86:14** (NAB) says, "O God, the arrogant have risen against me; a ruthless band has sought my life; to you they pay no need." This is exactly what happened with the prideful and ruthless religious leaders. They ignored all the ways in which Jesus was the Messiah who had been prophesied about. They ignored His words. They paid God no heed and dismissed their Savior.

Lesson 13, Day One

1. Answers will vary.
2. Answers will vary.
3. Answers will vary.
4. **A.** Judas Iscariot was in charge of the money and was stealing from the disciples' money box.

   B. No. Jesus often encouraged His followers to give to the poor and to care about them. He never contradicted Old Testament teaching. In Deuteronomy 15:11, the Israelite people were commanded, "You shall open wide your hand to your brother, to the needy and to the poor, in the land." Jesus taught this principle and encouraged His followers to recognize His own presence in the poor. Saint Rose of Lima said, "When we serve the poor and the sick, we serve Jesus. We must not fail to help our neighbors, because in them we serve Jesus."

In John 12:8, Jesus was pointing out Judas' hypocrisy. Judas was hiding under a cloak of piety, acting as if he was concerned for the poor, when really he simply didn't see the value of giving Jesus the honor that was due Him.

Lesson 13, Day Two

1. **Psalm 118:25** says, "Save us, we beg you, O Lord." As Jesus entered Jerusalem, He was preparing for the act that would save people from their sins.

   Zechariah 9:9: The prophet Zechariah predicted the way in which Jesus would enter Jerusalem five hundred years before it occurred: riding on a donkey.

2. When Jesus is the King of our hearts, He brings us peace through His very presence. Ephesians 2:14 says, "For He is our peace."

   Through the indwelling Holy Spirit, we can experience a peace that surpasses human understanding, as seen in Philippians 4:7: "And the peace of God, which passes all understanding, will keep your hearts and your minds in Christ Jesus." It is through Jesus that we can experience peace with God.

   Jesus' kingship has always been one of humility. We see this throughout His ministry in the gentle way He treated the most broken and fallen people in society. He never related to them as if He was looking down on them. Compassion and kindness were continually poured out as He served the most downtrodden people. His washing of the disciples' feet, a job normally left to household slaves, was another example of His humility. "Christ Jesus, who, though he was in the form of God, did not count equality with God a thing to be grasped, but emptied himself, taking the form of a servant, being born in the likeness of men. And being found in human form he humbled himself and became obedient unto death, even death on a cross" (Philippians 2:5–8).

3. **A.** "Holy, Holy, Holy Lord, God of hosts. Heaven and earth are full of Your glory, Hosanna in the highest. Blessed is He who comes in the name of the Lord, Hosanna in the highest."

   The Sanctus (Latin for *holy*) is prayed before receiving Jesus in the Eucharist. This is our preparation for the holiest part of the Mass. How can we respond in any way other than to cry "holy" and fall to our knees as we ponder such love, such sacrifice? What we read in Revelation 4:8 is the heavenly liturgy—worship in heaven. During the consecration of the host, heaven and earth meet in a mystical way. "In the earthly liturgy we share in a foretaste of that heavenly liturgy which is celebrated in the Holy City of Jerusalem toward which we journey as pilgrims, where Christ is sitting at the right hand of God, Minister of the sanctuary and of the true tabernacle" (CCC 1090).

B. In John 12:13, the people shouted, "God saves!" as Jesus walked by. That was exactly what He was arriving to do. Many of them were expecting a political salvation that would throw off the Roman occupation. The salvation Jesus would offer was to be spiritual, not political; His impending death on the cross was to save people from their sins.

During Mass when we pray the Sanctus (Latin for holy), we are recalling the salvation that Jesus purchased for us through His death on the cross. God saves. That's been His focus and mission ever since sin entered His beloved creation.

4. Answers will vary.

Lesson 13, Day Three

1. Jesus, by His death and Resurrection, was about to pay the price for the sins of the whole world, not just for the Jewish people. The chasm between the Lord and all of us was about to be bridged by Jesus, who would fulfill every promise, every feast, every ceremony. The old ways of relating to God and His Church would now pass away as Jews and Gentiles alike would be invited to embrace their Savior. Worship would be "in spirit and truth" and no longer reserved for the Temple alone. In the minds of the Jewish community of the time, Jesus was about to turn everything upside down.

2. A. "Unless a grain of wheat falls into the earth and dies, it remains alone; but if it dies, it bears much fruit." Jesus had to endure death in order to offer eternal life to all men. We are a part of the spiritual harvest that came because of Jesus' death.

B. Answers will vary.

3. A. Jesus didn't mean that our earthly lives don't have value. Nor was He advocating a lifestyle that displays a lack of care for self. He was drawing attention to the waste that occurs when we live just for earthly treasure, ignoring the fact that eternity is forever. He was warning against a life lived with no focus on eternity. Why? A love of leisure can cause a life to be wasted away on activities that bring pleasure but no eternal security. A love of power can cause a person to refuse to relinquish control to Christ, which is one of the requirements to enter heaven. A love of money and possessions can fool a person into thinking that he or she doesn't need God and that money gives all the security that is required. A love of popularity can hold a person back from giving his or her all to Jesus, because of a fear of what others might think.

Jesus is calling us to love Him so much that we'd be willing to do anything for Him. He's hoping that we'll grasp Him and let go of self-centeredness. He's calling us to a "self-forgetfulness" that can set aside our own desires in order to focus on what God wants and that allows us to meet the needs of others.

B. It is in no way permission for us to be self-destructive. Our lives are a precious gift from God, and we are to take care of our bodies and make healthy choices. But if we are asked to make a choice for God that means personal suffering, the right thing to do is to deny ourselves, take up the cross, and follow Him. Any act of self-denial, if done with the right motivation (love for God), will earn for us eternal reward.

Lesson 13, Day Four

1. **A.** Jesus was filled with dread as He looked ahead, knowing that His crucifixion was at hand. He knew that saving men from their sins was why His Father had sent Him to earth, but the suffering this would entail was overwhelming to contemplate.

   B. Jesus requested that God would glorify His (God's) name through Jesus' suffering.

   C. Answers will vary.

2. The Father spoke to Jesus at His baptism (Matthew 3:17) and at the transfiguration (Matthew 17:5). The Father spoke audibly as a clear sign of His blessing upon Jesus and as a way of setting Jesus apart. It was proof for us that Jesus was no ordinary man.

3. **A.** On the cross Jesus defeated Satan once and for all. Satan is a defeated foe. "Since therefore the children share in flesh and blood [this is us], he himself likewise partook of the same nature [describing Jesus taking on our human nature], that through death [on the cross] he might destroy him who has the power of death, that is, the devil, and deliver all those who through fear of death were subject to lifelong bondage" (Hebrews 2:14–15).

   B. Satan will be destroyed at the second coming of Christ, when he will be thrown into the lake of fire and brimstone, where he will be tormented day and night forever.

4. He who is within us (God in the person of the Holy Spirit) is stronger than Satan (1 John 4:4). We may feel weak in the face of Satan's attacks, but we have within us the same resurrection power that raised Jesus from the dead (Ephesians 1:18–20). If we ask God for His help, He will help us to resist all temptation. He promises to always provide a way out for us in the face of temptation (1 Corinthians 10:13).

Lesson 13, Day Five

1. The Jews feared the Pharisees and preferred being accepted by the in crowd more than they desired to be followers of the truth. In addition Jesus wasn't the kind of messiah that they had expected. They wanted a political leader who would overthrow Rome. Jesus' servant leadership was not what they expected or wanted.

2. Many people choose to worship the wrong things—money, power, reputation, comfort, and other people. They recognize there must be a God because of what they observe in creation but refuse to worship Him. People who repeatedly choose a god other than our merciful redeemer leave God, who is such a gentleman, standing at the closed door of their heart. He will never force Himself on anyone.

3. Answers will vary.

Lesson 15, Day One

1. **Jeremiah 31:3:** God's love for you is everlasting.
   Zephaniah 3:17: God delights in you. He rejoices over you. He sings over you.
   Romans 5:8 and **1 John 4:9–10:** He loves you so much that He sent Jesus to die in your place. He wanted to make sure that you would be able to spend eternity with Him. He knew that on your own, you'd never be able to reach Him. Someone needed to pay the price for your sin. That payment was death. ("For the wages of sin is death" [Romans 6:23].) It should have been your death that paid for your sins. Because of God's great love for you, Jesus died in your place and offered you a way back to God, your heavenly Father ("but the free gift of God is eternal life in Christ Jesus" [Romans 6:23]).
   Romans 8:38–39: God loves you unconditionally. Nothing you've done wrong or that you will do or that has been done to you can separate you from His love—nothing. God never turns His back on you, even if you choose to turn your back on Him. And if you refuse to abandon serious sin, even then, God is still waiting in all His love and glory for you to turn back to Him.

2. The devil put it into Judas' heart, because his desire has always been to thwart God's plan. The devil wanted to destroy Jesus. He has the same plan today. "The devil prowls around like a roaring lion, seeking some one to devour" (1 Peter 5:8).

3. **A.** Jesus knew that God the Father had given all things into His hands and that He had come from God and was going to God. Jesus knew who He was and whose He was.
   B. Jesus' service was not a degrading experience, regardless of how humble a task He performed. His dignity and identity were firmly rooted in God's Truth—He was the Son of God. Serving in such a humble way in no sense diminished Him.

4. **A.** Answers will vary.
   B. Answers will vary.

Lesson 15, Day Two

1. Jesus said that if He didn't wash Peter, Peter would have no part in Him.
2. Answers will vary.
3. **A.** Answers will vary.
   B. How can we display self-forgetful love? We can only forget ourselves and love with abandon if someone is loving and looking after us. That someone is God. His care and protection, His pouring of His own love into our hearts, enables us in turn to love and serve those around us.
4. **A.** They were arguing about which one of them was the greatest.
   B. Whoever wants to be great must be a servant, and whoever wants to be first must be willing to be a slave. Jesus is the example—He came not to be served but to serve and to give His life as a ransom for many.

Lesson 15, Day Three

1. No. In verse 22, it's clear that the disciples didn't know whom Jesus was talking about when He described being betrayed. When Jesus told Judas to do what he was going to do quickly, "no one at the table knew why he said this to [Judas]" (John 13:28).
2. **A.** God does not tempt us. The temptation to do evil comes from us. It comes from the desires within us.
   B. Judas was greedy and didn't want to follow a servant king. He perhaps wanted the Messiah to be a militant leader—one who would overthrow Rome's rule. He didn't recognize that the kingdom of God was within the hearts of men. He had seen Jesus' miracles and potential for power and was drawn to it. Clearly he didn't follow Jesus because of pure love for Him.
   C. Answers will vary.
   D. **Proverbs 4:23:** We must guard our hearts. The Hebrew word *leb*, translated "heart," means "the inner man, mind, will, and heart." This means we need to guard our mind, our will, and our emotions.
   2 Corinthians 10:5: We need to take every thought and make it captive to Christ. A thought in and of itself is not sinful. But what do we do with the thought once it pops into our heads? Do we play around with it? Do we dwell on it? Or do we lift it up to God, asking Him to take the sinful thought captive and remove it from our minds? We may have to do this over and over again

throughout the course of the day. The repeated action of "taking the thought captive to Christ" helps build a habit that will strengthen us to resist temptation in the future.

3. What intimacy Saint John described! He described himself as the disciple whom Jesus loved. He was lying close to the breast of Jesus.

4. In John 6:70–71, Jesus spoke the truth about Judas in a way that gave Judas the opportunity to repent and confess. In John 12:4–8, Jesus appealed to Judas to value Him above all else and recognize how amazing it was to have God present in their midst. In John 13, Jesus washed Judas' feet, showing love and offering cleansing. In John 13:10, He said, "you are clean, but not all of you."

Lesson 15, Day Four

1. **A.** The new commandment was to love one another, just as Jesus has loved.
   B. In the Old Testament, people were commanded to love one another as they loved themselves. Now they were told to love one another as Christ loved them. One is human love; the other is divine. It's supernatural.

2. **A.** We are to be known by our love.
   B. Fulfilling the new commandment to love as Jesus loved is only possible through the Holy Spirit. Without God we don't have the kind of supernatural love that loving like Jesus requires. God pours His love into our hearts through the Holy Spirit.

3. Jesus prophesied that Peter would deny Him three times before the cock crowed. That is exactly what happened.

4. **A.** We are to follow Christ's example and serve one another. We are to love as Jesus loved. This is the way people should recognize us as Christians.
   B. Answers will vary.

Lesson 15, Day Five

1. Jesus described a house with many rooms. It's a place that He is preparing for us. He was speaking of heaven. It describes the Father's house as our homeland. Conversion of heart enables us to return to the Father.

2. **A.** Heaven is the ultimate end and fulfillment of the deepest human longings, the state of supreme, definitive happiness. To live in heaven is to be with Christ. Those in heaven find their true identity, their own name.
   B. Jesus is the way to God the Father. If we want to be reconciled to God, it must be through Jesus. Jesus was claiming to be the sole Savior of the world.
   C. Answers will vary.

3. **A.** Sadness? Disappointment? After all the time that Jesus had spent pouring His life into His disciples, after all the miracles He had performed, after all the times He had spoken of His unity with God the Father, still Philip didn't recognize who Jesus really was.

   B. Jesus was claiming to be God. He was inviting them to look into His eyes, to touch His hands, to draw close to His presence, because in doing so, they were looking into God's eyes, touching God's hands, and drawing close to God's presence. Jesus is the visible image of the invisible God.

4. **A.** Jesus promised that whatever His followers asked in His name, He would do. The stipulation was that it had to be asked in His name. The purpose behind the answering of those future prayers was to glorify the Father.

   B. We are to ask in a way that is evidence of our faith in Jesus. This means that we ask for things that extend our desire to keep "the word and the commandments of Jesus…abiding with him in the Father." Asking in Jesus' name means asking for things that are consistent with God's will and character. "God will not grant requests contrary to His nature or His will and we cannot use His name as a magic formula to fulfill our selfish desires. If we are sincerely following God and seeking to do His will, then our requests will be in line with what He wants, and He will grant them."[92]

Lesson 16, Day One

1. We obey His commandments. In 1 John 2:5–6 we are called to love not just in word and speech but also in deed and truth.

2. **A.** God sent us the Holy Spirit to help us to be holy. The Holy Spirit instructs us so we know what God wants us to do, and He strengthens us from within so that we can resist temptation. The Holy Spirit dwells in the hearts of God's children. "Do you not know that your body is a temple of the Holy Spirit within you, which you have from God?" (1 Corinthians 6:19).

   B. The Counselor (the Holy Spirit) will be our teacher, bringing to our minds the things that God has taught us.

3. **A.** We find the peace the world gives when things are going the way we want them to go. Jesus gives us peace in the midst of difficult circumstances. It's an interior peace that cannot be taken away from us.

   B. Answers will vary.

4. Jesus wanted His disciples to understand that He knew exactly what was coming and that it was within the Father's will.

---

92 Life Application Study Bible, NIV, 1911.

5. The disciples were about to see Jesus tortured and killed. It was going to appear that evil had won—that Jesus hadn't been strong enough to prevent Satan's victory. It was going to appear that Jesus was not in control. He wanted the disciples to know that Satan had no power over Him. Jesus had said earlier that He would lay down His life in order to take it up again. He had told them that no one would have the power to take His life from Him.

Lesson 16, Day Two

1. Jesus is the vine. The Father is the vinedresser. We are the branches.
2. **A.** The branches that don't bear fruit are taken away.
   B. The branches that do bear fruit are pruned so that they can bear more fruit.
3. **Hebrews 12:5–11:** God disciplines us out of love, just as earthly parents discipline their children. Love inspires the discipline. If we miss this point, we will often mistake difficult circumstances, allowed by God for our good, for persecution by God or for His anger. No one enjoys being disciplined, but God sometimes does this so that we can become holy. If we are willing to be trained by God, then we'll experience the fruit of righteousness in our lives.
   James 1:2–4: We are called to rejoice in the midst of trials. This doesn't mean that we are thrilled about whatever is causing us pain. Pain, sickness, and death are the result of sin in our world. It's normal to desire healing and comfort. We must never forget, however, that God sees the big picture. Sometimes He doesn't remove the trials in our lives; instead He gives us the strength to get through them. If we'll accept this without anger and bitterness, then He can do amazing things in our hearts. Trials produce in us steadfastness and many other beautiful fruits if we respond to them as God desires.
4. We may accomplish things without Christ's help, but they won't be the things that have value in eternity. What God wants to see in us is a dependence on Him, an acknowledgment that it is the Holy Spirit in us that produces anything of eternal worth. God has good works set aside for each of us to do (Ephesians 2:10). He calls His children to do works that are often beyond our natural ability and strength. Only as we rely on Christ will we be able to know and live out the purposes that God has for each of us.
5. The fruit is "the holiness of a life made fruitful by union with Christ" (CCC 2074). Through the inner working of the Holy Spirit, Christ loves others through us. The fruit that is produced as we allow God to prune us is love, joy, peace, patience, kindness, goodness, faithfulness, gentleness, and self-control.

Lesson 16, Day Three

1. The burning of branches symbolizes the fire of divine judgment. To avoid it we need to abide in Christ and bear the fruit that comes from obeying Him. The prophet Ezekiel wrote about this, describing the inhabitants of Jerusalem as a vine that broke faith, didn't bear fruit, and as a result was destroyed by fire.

2. As we learned in lesson 15, our prayers need to be asked "in Jesus' name," which means that we want what He wants, when He wants, and how He wants it. Submission to God's will is essential in the life of a Christian. Sometimes we ask for things with impure motives (James 4:3). God sees our heart as we pray and faithfully gives us what is truly best for us.

3. We abide in the love of Christ by believing in and obeying Him. God abides in us when we confess Jesus as the Son of God (1 John 4:15). Jesus asks us to pray, and this is an essential aspect of abiding in Him. In 1 John 3:23, we're reminded that Jesus commands us to love each other. One way we draw close to Christ is by loving those He places in our lives (1 John 4:12). We abide in Christ when we study Scripture (John 15:7). We also abide in Christ through the sacrament of the Eucharist (John 6:56). The intimacy that comes from the body, blood, soul, and divinity of Christ dwelling within us is real.

4. The joy comes from the certainty that we are loved by God.

Lesson 16, Day Four

1. **A.** The "new commandment" of Jesus is to love as He has loved us.

   B. Leviticus 19:18: This is a command to love your neighbor as yourself, to treat others as you would like to be treated.

   Luke 6:32–36: Not only are we to love our neighbors; we are to love those who hurt us and hate us. We are to love our enemies and expect nothing in return. (Note: This is not a directive to stay in an abusive relationship. You were not created by God to be a punching bag. You may need to love from a distance. From a place of safety, you can want what is best for the other person. You can forgive and want him or her to repent and then find God's mercy.)

   John 15:12–13: This verse intensifies the command by giving Jesus as our example of how to love. How did He show us that we should love? Sacrificially. He held nothing back and laid down His life for us.

2. **A.** Answers will vary.

   B. Love is infused into us through the indwelling Holy Spirit. The Holy Spirit within us gives us the strength to act in a loving way, even when it's difficult and goes against our natural instinct. "We love, because he first loved us" (1

John 4:19). As we fill up with God's love, we find an unending source of love that we can pour into the lives of others.

Lesson 16, Day Five

1. It can be hard to understand what Jesus meant by "world" in this passage. In Scripture this word is used to describe God's creation. John 3:16 says, "God so loved the world that He gave His only-begotten Son, that whoever believes in Him should not perish but have eternal life." Yet later in Scripture, we read, "Do not love the world or the things in the world. If anyone loves the world, love for the Father is not in him" (1 John 2:15). Are we to understand that God loves the world, but we are not to love the world? No.

   The Bible uses the word "world" in several different ways. When Jesus speaks of the world in John 15:18–25, He is describing fallen humanity. He is describing the "negative influence exerted on people by communal situations and social structures that are the fruit of men's sins" (CCC 408). It's men ignoring God and living life according to what seems right, which may or may not coincide with what God says is right. It's a description of "the whole world [which] is in the power of the evil one" (CCC 409).

2. **Romans 12:14:** We are to bless those who persecute us. We can do this through our words or by refraining from telling others how we have been mistreated. We can pray for those who hurt us. We can choose not to seek revenge, leaving judgment to God.

   1 Peter 4:12–16: We should recognize that it is a privilege to be identified with Christ and to share in His suffering.

3. Jesus' listeners have no excuse because they have heard His words and seen His works—works of mercy and miracles that only God could do. "Revelation entails the responsibility of embracing it. Had Jesus not spoken the truth to the world, its culpability would be lessened; since he did, however, scoffers and unbelievers face the dreadful consequences of rejecting the voice of the living God."[93]

4. God has sent the Holy Spirit.

Lesson 17, Day One

1. Answers will vary.
2. **A.** Jesus promised to send the Holy Spirit.

---

93 *Ignatius Catholic Study Bible, RSV, 192.*

    B. When the Holy Spirit dwells in our hearts, we never need to feel lonely or that no one truly knows and understands us. We are known. We are understood. God is with us, within us, through the indwelling Holy Spirit.

3. Jesus said that the Holy Spirit would convict the world of sin, righteousness, and judgment.

Lesson 17, Day Two

1. The Holy Spirit is not a separate source of truth. He does not differ from God the Father or Jesus the Son. The Holy Spirit only speaks what He hears from Jesus, and all Jesus has, He's received from the Father.

2. Jesus was speaking of His death ("you will see me no more") and then His Resurrection ("you will see me").

3. Limitless joy awaits us in heaven. While here on earth, we will have difficulties and troubles. We can receive great comfort by meditating on what heaven will be like. God will wipe away our tears; there will be no cause for sadness. Death will no longer destroy. No one will be hungry or thirsty. We'll be filled with joy forever!

4. Answers will vary.

Lesson 17, Day Three

1. Jesus was no longer going to speak in parables or use illustrations such as the true vine (John 15:1) to explain God the Father. He was going to speak directly to them.

2. The Father tenderly loves us because we have loved Jesus and believe that He came from the heavenly Father (John 16:27). Before Jesus' death on the cross in our place, the average man had a relationship with God that lacked the intimacy we can now experience. Even Moses, who was certainly very close to God, was told, "Do not come near; put off your shoes from your feet, for the place on which you are standing is holy ground" (Exodus 3:5). Jesus brings us into God's presence because His death on the cross paid for our sins.

   Because Jesus has reconciled us to the Father through His atoning death on the cross, we can now call God *Abba*. This is an Aramaic term for "Daddy"—an intimate way of speaking to one's father. We are able to approach God directly for our needs. He loves us tenderly, as a father loves his child.

3. Answers will vary.

4. We need fortitude:

5. Fortitude is the moral virtue that ensures firmness in difficulties and constancy in the pursuit of the good. It strengthens the resolve to resist temptations and to overcome obstacles in the moral life. The virtue of fortitude enables one to

conquer fear, even fear of death, and to face trials and persecutions. It disposes one even to renounce and sacrifice his life in defense of a just cause. "The Lord is my strength and my song." (CCC 1808)

Lesson 17, Day Four

1. **John 17:3** describes eternal life as knowing the only true God and knowing Jesus. This knowledge goes beyond a cerebral understanding of God's identity. It's speaking of an intimate knowledge that comes from a relationship. The Greek word translated as "know" is *ginōskō*, which means "to know through personal experience." This is also the word that Mary used when she asked the angel Gabriel, "How will this be since I do not know [ginōskō] a man?" This knowledge should be something that grows throughout our lifetime. We should know God more intimately at the end of our lives than we do today. It's an adventure—there is always more to be discovered about Him.

2. Answers will vary.

3. **A.** Those who are baptized are given "a share in the common priesthood of all believers" (CCC 1268). The baptized are to share with others what God has done to make a difference in their lives. "This is who I was before Christ intersected my life...and this is how I've changed!"

   B. The apostles were chosen to both witness Jesus' Resurrection and then to become the foundation stones of the Church.

   C. The apostles appointed successors to carry on their work. Today that office is held by the bishops. The Church teaches that "the bishops have by divine institution taken the place of the apostles as pastors of the Church, in such wise that whoever listens to them is listening to Christ and whoever despises them despises Christ and him who sent Christ" (CCC 862).

Lesson 17, Day Five

1. Jesus was praying for people in the future, who would believe in Him as the Gospel was passed from generation to generation. He was praying for us.

2. Jesus prayed that His followers would be one, as God the Father, God the Son, and God the Holy Spirit are one. He prayed for unity among believers and that we would know the magnitude of God's love for us, the same love He has for Jesus.

3. We can listen to one another, desiring to grow in understanding. This differs from listening while at the same time preparing to convince the other person of the validity of our beliefs. We can acknowledge the doctrines we agree upon, which are many. We can verbally recognize the things done well (for example: great service projects, wonderful programs, excellent presentation). We can

look for opportunities to serve together. We all agree that as Christians we are called to minister to the marginalized and suffering people in society. We should pray together. We should all pursue renewal within the Church and personal conversion of heart.

4. The Catholic Church accepts members of the Protestant Church with respect and affection as brothers. CCC 819 states, "'many elements of sanctification and of truth' are found outside the visible confines of the Catholic Church: 'the written Word of God; the life of grace; faith, hope, and charity, with the other interior gifts of the Holy Spirit, as well as visible elements.'"

Lesson 19, Day One

1. This garden was called Gethsemane. Jesus went there to pray. He asked His disciples to join Him in prayer. This is where Jesus, full of sorrow and distress, fell to the ground and asked His Father (Abba) to let this cup of suffering pass from Him. He also reaffirmed His commitment to embrace His Father's will, even if it meant enduring the cross (Mark 14:36). Jesus was in such agony that His sweat became like drops of blood.

2. While Jesus knew that Judas was to betray Him, the revelation was shocking to the disciples. Initially they must have been confused. Why would Judas be with all of Jesus' enemies? When Judas' motives were made clear, they probably felt anger, disbelief, and fear. Jesus' heart must have broken. Did He wonder if Judas might change his mind at the last minute? But no, the betrayal was not avoided. It's painful enough to be attacked or hurt by an enemy. When it is done by a friend, the sorrow can be devastating.

3. They drew back and fell to the ground. Saint Augustine had this to say about the event: "Why did they not lay hold of him but fell back to the ground? Because that was what he wished, who could do whatever he wished. Had he not allowed himself to be taken by them, they would have been unable to effect their plan, but neither would he have done what he came to do."[94]

4. Jesus healed the servant's ear. Reflect on the fact that the servant of the high priest knew without a doubt that Jesus was no ordinary man, let alone a vicious criminal. The healing of Malchus' ear was one last miracle, one last opportunity for people to repent.

Lesson 19, Day Two

1. Jesus allowed them to bind Him. Had He decided He wanted to be free, He could have freed Himself. At other points in Scripture, we read that people tried to seize

---

94 Saint Augustine, *In Ioannis Evangelium Tractatus*, 112-113.

or stone Him, but He hid or slipped away. Jesus was in control every minute of His trial and crucifixion. Nothing was taken from Him; He gave Himself freely. At any moment He could have appealed to His Father, and the Father would have sent Jesus "more than twelve legions of angels" (Matthew 26:53).

2. Jesus' first religious trial was with Annas, the father-in-law of Caiaphas, the high priest that year.

3. In Matthew 26:59, we read that the chief priests and the council sought false testimony against Jesus but found none. Many false witnesses came forward, but no one said anything deserving of death. Finally two witnesses distorted Jesus' words in John 2:19. Jesus broke His silence and accepted fully the charge of being Israel's Messiah—the Son of God. Their response was to spit in His face, to strike and slap Him.

4. **A.** In John 18:17, Peter was asked, "Are not you also one of his disciples?" He said, "I am not." In John 18:25, when Peter was warming himself by the fire in the company of the servants and officers, they asked him if he was one of Jesus' disciples. He said he wasn't. In John 18:26, one of the relatives of the servant whose ear Peter had cut off said, "Did I not see you in the garden with him?" Peter denied it.

    Fear took hold in Peter's heart. It overruled his best intentions to stay faithful to the point of death. His eyes shifted to the circumstances at hand, much as they had when he was walking on the water toward Jesus. The minute his eyes shifted to the wind and off of Jesus, he began to sink (Matthew 14:29–30).

    B. Answers will vary.

    C. Jesus turned and looked straight at Peter. His penetrating gaze caused a bitter grief and overwhelming regret to fill Peter's heart. It was the look of One who knew Peter's heart and loved him in spite of his denial.

Lesson 19, Day Three

1. **A.** The Jewish leaders didn't enter so that they wouldn't be defiled. If they were defiled, they wouldn't be able to eat the Passover. "Jewish tradition at the time laid down that anyone who entered a Gentile or pagan house incurred seven days' legal defilement (see Acts 10:28); such defilement would have prevented them from celebrating the Passover."[95]

    B. Ironically, they were concerned about missing Passover due to defiling themselves through contact with the Gentiles, while at the same time plotting the death of the Lamb of God.

---

95 Navarre Bible: Saint John's Gospel, RSV, 179.

2. Israel was occupied by the Romans, and the Jewish religious leaders didn't have the right to execute anyone (John 18:31). They needed to convince the Roman authorities that Jesus was deserving of death. Pilate alone had the authority to issue and execute a capital offense.[96]

3. Jesus had to be accused of political revolt. Religious charges meant nothing to the Romans. Keeping the peace was of the utmost importance to Pilate. If there was unrest or revolt, his job was at risk.

   "Not daring to stone [Jesus], [the Jewish religious leaders] will shrewdly manage to turn a religious charge into a political question and have the authority of the Empire brought to bear on their side; they preferred to denounce Jesus to the procurator as a revolutionary who plotted against Caesar by declaring himself to be the Messiah and King of the Jews; by acting in this way they avoided risking the people's wrath and ensured that Jesus would be condemned by the Roman authorities to death by crucifixion."[97]

Lesson 19, Day Four

1. **A.** Pilate asked Jesus if He was the King of the Jews. He didn't want anything to threaten his job security.

   B. "Herod was appointed King of the Jews by the Roman Senate in 40 B.C. to replace the collapsing dynasty of Jewish priestly rulers. He took power in Jerusalem in 37 B.C. and reigned until his death…As a ruler, he was extremely harsh and inflexible. He enjoyed little favor with the Jews since he remained loyal to the Roman emperor and was not a rightful Davidic leader."[98] He, too, was concerned with job security and maintenance of power.

2. **A.** Jesus is King over a spiritual kingdom, not a worldly one. In His kingdom the greatest among the people is a servant. The King comes to give his life as a ransom for many. This stands in stark contrast to the Gentile rulers who lord their authority over people and oppress them in order to remain in power.

   B. Jesus responded to Pilate in John 18:37 by saying, "You say I am a king. For this I was born and for this I came into the world, to testify to the truth. Everyone who belongs to the truth listens to my voice." Jesus reveals something about His kingdom and how it differs from the world when He talks about the authority of Truth. He is the King of Truth. The religious leaders preferred

---

96 Ignatius Catholic Study Bible, RSV, 151.

97 Navarre Bible, Saint John's Gospel, RSV, 179.

98 Ignatius Catholic Study Bible, RSV, 9.

lies to the truth. They "preferred darkness to light, because their works were evil" (John 3:19).

3. **A.** Answers will vary.

   B. Jesus said, "I am the way, and the truth, and the life." If Pilate sincerely wanted to know truth, he just needed Jesus.

4. Answers will vary.

   Proverbs 2:3–4 encourages us to cry out for truth, to look for it as for silver. We get so busy pursuing other things. Are we neglecting what is most important?

Lesson 19, Day Five

1. Pilate knew that the Jewish leaders were envious of Jesus and that there was more to this trial than met the eye. Pilate's wife had a dream, which she felt was a divine warning not to convict Jesus, who was a righteous man.

2. **A.** Pilate sent Jesus to Herod when he realized that Jesus was from Galilee and therefore under Herod's jurisdiction.

   B. Herod wanted Jesus to show him a sign. Jesus didn't and was, in fact, completely silent. He refused to enter into a pointless discussion with a man who was not seeking truth.

3. Answers will vary.

Lesson 20, Day One

1. Jesus was scourged. A crown of thorns was pushed into His scalp. He was clothed in a purple robe (imagine what it felt like for fabric to rub on and stick to Jesus' bleeding wounds). He was struck by the soldiers' hands.

2. When Jesus slumped to the ground, covered in blood, the soldiers thought it was humorous that this man had claimed to be a king. They put a robe on His raw back and made a crown of branches with long thorns. They dug the thorns into Jesus' head, which would have caused even more bleeding. Then they took the stick they had placed in His hands as a scepter and used it to beat Him, driving the thorns deeper still into His head. All the while they laughed and mocked Him. "Hail, King of the Jews!"

3. Answers will vary.

Lesson 20, Day Two

1. Pilate said that he found no crime in Jesus three times (John 18:38, 19:4, 19:6).

2. The religious leaders charged Jesus with blasphemy. The Catechism states that blasphemy is speech, thought, or action involving contempt for God or the Church

or for persons or things dedicated to God. They believed that in claiming to be the Son of God, Jesus had shown contempt for God. The irony is that Jesus was God, standing in front of them unrecognized, and they were showing Him contempt and hatred. Who were the true blasphemers?

3. Pilate recognized that there was more to this situation than met the eye. He knew that the Jewish leaders were envious of Jesus. He had also been warned by his wife that he should have nothing to do with the execution of this righteous man. She'd had a dream about Jesus that affected her deeply.

4. Jesus was in control. He wasn't forced to die—He laid down His life willingly and according to God's plan. God can take all man's choices into account and still accomplish His divine purposes.

Even when our circumstances seem out of control, God is always present, always guiding, always in control. Nothing takes Him by surprise. Even when we don't see evidence of Him being with us or working good in our situation, He is there. He doesn't watch us passively. He is actively involved in our lives. No person, no matter how evil, can thwart God's sovereign power.

Lesson 20, Day Three

1. **A.** The Jewish people said, "Away with him, away with him, crucify him," and, "We have no king but Caesar."

   B. The Church does not blame the Jews for Jesus' death. CCC 597 says: We cannot lay responsibility for the trial on the Jews in Jerusalem as a whole, despite the outcry of a manipulated crowd and the global reproaches contained in the apostles' calls to conversion after Pentecost…As the Church declared at the Second Vatican Council: "Neither all Jews indiscriminately at that time, nor Jews today, can be charged with the crimes committed during his Passion… [T]he Jews should not be spoken of as rejected or accursed as if this followed from holy Scripture."

2. According to CCC 598:

   The Church has never forgotten that "sinners were the authors and the ministers of all the sufferings that the divine Redeemer endured."…Since our sins made the Lord Christ suffer the torment of the cross, those who plunge themselves into disorders and crimes crucify the Son of God anew in their hearts (for he is in them) and hold him up to contempt. And it can be seen that our crime in this case is greater in us than in the Jews. As for them, according to the witness of the Apostle, "None of the rulers of this age understood this; for if they had, they would not have crucified the Lord of glory." We, however, profess to know him. And when we deny him by our deeds, we in some way seem to lay violent hands on him.

3. Answers will vary.
4. Answers will vary.

Lesson 20, Day Four

1. Answers will vary.
2. Jesus wore our sins when He hung on the cross.
3. **A.** Jesus said, "Father, forgive them; for they know not what they do."
   B. Answers will vary.
4. The Blessed Mother, Mary; Mary (wife of Clopas); Mary Magdalene; and the apostle John.
5. Jesus honored His mother by entrusting her to the care of John. The apostle John represented all of Jesus' followers, to whom Jesus gave His mother. Because of this Mary is our spiritual mother. She prays for us and accompanies us. We have a spiritual family. Mary is our mother, Jesus is our Brother, and God is our Father.

Lesson 20, Day Five

1. "The blood and water that flowed from the pierced side of the crucified Jesus are types of Baptism and the Eucharist, the sacraments of new life" (CCC 1225). "The symbolism of water signifies the Holy Spirit's action in Baptism" (CCC 694). Jesus' blood both nourishes us (in the Eucharist) and ransoms us (1 Peter 1:18–19).
2. **A.** We are crucified with Christ through Baptism. We are submerged in water like a body is surrounded by the grave, and then, we are lifted out of the water to a new life with God just as Jesus' body was resurrected. In our daily lives, we are "crucified with Christ" when we die to our desires or our sinful patterns of behavior. We die to the old, selfish way of doing things and choose to live the way God wants us to live.
   B. Christ lives in us through the indwelling Holy Spirit.
   C. Jesus showed His love for the world collectively and for me individually when He died on the cross in our place. "No man, not even the holiest, was ever able to take on himself the sins of all men and offer himself as a sacrifice for all. The existence in Christ of the divine person of the Son, who at once surpasses and embraces all human persons, and constitutes himself as the Head of all mankind, makes possible his redemptive sacrifice for all" (CCC 616).
3. Mary of Bethany had taken a costly ointment of pure nard (the equivalent of a year's wages) and poured it on Jesus' feet. Jesus said that she had done a beautiful thing and that it prepared Him for burial.

Lesson 21, Day One

1. **A.** John referred to himself as the disciple whom Jesus loved.

   B. To consider himself beloved is a beautiful testimony to John's relationship with Jesus. He knew he was loved, personally and intensely. Jesus had proven His love to John on the cross. John would never forget it. We, too, are the beloved. Jesus died for each of us because of His love for us. He wants us to see ourselves as loved, cherished, and delighted in. Because of His work on the cross, we are forgiven. He sees inside us—into our hearts—into all that we want to be for Him. As beloved daughters of God, we are full of grace (John 1:16), temples of the Holy Spirit (1 Corinthians 6:19), new creations (2 Corinthians 5:17).

2. John's waiting indicates a deference to Peter, suggesting Peter was already considered the leader of the disciples.

3. Mary Magdalene thought someone had taken Jesus' body. When the disciples saw that "the cloth that had covered his head [was] not with the burial cloths but rolled up in a separate place" (John 20:7), they knew no one had stolen Him. This led them to think back on Jesus' words of rising from the dead, recorded in Matthew 16:21 and 27:63.

4. **A.** Mary Magdalene recognized Jesus when He called her by name. What a beautiful and hope-filled testimonial that Jesus first appeared to her, a notorious sinner.

   B. Jesus asked Mary Magdalene to say, "I am ascending to my Father and your Father, to my God and your God."

   C. We are able to call ourselves God's daughters—we can call Him *Abba*, which means "Daddy"—because Jesus redeemed us. His death and Resurrection radically changed man's relationship with God. God wants me to see myself as His beloved daughter, adopted into His family. He "sent the spirit of His Son into our hearts, crying, 'Abba! Father!'" (Galatians 4:6)

Lesson 21, Day Two

1. Jesus could pass through walls. He was able to appear as He'd like to—as a gardener or in another guise. People did not instantly recognize Him, so His appearance had to have been altered. His body was not limited by time and space. It was a real body; Jesus ate when He was with them. He had flesh and bones. It was His same body that had been crucified—He showed them the wounds in His hands and feet. His wounds bring to mind Isaiah 49:16: "Behold, I have graven you on the palms of my hands."

2. Jesus breathed the Holy Spirit on them. This event anticipated Pentecost, which would take place in fifty days. At that point they'd receive the fullness of the indwelling Holy Spirit. Jesus did not leave His disciples orphans. He fulfilled His promise to remain with them until the end of time (John 14:18) by sending the Holy Spirit.

3. Jesus gave the disciples the power to forgive and retain sins.

4. The reason the apostle John wrote his Gospel was so that his readers might believe that Jesus is the Christ and that because they believe, they might have life in His name.

Lesson 21, Day Three

1. Another name for the Sea of Tiberias was the Sea of Galilee. Jesus had told the disciples to go to Galilee and wait for Him there.

2. **A.** Peter not only said that he wouldn't deny Christ (which he did), he said, "Even though [the other disciples] all fall away, I will not." Ah...pride. How easily it ensnares us. These words probably haunted him. He had said them in front of the disciples and then had publicly denied Jesus three times. How could he then stand up and lead them? He probably felt unqualified to lead.

   B. God's grace is what we need in our areas of weakness. It's the power of Christ that enables us to be faithful—not our own strength. We are strongest when we are relying on the Lord, recognizing that without Him, we are weak. When we observe people fall in areas in which we are determined to stay faithful, we need to have a spirit of humility that says, "There but for the grace of God go I."

3. The Church is universal—it is open to all people. There is no exclusion based on race or nationality. The disciples were called to go and make disciples of all nations.

4. The last time Peter was in front of a charcoal fire, he denied Jesus three times.

Lesson 21, Day Four

1. The first and second time that Jesus asked Peter if he loved Him, He asked if Peter loved Him with a divine love. Peter responded by saying that he loved Jesus but with the love of friendship. His previous self-assurance was gone; Peter showed humility in recognizing that his love had shown a limit when he denied Jesus. The third time, Jesus asked Peter if he loved Him with the love of friendship, and Peter said that he did.

2. Agape love, God's love, divine love, has been poured into our hearts through the Holy Spirit. (The Greek word for love used in Romans 5:5 is *agape*.) The Catechism says that the theological virtue of love is infused into our souls.

3. Peter denied Jesus three times publicly and was given the chance to reaffirm his love for Him three times publicly.

4. Jesus gave Peter the job of shepherding the entire Church as its first pope. He delegated authority as the Good Shepherd to Peter, the shepherd of the Church. He asked Peter to spiritually feed the flock of His followers entrusted to his care.

Lesson 21, Day Five

1. **A.** Answers will vary.

   B. We cannot worship someone we know nothing about. Our children need to learn from us that God is more real and relevant than any other wonderful thing in our world. Often the first hurdle we need to jump is the feeling that talking about spiritual matters with our children is weird. We picture the look on their faces and the comments they will make when we start talking in a way that we haven't talked before. Perhaps you feel that it is too late—that if you had started talking this way from the very beginning, they wouldn't balk, but now, it would just be too strange. Remember, there will never be a time in your child's life when you will have more influence than right now. There is no better time than the present to begin to focus on spiritually shepherding your child's heart. This is your most important task.

   Summer is a perfect opportunity, because you will most likely have your children with you more. If you don't do it already, you could begin to pray before meals. Pray before bedtime. Read to your child daily if he or she is young, and choose books with a spiritual message or a children's Bible. *The Jesus Storybook Bible* is an excellent resource for young children. Bring Christian music and programs into your home. Search out good spiritual experiences for your kids—camps, retreats, youth ministry programs. Talk about answers to prayer that you have experienced. Talk about how much God loves them and how He has a plan for each one of their lives. Offer to pray for them in areas that are concerning them. Faithfully pray for them each day—that their hearts will be softened and open to God's love.

2. **A.** Answers will vary.

   B. Love draws a soul to Christ far more than judgment. Take the time to truly love and listen. Learn her struggles, hopes, joys, and fears. Enter her life and be of practical help when needed. True love doesn't just serve—it also tells the truth. If you know that a person's emptiness and longing for fulfillment can be satisfied in Christ, it's loving to share that truth. Certainly timing and the right words are essential, but so often, we don't speak because we're afraid. You can show true love by inviting her into your heart and home and to Mass.

    C. Answers will vary.

3. Jesus said to him, "If it is my will that he remain until I come, what is that to you? Follow me!" (John 21:22). Jesus was telling Peter to keep his eyes fixed on what God had asked of him, not looking to the left or the right and comparing his call to others'.

Prayer Pages

walking with purpose

Throughout this day,

may I pour myself out in humble service.

May I be full of You, God, and empty of selfish

desires and malicious intentions. May I drink deeply

of Your spirit, God, so that kindness and peacefulness flow

through all my words and actions. May I be loud in praise of

others and silent to their faults. May joy and laughter

well up from deep within me, washing over sadness

and disappointments that surely will come.

May each and every day be Your day,

God, and may all who see me see

only Your Son. Amen.

Prayer Requests

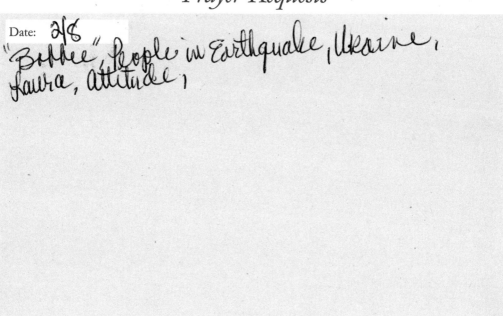

Date: 2/8

"Bobbee", People in Earthquake, Ukraine, Laura, Attitude,

Date:

Prayer Requests

Date:

Date:

Prayer Requests

Date:

Date:

Prayer Requests

Date:

Date:

Prayer Requests

Date:

Date:

Prayer Requests

Date:

Date:

Prayer Requests

Date:

Date:

Prayer Requests

Date:

❋ ❋ ❋ ❋ ❋ ❋ ❋ ❋ ❋ ❋ ❋ ❋ ❋ ❋

Date:

❋ ❋ ❋ ❋ ❋ ❋ ❋ ❋ ❋ ❋ ❋ ❋ ❋ ❋

Prayer Requests

Date:

Date:

Prayer Requests

Date:

Date:

Prayer Requests

Date:

Date:

"For to the one who has, more will be given"
Matthew 13:12

The Journey Doesn't End Here

~ Christ's Love Is Endless ~

Walking with Purpose is more than a Bible study, it's a supportive community of women seeking lasting transformation of the heart. And you are invited.

Walking with Purpose believes that change happens in the hearts of women – and, by extension, in their families and beyond – through Bible study and community. We welcome all women, irrespective of faith background, age, or marital status.

Connect with us online for regular inspiration and to join the conversation. There you'll find insightful blog posts, videos, and free scripture printables.

For a daily dose of spiritual nourishment, join our community on Facebook, Twitter, Pinterest and Instagram.

And if you're so moved to start a Walking with Purpose study group at home or in your parish, take a look at our website for more information.

walkingwithpurpose.com

walking with purpose
~ SO MUCH MORE THAN A BIBLE STUDY ~

✳ DEEPEN YOUR FAITH ✳ OPEN YOUR ARMS ✳ ✳ BROADEN YOUR CIRCLE ✳

When your heart opens, and your love for Christ deepens, you may be moved to bring Walking With Purpose to your friends or parish. It's rewarding experience for many women who, in doing so, learn to rely on God's grace while serving Him.

If leading a group seems like a leap of faith, consider that you already have all the skills you need to share the Lord's Word:

- Personal commitment to Christ
- Desire to share the love of Christ
- Belief in the power of authentic, transparent community

The Walking With Purpose community supports you with:

- Training
- Mentoring
- Bible study materials
- Promotional materials

Few things stretch and grow our faith like stepping out of our comfort zone and asking God to work through us. Say YES, soon you'll see the mysterious and unpredictable ways He works through imperfect women devoted to Him.

Remember that if you humbly offer Him what you can, He promises to do the rest.

"See to it that no one misses the grace of God" Hebrews 12:15

Learn more about bringing Walking with Purpose to your parish. Visit us at walkingwithpurpose.com

Walking with Purpose Devotionals

Daily affirmations of God's love

Rest: 31 Days of Peace

- A beautiful, hardcover, pocket-sized devotional to take wherever you go.

- 31 Scripture-based meditations that you can read (and re-read) daily.

- Become saturated with the truth that you are seen, known, and loved by a God who gave everything for you!

Be Still: A Daily Devotional to Quiet Your Heart

- Grow closer to the Lord each day of the year with our 365-day devotional.

- This beautifully designed hardcover devotional collection will renew your mind and help you look at things from God's perspective.

- Apply what you read in *Be Still*, and you'll make significant progress in your spiritual life!

shop.walkingwithpurpose.com

walking with purpose

SO MUCH MORE THAN A BIBLE STUDY

Journal Your Prayers & Grow Closer to God

The Walking with Purpose *Praying from the Heart: Guided Journal* is a beautiful, comprehensive prayer journal that provides a private space to share your thoughts and feelings with the Lord.

Journaling your prayers lets you express a greater depth of intimacy toward God, and it will help you cultivate the practice of gratitude. Journaling will motivate you to pray regularly, too!

Praying from the Heart lays flat for easy writing, and is fashioned after the way that author Lisa Brenninkmeyer journals her own prayers. You'll love the heavyweight paper, luxurious leatherette cover, and many other special details.

shop.walkingwithpurpose.com

walking with purpose
SO MUCH MORE THAN A BIBLE STUDY

FEARLESS & FREE
EXPERIENCING HEALING AND WHOLENESS IN CHRIST

Fear is a powerful emotion, and part of the human condition. Life isn't easy. But we were never meant to go it alone. God has wired us for connection – to Him.

Do you long to be grounded in a love that will never fail you?

Fearless and Free is for any woman confronting the reality of her fears. When suffering slams into you and leaves you reeling, or you feel great one day, and down on the mat the next, turn to this Scripture study.

Do you long for healing and wholeness? Would you like to be grounded in a love that will never fail?

In these six compassionate lessons, you'll learn to:

- **WAKEN** to the reality of who you are in Christ,

- **WRESTLE** with the battle in your mind, and conquer the enemy who seeks to steal your true identity.

- Be strengthened as a **WARRIOR** to reclaim your footing and move forward in life.

Fearless and Free is not about surviving; it's about flourishing in Christ's love, the One who truly loves you completely and without end.

Learn more about *Fearless and Free* at walkingwithpurpose.com

The guided tour of God's love begins here.

Opening Your Heart: The Starting Point begins a woman's exploration of her Catholic faith and enhances her relationship with Jesus Christ. This Bible study is designed to inspire thoughtful consideration of the fundamental questions of living a life in the Lord. More than anything, it's a weekly practice of opening your heart to the only One who can heal and transform lives.

Explore these topics and more:

- What is the role of the Holy Spirit in my life?
- What does the Eucharist have to do with my friendship with Christ?
- What are the limits of Christ's forgiveness?
- Why and how should I pray?
- What is the purpose of suffering?
- What challenges will I face in my efforts to follow Jesus more closely?
- How can fear be overcome?

A companion video series complements this journey with practical insights and spiritual support.

Opening Your Heart is a foundational 22-lesson Bible study that serves any woman who seeks to grow closer to God. It's an ideal starting point for women who are new to Walking with Purpose and those with prior practice in Bible study, too.

To share Walking with Purpose with the women in your parish, contact us at walkingwithpurpose.com/contact-us.

walkingwithpurpose.com

walking with purpose

blaze for Tween/Teen Girls!

Do you want to help girls grow in confidence, faith and kindness?

The Lord is calling for women like you to speak truth into the hearts of young girls – girls who can be easily confused about their true worth and beauty.

BLAZE is the Walking with Purpose ministry designed especially for tween/teen girls. It makes the wisdom of the Bible relevant to the challenges girls face today, and teaches them to recognize the difference between the loving voice of their heavenly Father and the voices that tell them they aren't good enough.

You can be a positive influence on the girls you know by starting a BLAZE program for any number of girls in your parish, school or home (or use one-on-one)!

The 20-week **BLAZE Core Program** includes a Leader's Guide and fun BLAZE kits. Each kit contains a pack of Truth vs. Lie cards, materials for icebreaker activities, take-home gifts and the BLAZE Prayer Journal.

You might also like **Between You and Me**, a 40-day conversation guide for mothers and daughters to read together. The daily reflection, journaling opportunities, discussion questions, and prayer prompts will help take your relationship to a new level of honesty and intimacy.

Discovering My Purpose is a six-lesson Bible study designed to open girls' eyes to their unique purpose, gifts, and God's love. It includes the **BLAZE Spiritual Gifts Inventory**, a fabulous tool to help girls discern where God is calling them to be world-changers.

Learn more at walkingwithpurpose.com/BLAZE

"BE WHO GOD MEANT YOU TO BE
AND YOU WILL SET THE WORLD ON FIRE."
SAINT CATHERINE OF SIENA

walking with purpose

Transformative Catholic Bible Studies

Walking with Purpose Bible studies are created to help women deepen their personal relationship with Christ. Each study includes many lessons that explore core themes and challenges of modern life through the ancient wisdom of the Bible and the Catholic Church.

Opening Your Heart

A thoughtful consideration of the fundamental questions of faith – from why and how to pray to the role of the Holy Spirit in our lives and the purpose of suffering.

Living In the Father's Love

Gain a deeper understanding of how God's unconditional love transforms your relationship with others, with yourself, and most dearly, with Him.

Keeping In Balance

Discover how the wisdom of the Old and New Testaments can help you live a blessed lifestyle of calm, health, and holiness.

Touching the Divine

These thoughtful lessons draw you closer to Jesus and deepen your faith, trust, and understanding of what it means to be God's beloved daughter.

Discovering Our Dignity

Modern-day insight directly from women of the Bible presented as a tender, honest, and loving conversation—woman to woman.

Beholding His Glory

Old Testament Scripture leads us directly to our Redeemer, Jesus Christ. Page after page, God's awe-inspiring majesty is a treasure to behold.

Beholding Your King

This study of King David and several Old Testament prophets offers a fresh perspective of how all Scripture points to the glorious coming of Christ.

Grounded In Hope

Anchor yourself in the truth found in the New Testament book of Hebrews, and gain practical insight to help you run your race with perseverance.

Fearless and Free

With an emphasis on healing and wholeness, this study provides a firm foundation to stand on, no matter what life throws our way.

Reclaiming Friendship

Let God reshape how you see and experience intentional relationships, deal with your past friendship wounds, and become a woman who is capable of the lifelong bond of true friendship.

Ordering Your Priorities

An immensely practical study that will help you put the most important things first. Discover not only what matters most in life, but also how to prioritize those things!

Choose your next Bible study at
shop.walkingwithpurpose.com

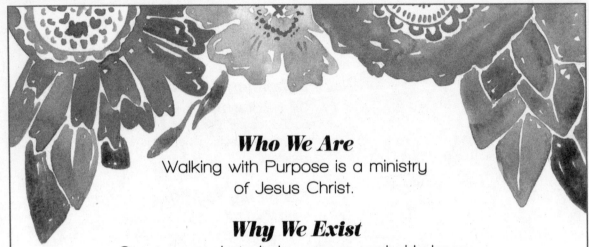

Who We Are
Walking with Purpose is a ministry
of Jesus Christ.

Why We Exist
Our purpose is to help women and girls know
Jesus Christ personally by making Scripture and the
teachings of the Catholic Church relevant and applicable.

Our Mission
Our mission is to help every Catholic woman and girl in
America encounter Jesus Christ through our Bible studies.

Our Vision
Our vision for the future is that, as more Catholic
women deepen their relationships with Jesus Christ,
eternity-changing transformation will take place in their
hearts – and, by extension – in their families, in their
communities, and ultimately, in our nation.

walking with purpose
SO MUCH MORE THAN A BIBLE STUDY

You can support our mission through a tax-deductible gift.
Learn more at walkingwithpurpose.com/donate